PERU

Copublished with Hoover Institution Press,
Stanford University, Stanford, California

POLITICS IN LATIN AMERICA
A HOOVER INSTITUTION SERIES

General Editor, **Robert Wesson**

PERU

The Evolution of a Crisis

JAMES D. RUDOLPH

Foreword by Cynthia McClintock

PRAEGER

Westport, Connecticut
London

HOUSTON PUBLIC LIBRARY

Library of Congress Cataloging-in-Publication Data

Rudolph, James D., 1947–
    Peru : the evolution of a crisis / James D. Rudolph ;
foreword by Cynthia McClintock
        p.   cm. — (Politics in Latin America)
    Includes bibliographical references (p.   ) and index.
    ISBN 0-275-94146-6 (alk. paper)
    ISBN 0-275-94181-7 (pbk : alk. paper)
    1. Peru—Politics and government—1919– 2. Peru—Economic
conditions—1918– 3. García, Alan.   I. Title. II. Series.
F3448.R84 1991
985.06′3—dc20   91-23655

British Library Cataloguing in Publication Data is available.

Library of Congress Catalog Card Number: 91-23655
ISBN: 0-275-94146-6 (hb.)
      0-275-94181-7 (pb.)

First published in 1992

Praeger Publishers, 88 Post Road West, Westport, CT 06881
An imprint of Greenwood Publishing Group, Inc.

Printed in the United States of America

The paper used in this book complies with the
Permanent Paper Standard issued by the National
Information Standards Organization (Z39.48–1984).

10 9 8 7 6 5 4 3 2 1

Para Paulita
Que conozca un Perú mejor

Contents

Photographs follow p. 76.

Foreword

The decade of the 1980s was perhaps harsher for Peru than for any other Latin American country. While for most of the twentieth century Peru was relatively prosperous and peaceful by Latin American standards, during the 1980s living standards plummeted and the continent's most ruthless guerrilla group, Sendero Luminoso, expanded inexorably. The intensity of human suffering in Peru became evident to the world when cholera, a disease not seen in Latin America for a century, assumed epidemic proportions.

From the perspective of advocates of democracy, one of the saddest dimensions of Peru's social and economic crisis was that it occurred under two successive freely and fairly elected governments. Peruvian citizens pinned high hopes first upon President Fernando Belaúnde (1980–1985) and then upon the charismatic President Alan García (1985–1990), but both times these hopes were dashed.

In *Peru: The Evolution of a Crisis,* Jim Rudolph provides a superlative examination of the country's downward spiral. Having lived and worked in Peru for more than five years, Rudolph intimately knows recent events in Peru; about one-third of the book is a rich and thoughtful analysis of the rise and decline of Alan García's popularity and power. Trained as a historian, Rudolph also illuminates aspects of Peru's past that are critical to understanding its current crisis.

This sober and factual account is the only work available that takes a comprehensive perspective to Peru's decade-long crisis, interrelating problems of geography and economics as well as history and politics. It will be extremely valuable to all those who want to understand how and why this tragic crisis occurred.

Cynthia McClintock
George Washington University

Preface

The volume that follows had its germination in 1985, when Robert Wesson asked me to write a book on Peru for the Hoover Institution's Politics in Latin America series. My initial intention was to examine the political institutions associated with democracy (Congress, political parties, labor unions, and so on) with an eye toward evaluating the prospects for the consolidation of Peru's fledgling democratic rule. As I neared completion of that study, however, and as the atmosphere of optimism that had greeted Alan García's assumption of power gave way to one of ever-deepening crisis, it became apparent that, in Peru, the consolidation of democracy was not the burning issue in the 1980s that it was within the diplomatic and academic communities in the United States.

By no means is this meant to imply that I believe Peruvians, by nature, to be somehow undemocratic. An overwhelming majority, in fact, favor a democratic form of government. Peruvians took pride in their democratic record of the 1980s; this pride became overshadowed, however, by fear and anxiety rooted in the rampant growth of an economic, social, and political crisis, known to Peruvians simply as *la crisis,* throughout the decade. This socioeconomic crisis became so salient in any discussion of Peruvian politics during the late 1980s that I felt compelled to refocus my study to facilitate an understanding of the crisis. I chose a historical narrative format to examine the historical roots of Peru's crisis; while Alan García is the object of vehement criticism in this book—the principal villain, as it were—the country was already in dire straits when he assumed office in 1985.

My objective is to provide an overview of Peru's multifaceted crisis. Readers looking for a more detailed understanding of specific aspects of the crisis should consult the bibliography. I tried to include the most important investigations, with an emphasis on recent English-language studies, though surely there are some that I have omitted. This study makes no pretense of being based in comparative theory—even though readers may find that one or more of its conclusions can be applied to other Latin American countries that were suffering their own crises as they entered the last decade of the twentieth century.

I want to thank the countless number of friends and colleagues, in Washington and in Lima, who encouraged me to complete this book. Special thanks are due to Robert Wesson, whose supportive telephone calls and advice were invaluable, and to my loving wife, Sylvia, whose nurturing and exceptional patience throughout the duration of this project were indispensable. I also want to thank Alejandro Balaguer and Vera A. Lentz for giving me permission to include their fine photographs, as well as David Scott Palmer, Cynthia McClintock, Lorenzo Rosselló Truel, Meredith Rosenberg, and Jaysuño Abramovich for their most beneficial comments on the draft manuscript. Any errors that remain herein are, naturally, solely my responsibility.

Peru: Departmental Subdivisions

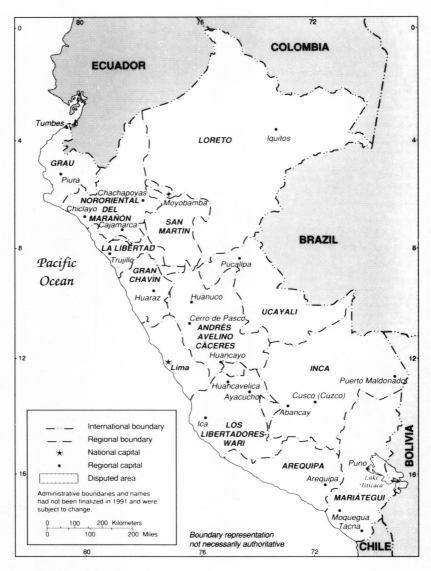

Peru: Regional Subdivisions

Courtesy of Rex A. Hudson, ed., Peru: A Country Study, *Library of Congress, 1992.*

INTRODUCTION

Crisis: A situation whose outcome decides whether possible bad consequences will follow.

Webster's New World Dictionary

Peru in 1990 was, by almost any standard, a country in the midst of a crisis. Economically, a decade and a half of persistent recession had recently worsened into Peru's deepest depression of the twentieth century, with gross domestic production (GDP) declining 14 percent in 1989 alone; at the same time, hyperinflation, measured at nearly 3,000 percent in 1989, so ravished Peru's currency, the inti, that it was scheduled to be replaced in 1991, only five years after it had been created. The social crisis was most evident in a growth of poverty to levels that could appropriately be termed obscene: by 1990, it was estimated that a third or more of Peru's population was unable to supply its basic nutritional needs. The immense power of the apparently limitless profits from narcotics trafficking to corrupt an ever broader segment of the population—a power that only grew with the deepening of the economic crisis—led many Peruvians to talk about a society-wide moral crisis as well.

Peru's political crisis, like the economic and social, was multifaceted. A rapidly growing insurgency—spearheaded by Sendero Luminoso, or Shining Path—was the most visible aspect of a crisis so pervasive that it increasingly questioned the very legitimacy of Peru's political and governmental structures. State institutions had deteriorated to the point that they were routinely unable to provide electrical, water, sanitary, educational, health, police, and judicial services. The condition of the political parties in late 1990 was little better. The right was devastated by the failure of what had been the promising presidential campaign of Mario Vargas Llosa, while APRA (Alianza Popular Revolucionaria Americana) was hit almost as hard by the failure of Alan García's government, and the left, which as recently as 1988 looked like a sure bet to capture the presidency in 1990, was in fact weaker and more divided than it had been in over a decade. The astonishing 1990 electoral victory of Alberto Fujimori, an utter political novice, was the result of a widespread popular vote *against* the political system.

Perhaps the most disturbing aspect of Peru's political crisis in 1990 was the widespread pessimism about the country's future prospects, a mood that contrasted markedly to the hopes that greeted presidents Fernando Belaúnde Terry in 1980 and Alan García Pérez in 1985. For many, a decade of mounting difficulties had taken the shine off the once-radiant democratic system. A return to military rule or, worse still, the coming to power of Sendero Luminoso are, no doubt, the most "possible bad consequences [that might] follow" Peru's crisis. Few in Peru hoped for such an outcome, however.

This text will use a historical narrative as its principal vehicle in the search for an answer to how Peru got into such a quandary. Before leaping back to the Pre-Incan period in our chronicle of Peru's extraordinary past, however, it behooves us to look at a number of highly pertinent aspects of Peru's geography and population in order to define some parameters of politics in Peru.

1

THE GEOGRAPHIC AND DEMOGRAPHIC SETTING

Peru is located in the west-central portion of South America, between 68 and 82 degrees west longitude and from just below the equator to nearly 19 degrees south latitude. Peru's land area of 1,285,216 square kilometers makes it the third largest nation on the continent, after Brazil and Argentina. In 1986, its population, which then reached the 20 million mark, was exceeded only by those of Colombia, Brazil, and Argentina, and was growing at an annual rate of 2.5 percent, or 500,000 persons. By 1990, Peru had reached a population of 22 million. Overall population density is relatively small, but Peru's rugged and spectacular geography, which has made it a visual delight for tourists, also makes a large part of the national territory unfit for permanent human settlement. As such, the vast majority of the population is concentrated within the scant 15 percent of the land that is suitable for agricultural exploitation.

THE LAND

Peruvian geography, among the most dramatic and awe-inspiring on earth, has proven to be a major obstacle to the nation's political and economic development. The Andes mountains, which run the length of the country from north to south, constitute a towering barrier to the lowlands on either side to such an extent that people from both sides were barely accessible to one another until the advent of air travel. The few highways and railways that penetrate the *sierra* (mountains) are engineering marvels, but they require nearly constant attention, due to avalanches and mud slides that periodically ravage these important means of national integration. To the east, the *selva* (jungle) presents its own set of challenges. Roads, commonly victimized by torrential rains, have only recently begun to penetrate Peru's vast Amazon Basin, where vast rivers continue to provide the primary means of transportation. The *sierra* and the *selva,* which together constitute nearly 90 percent of the national territory and fully half of Peru's population, commonly seem a world away from the political capital of Lima, which is located in the narrow coastal strip, or *costa,* wedged between the Andes and the Pacific Ocean.

The existence of three distinct regions—the *sierra, selva,* and *costa*—point out that Peru's geography is as varied as it is difficult. Although some geographers consider the Pacific to be a fourth region, as Peru claims the maritime region within 200 nautical miles of its coast as national territory, it will not be treated as such here. The steep eastern slope of the Andes, popularly known as the *ceja de la montaña* or *ceja de la selva* (both terms mean "the eyebrow of the jungle"), is also sometimes referred to as a separate region, but will be considered in this volume as part of the *selva.*

The *Sierra*

The *sierra* occupies approximately 30 percent of the national territory and in 1981 was home to some 39 percent of Peru's population. Once the center of the Inca empire, the *sierra* today continues a dramatic decline that began with the Spanish conquest. The region's economic mainstays, mining and agriculture, have long been stagnant or in decline. A high rate of out-migration caused by poverty and, in recent years, escalating violence, has cost the region its relative population standing. As recently as 1940, the *sierra* had held two-thirds of the national population.

The Peruvian Andes are only some 100 kilometers wide at the northern border with Ecuador but fan out to a width of 320 kilometers at Peru's southern border. They constitute a geographic region that is highly complex, with an intermittent high plateau, or *altiplano,* which rises gradually from some 2,000 meters in the north to over 3,500 meters in the south and is interrupted by steep canyons and towering mountain ranges that conceal hundreds of small glacial lakes and agricultural valleys. Near the southern border, the *altiplano* becomes quite broad and rises to some 3,800 meters before giving way to Lake Titicaca, the world's highest navigable lake, which Peru shares with Bolivia. The Cordillera Occidental defines the steep transition from the *costa* and is the only continuous north-south range. Intermittent ranges to its east include the Cordilleras Oriental and Vilcabamba in the south and the Cordilleras Azul and Blanca in the north. The spectacular Cordillera Blanca contains Peru's highest peak, El Huascarán, at 6,729 meters, in addition to a dozen other peaks that surpass the altitude of the highest point in North America, Alaska's Mt. McKinley.

Although the *sierra* encompasses a majority of Peru's arable land, most consists of high-altitude *puna* grasslands, which supports only a relatively small number of grazing animals and is not suitable for crops. Cultivable land, the scarcity of which has been a major cause of out-migration, constitutes only about 18,000 square kilometers, or 4.5 percent of the region's total area.[1]

Average temperatures in the *sierra* vary considerably with altitude, but, given its proximity to the equator, there is little seasonal variation in local average temperatures. Rather, the seasons are defined by precipitation. May through August are dry, while September through April see the rains (snow at higher altitudes) that nearly all *sierra* agriculturists rely on for their livelihood. Coastal farmers, with irrigation systems tapped into rivers that rise in the Andes, also depend on adequate rainfall and snowmelt in the *sierra*. Thus, periodic droughts, which bring disaster to the highlands, also profoundly affect the coast. Too much rain can yield disaster in the *sierra* as well, as flash floods and mud slides commonly wash away crops, roads, and, at times, entire villages, especially during the height of the rainy season in March.

The majority of the 7 million inhabitants of the Peruvian *sierra* are rural; many are largely isolated from the rest of the nation as a result of both cultural and physical barriers, as well as the region's poor communication and transportation links. An increasing number of *sierra* residents are urban, however. Arequipa, Peru's second largest city, has absorbed vast numbers of migrants from the southern *sierra* in recent years, and by 1990 had more than a half million residents. Cuzco and Huancayo, the region's second and third cities, had grown to about 200,000 by that time.

The *Selva*

The *selva*, often referred to as the *montaña*, occupies 57 percent of the national territory, but in 1981 it contained only 11 percent of its population. Most of its population is concentrated in the *ceja de la montaña*, a transitional subregion lying between 1,000 and 2,000 meters that consists of the steep eastern slopes of the Andes and their lush valleys, which are home to most of the region's agriculture. The fertile soils of the *ceja* produce a variety of crops, but by far the most important is coca, a bush with leaves that have long been chewed in the *sierra* as a means of coping with the combined effects of high altitude and hunger, and which today have acquired a vastly increased value as the raw material for cocaine. The inaccessibility of the *ceja*, due to its rugged terrain and the heavy rainfall that plays havoc with its transportation links, has aided in the rapid growth of this illicit industry that, attracting a large number of immigrants during the 1980s, became the most important economic activity in Peru.

The *selva* below 1,000 meters, Peru's Amazon Basin, is a vast jungle with leached soils that support little agriculture. This fact, together with disease, high temperatures and humidity, swarms of insect pests, and the difficulty of transportation, continue to present serious obstacles to human settlement, despite increased government colonization efforts of recent decades. Economic opportunities in the region remain severely limited. Its heyday came during a short-lived rubber boom at the turn of the twentieth century. Oil has been pumped from the northern *selva* since the 1970s, but only in small quantities that have belied optimistic early projections. The discovery of significant deposits of gold in the early 1980s created a minor boom in the southern *selva*. Tourism has become an important source of income in Iquitos, the region's largest city. Although nearly 4,000 kilometers from the mouth of the Amazon, Iquitos also receives regular visits from oceangoing ships.

The Amazon and its tributaries, of course, are the region's major geographic feature. The Marañón and the Ucayali, Peru's two longest rivers, drain the northern and central *sierra,* respectively, and become the Amazon when they merge southwest of Iquitos. The Madre de Dios River drains the southern *sierra,* but does not enter the Amazon in Peru, exiting instead into the northern Bolivian jungle. Pucallpa, in the central *selva* along the Ucayali River, and Puerto Maldonado, in the south along the Madre de Dios River, are the region's second and third largest cities.

The *Costa*

The *costa* occupies only 11 percent of the Peru's territory. Endowed with the nation's most important economic resources as well as its capital, however, it is home to fully half of Peru's total population. The region, which is some 200 kilometers wide at its northern extreme but soon narrows to a strip less than 100 kilometers wide, is extremely arid. Many parts go for years without receiving rain. The dry climate of the *costa* is controlled by the Humboldt Current in the Pacific waters offshore. At uneven intervals, most recently in 1972 and in 1983, this cold current is interrupted by a warm stream from the north known as El Niño, which can cause extremely destructive rainstorms and also ruin the region's fishing economy.

The *costa* consists largely of sand dunes, which are interrupted by 36 rivers that traverse the narrow region on their brief journeys from the Andes to the Pacific. No less than 30 rivers on the eastern slope of the Andes are longer than the Río Santa, Peru's longest Pacific-flowing river. The coast's short river valleys constitute oases into which the large coastal population is concentrated. Vast irrigation systems, many dating from pre-Incan civilizations, have converted a number of them into the most fertile agricultural lands in Peru. The largest of these areas, in the north around Trujillo and Chiclayo, produce sugarcane, rice, and cotton. Agricultural valleys in the central *costa,* around Lima, consist largely of dairy and truck farms. Cotton, olives, and grapes are grown in the smaller, southern valleys.

The northern *costa,* around Talara and its offshore environs, is the nation's most important oil-producing region. The Pacific has also brought Peru wealth in the form of guano, bird droppings that during the nineteenth century were mined as fertilizer from vast deposits on the Chincha Islands off the central coast, and fish products, including anchovies. Although it fell on hard times during much of the 1970s and 1980s, Peru had the world's most important fishing industry as recently as the late 1960s and early 1970s. The Marcona ore deposits also make the *costa* an important mining region. Finally, the large majority of Peru's manufacturing capability is concentrated in the coastal cities of Lima and, to a lesser extent, Chimbote.

The coastal cities of Lima, Trujillo, Chiclayo, and Chimbote constitute four of Peru's five largest cities. The burgeoning capital city of Lima, which long ago overflowed from the valley of the Río Rímac into the surrounding hills and sand dunes and by the 1980s had spilled into the two adjacent river valleys, is the dominant city. The estimated 7 million residents of metropolitan Lima–Callao in 1990 represented no less than 30 percent of the national population. The myriad problems associated with this growing demographic concentration in Lima present great challenges to the government, not the least of which is the provision of employment opportunities and basic social services to the mass of mostly poor and uneducated recent arrivals. At the same time, the rapid migration to Lima and other cities offers a solution, in part at least, to the challenge of integrating a highly dispersed and diverse population into the Peruvian nation.

POPULATION DYNAMICS

Estimates of the size of Peru's population at the time of the Spanish conquest vary radically from 3 million up to 30 million, but 6 million is the most commonly cited figure. The subsequent demographic catastrophe is not in dispute, however. By the end of the sixteenth century, Peru's population was estimated at only slightly more than 1 million; a century later, at 600,000.[2] The 6 million figure was not reached again until well into the twentieth century. A dramatic decline in the death rate produced a rapid growth from the 6.2 million persons recorded by the 1940 census. The rate of population growth peaked during the early 1960s at 2.9 percent annually, then began a gradual descent. By 1990 the growth rate had slowed to 2.5 percent and, having surpassed the 20 million mark during the mid-1980s, the population had more than tripled since 1940. Average life expectancy had increased from 37 to 59 years during the interim. By the end of the century, Peru's population was projected to grow to 28 million, and its growth rate was projected to slow further to 2.2 percent.[3]

Per capita income had been in decline since 1974, and by 1990, Peru was among the poorest nations in Latin America. In 1985, the Washington-based Population Reference Bureau measured Peru's per capita income at $1,040, which was by far the lowest figure of any major country in the region. Among nations having over 10 million inhabitants, Colombia, at $1,410 per capita, was closest to Peru. Despite improvements during the previous half century, Peru's life expectancy was lower than that of any other nation in Latin America, save Haiti and Bolivia, while its infant mortality rate, 99 per 1,000 live births, was exceeded only by those same countries.[4] Measures of the population's average daily intake of calories and protein vary, but all find nutritional levels far below those recommended by the World Health Organization. Only 30 percent of the national population has access to sewage treatment services, and only 49 percent to potable water.[5] Public health services are inadequate; a study in 1985 found that half the population lacked access to any health care facility. The major causes of death—influenza, pneumonia, enteritis, and diarrheal disorders—are associated with the persistence of widespread poverty.

The overall educational level of the population has shown a marked improvement in recent decades. Between 1961 and 1981, the level of literacy among those five years of age and older had increased from 61 to 79 percent. By 1981, 31 percent of Peruvians had completed secondary education, compared with only 8 percent in 1961. These figures were likely to improve further, as some 90 percent of primary-aged and 57 percent of secondary-aged children, according to the 1981 census, were attending school.

In 1986, Peru had a total of no less than 46 universities—19 private and 27 run by the state—with some 350,000 students. The three largest were all in Lima: the Universidad Nacional Mayor de San Marcos and the Universidad Nacional Federico Villareal, both public, and the private Universidad de San Martín de Porras. A mere 30 percent of Peru's university students would ever graduate, however, and there were only scant jobs awaiting these fortunate few.[6]

These overall data fail to reveal the wide disparities in socioeconomic levels that exist among Peru's three regions. Per capita incomes in the southern *sierra* averaged about one-sixth of those in metropolitan Lima–Callao. Life expectancy in the *costa* was fully 12 years more than in the *sierra* and 8 years more than in the *selva*. The infant mortality rate, only 46 per 1,000 in the *costa*, was 128 in the *selva* and 156 in the *sierra*. Data from the 1981 census measured the privileged position of the *costa*, and Lima in particular, in a variety of other manners. Seventy-three percent of all the nation's doctors were found to be in Lima, giving it a ratio of about

one doctor per 500 inhabitants. In contrast, the two poor *sierra* departments of Apurímac and Huancavelica had a total of only 25 doctors between them, for a ratio of one doctor per 29,000 inhabitants. The literacy
rate, 92 percent in Lima, was only 55 percent in Ayacucho. Seventy percent of all illiterates lived in the *sierra*. With respect to access to basic services, 15 percent of all homes in Lima lacked sewage, electricity, and
potable water; in Ayacucho, 81 percent of homes lacked these amenities.

Data compiled on a nationwide basis that demonstrate Peru's status as
a poor nation, then, hide the coexistence of a Lima-based elite, whose
overall standard of living approximates that of the industrialized world,
with a large, rural-based underclass that includes some of the poorest people on earth. This vast socioeconomic cleavage, accentuated by the physical barriers presented by the rugged Andean *sierra,* has led to the common
description of Peru as a "dual society."[7] Modern Peru is concentrated in
Lima, which in many respects continues to act in its role as the colonial
capital founded more than four and a half centuries ago. The poverty-
ridden population of the *sierra,* for its part, retains much of its identity as
a conquered people.

This deep division in Peruvian society continues to be reinforced by
fear and ignorance. *Limeños* today retain many psychological remnants
of the Spanish conquerors' fear that, as they stood with their backs against
the Pacific, the *serrano* population (those from the *sierra*) would descend
upon them to take revenge. Like Lima-based Spanish colonial officials
who were more familiar with the Iberian peninsula than with the Peruvian *sierra,* it is common today to find upper-class *limeños* who feel at
home in Miami, New York, or Madrid, but only rarely, if ever, visit the
Andean interior of their own nation. The integration of the Peruvian population into a single political and economic unit, one in which all can
share in benefits from participation in the nation-state, has proven to be
elusive. The creation of a common sense of Peruvian nationhood remains
one of the great challenges that faces the Peruvian political system.

ETHNICITY

The ethnic composition of the Peruvian population includes Amerindians, mestizos, whites, blacks, and Asians. Blacks and Asians (Chinese
and Japanese) live primarily in coastal cities and, together, comprise less
than 5 percent of the population. Blacks are descendants of slaves brought
from Africa between the late sixteenth and mid-nineteenth centuries.
They were a large segment of the coastal population during colonial
times, but miscegenation subsequently reduced their numbers as an identifiable ethnic group. The ancestors of a large number of Peru's Asian
population had immigrated as railroad and guano workers between the
mid-nineteenth and early twentieth centuries.

Beyond these two groups, ethnic classification is imprecise and is based on social and cultural distinctions as much as it is on "racial type." Peruvians are overwhelmingly mestizo, a term that most often refers to a mixture of Indians, whites, and, to a lesser extent, blacks. Many Peruvians of mixed blood, nevertheless, are considered ethnic Indians within their communities. Even more common are persons who are Indians by descent but are considered to be mestizos when they adopt aspects of Hispanic culture, such as the Spanish language or western dress, or when they move into a Hispanicized urban area. Although *cholos,* as such persons are commonly known, may continue to be referred to disparagingly, their social position within the wider society is clearly improved. They have "passed" from the subordinate social status that may, in the end, be the least ambiguous manner in which to distinguish the indian.

The last Peruvian census that attempted to classify persons according to ethnicity was in 1940, when 53 percent of the population was found to be white or mestizo and 46 percent was found to be Indian. In 1972, respondents were asked to state their language capabilities. Almost 69 percent declared themselves to be monolingual in Spanish; 13 percent spoke only a native American language; and an additional 18 percent spoke both Spanish and a native American language. Bilingual speakers included people of all ethnic groups.

The vast majority of Amerindians spoke Quechua, the language of the Inca empire. The 1979 Constitution declared Quechua, along with Spanish, to be an official national language. Quechua speakers, estimated to total nearly 3 million Peruvians, were found primarily in the central *sierra.* Aymara, the language of the ancient Tiahuanaco culture centered in the Bolivian *altiplano,* was Peru's second indigenous language. Aymara speakers were concentrated in the southern *sierra* around Puno. Lastly, some 200,000 to 250,000 indigenous peoples, divided among more than 50 different language and ethnic groups, were located in the Peruvian *selva.* Most were extremely isolated; their numbers were greatest along the Marañón River.

Ethnicity is also poorly defined between whites and mestizos. Many mestizos "pass" into the white ethnic category by virtue of their acquisition of wealth and prestige. As a result, whites, who used to be touted as comprising 10 to 15 percent of the population, have become increasingly difficult to distinguish as a separate ethnic group. By the 1980s, many Peruvians had stopped referring to themselves in ethnic terms but, rather, made a distinction instead between *criollo* culture, associated with lighter-skinned, coastal peoples, and *serrano* culture, associated with comparatively dark-skinned people. Migration patterns had resulted, nevertheless, in the growing presence of *serrano* culture within the Peruvian *costa.*

SOCIAL CLASSES

To a certain extent, then, Peru's vast socioeconomic inequality parallels ethnic cleavages. Inequality can also be seen in terms of the nation's geographic regions. Perhaps the most useful way of looking at Peruvian social relations, however, is in terms of class structure. In this respect, Peru is not atypical of nations of the Third World that have a tiny elite, a small but diverse middle class, and a vast lower class living in various degrees of poverty. Income distribution data serves to reveal this class structure. In 1961, the top 1 percent of the nation's income earners took in 30.5 percent of all income. The next 19 percent garnered 36.3 percent of national income, leaving a total of 33.2 percent for the remaining 80 percent of the population.[8] Subsequent studies found that government-fostered efforts to improve income distribution between 1963 and 1975 resulted in only minor transfers of wealth downward, and that these were concentrated in the top quarter of the income scale.[9] Because the deterioration of real incomes after 1975 was especially pronounced among those groups within the middle class that had only recently witnessed relative gains, the data for 1961 should offer a rough approximation of Peru's income distribution in 1990.

The Elite

Although their share of national income did not change significantly, the composition of the Peruvian elite did change dramatically during the past quarter century. The wealth of Peru's prior oligarchy, traditionally said to have consisted of 44 families, had been based largely on two types of landholdings. Coastal sugar and cotton plantations produced goods primarily for export markets and were the most modern and dynamic agricultural endeavors in Peru. Landholdings of the *sierra* elite consisted of vast haciendas that depended on the exploitation of Indian labor to raise cattle and grow a variety of crops for the domestic market. By the early 1960s, however, the traditional *sierra* haciendas were rapidly decaying, and the elites of both regions began diversifying their wealth into commercial, industrial, and financial concerns that had emerged in the coastal cities following World War II.

The agrarian reform during the military government of Juan Velasco Alvarado (1968–1975) destroyed what was left of the landholding basis of the Peruvian elite. The military regime, however, also fostered the emergence of a new elite that was based in part on capital that had been salvaged by the traditional oligarchy. The new elites were Lima-based owners of financial institutions, medium-sized mining concerns, urban real estate, firms (particularly in construction) that bid on government contracts, and industrial and commercial firms involved in imports and exports. The wealthiest people controlled conglomerates with holdings in a number of these areas. Peru's largest conglomerate throughout the 1980s was overseen by a partnership between Dionisio Romero and Juan Francisco Raffo, whose families had immigrated from Italy during the late nineteenth century. The holdings of the Romero–Raffo group included majority interest in Peru's largest private bank, the Banco del Crédito, as well as the nation's largest insurance company, vast property holdings, and a number of firms that produced vegetable oils.[10]

During the early 1980s, a shadowy and dangerous new basis for elite status—narcotics trafficking—emerged into Peruvian society. By 1990, the nation's illicit manufacturing and distribution of *pasta de coca* (a semirefined base halfway through the process of manufacturing cocaine) was estimated to net anywhere from $600 million to $1.5 billion annually. By and large, the most important traffickers were foreigners, although among the Peruvian traffickers there were a number who constituted fabulously wealthy "elites," whose illicit gains were sent overseas, invested in local real estate, or used to spread corruption among Peru's judiciary, law enforcement agencies, and other government officials. The power of this new face of the Peruvian elite to corrupt officials at all levels of government made it a major threat to the viability of the political process. This was in marked contrast to the political role that the traditional oligarchy had played in propping up national political structures (see Chapter 6 in this volume).

The Middle Class

The middle class, having been extremely small in numbers before the 1960s, is a relatively new phenomenon in Peru. It is a heterogeneous category that ranges from highly paid managers of major business interests and government agencies to small shop owners and the skilled upper reaches of the industrial labor force. By the 1980s, it captured as much as 20 percent of the total population. The middle class is plugged into modern Peru: like the elite, the people are predominantly urban, educated, and Spanish speaking. Unlike the new elite, however, members of the middle class witnessed a decline in their standard of living during the post-1975 economic crisis. Their gains during the previous decade had been made largely at the expense of the decaying traditional oligarchy. A nationalistic political orientation also distinguishes the middle class from the new elite, whose internationalism derived from their foreign trading and financial links.

The growth in the size of the middle class in recent decades was closely associated with an increase in government employment. By 1990 the heart of the middle class lay among the more than 800,000 persons employed in state agencies, government-owned corporations, schools, and the military. More than half of all public-sector employees were based in Lima. Professionals, managers, owners of small-and medium-sized farms and business concerns were among the elements of the middle class employed in the private sector.

As their fortunes declined during the late 1970s and the 1980s, many wage earners at the lower end of the middle-class income scale assumed an increasing identification with the proletarian lower class. What were to become some of the nation's most militant labor unions were formed among such traditionally middle-class, white-collar workers as bank employees, teachers, and public-sector bureaucrats. The economic crisis also reversed many of the gains that had been made by the organized labor elite during the early 1970s.

The Lower Class

The lower class, making up some 80 percent of the total population, is at least as diverse as the middle class. It encompasses the lower end of the income scale in modern Peru and virtually the entire spectrum of Peru's traditional, agrarian-based society. In the modern sector, it includes petty government officials; the bulk of police officials; conscripts and enlisted ranks within the military; a large majority of the industrial labor force; workers in mines, sugar cooperatives, and other export-oriented concerns; and the vast army of people, estimated at some 85 percent of the work force in 1990, that were either unemployed or underemployed. Many of the latter work marginally as street vendors or in some other capacity within the informal (that is, unregulated and untaxed by the state) economy that has grown into giant proportions in Lima and other cities. The traditional sector includes small private farmers and campesinos working under a variety of communal land tenure arrangements, landless rural laborers, itinerant traders and artisans, and domestic employees, to name some of the significant occupations among this segment of the lower class.

The Peruvian lower class has also undergone dramatic change during the past two decades. Many of the programs of the Velasco regime were ostensibly aimed to benefit the poor, but the lower class saw little, if any, increase in their meager share of national income during the period. Nevertheless, the military regime did provide a measure of hope to the lower class, and it encouraged a level of political activism and organizational capability during the 1970s that these people had never known previously. The most significant change in the composition of the lower class involved movement from the traditional into the modern sector. The marked shift of Peru's labor force from agriculture into the service sector—especially into urban marginal occupations associated with the informal economy—has had a profound effect on the nation's social order.

SOCIAL DYNAMICS: URBANIZATION AND INTERNAL MIGRATION

The process of urbanization in Peru dates from the establishment of Lima and regional colonial outposts in the wake of the Spanish conquest. During the mid-twentieth century, however, the pace of urbanization exploded. Between 1940 and 1981, Peru's urban population grew from being one-third to two-thirds of the national total. When the fact is taken into account that the total population nearly tripled during that period, the growth of Peru's cities becomes truly astonishing.

Lima, with a population in the mid-1980s that represented half the entire urban population of Peru and a nearly tenfold increase over the 645,000 inhabitants recorded in 1940, was the major focus of the urbanization process. Whereas in 1940, Lima contained about one in ten Peruvians, by 1990, it was home to nearly one-third of the national population total. The capital city, having the preponderance of the nation's industrial capacity as well as its best health and educational facilities, became the principal pole of attraction for a great wave of internal migration that took place during those years. The 1981 census found that fully 41 percent of Lima's population was born outside the national capital. The majority of Lima's migrant population came from the *sierra*. Not surprisingly, the areas with the highest rates of out-migration (the departments of Apurímac, Ayacucho, and Huancavelica) are among the poorest parts of the central *sierra*. This pattern of migration was reflected in great regional disparities in population growth. Between 1940 and 1981, Lima's annual growth rate averaged 4.9 percent; the annual average in the *sierra* during that time was a mere 1.2 percent.[11]

Other cities received large inflows of migrants as well. In the *costa,* Piura, Chiclayo, Chimbote, Trujillo, and Tacna were most significant. Nearly 55 percent of Trujillo's population in 1981 consisted of migrants; the comparable figure was 60 percent in Chimbote, a city that had grown from barely 4,000 to over 200,000 inhabitants in a mere 40 years. A number of departmental capitals in the *sierra* were also important recipients of migrants: Arequipa, Huancayo, and Cuzco were each growing at about 6 percent annually.[12]

Although Lima's growth rate slowed to 3.7 percent during the late 1970s, it continued to receive the largest inflow due to the vast size differential between it and the comparatively small cities that were growing more rapidly. The onset of economic decay no doubt put brakes on the "pull factor" that brought migrants to the capital city in search of economic opportunity. The 1980s saw the emergence, nevertheless, of a new "push factor," as large numbers of persons fled the deadly conflict in the *sierra* in which civilians were more often victims than were either the Sendero Luminoso (Shining Path) guerrillas or the military and police forces they were battling.

The absorption of this vast inflow of migrants into Peru's cities presented a number of challenges, both to urban authorities and to the migrants themselves. The need to house the new arrivals was met by the erection of shanty towns, known as *pueblos jóvenes* (young towns) or *barriadas,* on lands on the cities' outskirts that were invaded by migrants and other segments of the urban poor. Early land invasions in the 1940s were resisted by authorities. As time went on, however, authorities began to cooperate in initiating squatter settlements, which came to be viewed as a practical solution to the growing need for low-income urban housing.

Residents of *pueblos jóvenes* paid no rent and were gradually able to convert their flimsy initial shacks, constructed of reed mats, into permanent brick or concrete structures. Schools, electricity, potable water, and other public services most often remained woefully inadequate, however. By the 1980s, nearly 40 percent of Lima's population lived in one of about 500 *pueblos jóvenes* that ringed the city. In Chimbote, the figure was 80 percent or higher.

This rapid urbanization process was closely associated with the development of a vast underground, or informal, economy that operated outside the purview of the organizational and regulatory mechanisms of society. By the early 1980s, the informal sector was estimated to have absorbed between one-third and two-thirds of Peru's total urban labor force.[13] In Lima, the informal sector included nearly the entire network of public transportation; the majority of construction activities; thousands of small manufacturing firms, including the makers of most of Peru's clothing, shoes, and furniture; and a wide variety of ambulatory services and retail commercial establishments found on streets throughout the city. Although a few, such as bus, cab, and manufacturing plant owners, were relatively well rewarded for their participation in the informal economy, nearly all this sector of the work force made incomes so small that they were considered underemployed. They clearly remained on the margins of urban society.

Urban migration, then, did not change the historical reality of a privileged minority coexisting with a marginalized majority. Rather, it simply brought the "two Perus" into closer proximity. In the words of historian David Werlich, "the *barriadas* brought the problems of underdevelopment literally into the backyard of the modern sector of society. The privileged classes no longer could ignore them."[14]

In fact, however, the social needs of the new urban poor continued to be largely ignored. Although the poor were physically integrated, they found that they were barred from economic opportunity within the small formal economic structures. By creating marginal employment for the urban poor, then, the parallel, informal economy served to reinforce society's age-old dualism. By the 1970s, Lima had become a city divided between a relatively privileged formal sector minority and a largely poor informal sector, in which up to two-thirds of the population lived essentially without benefit of the organizational capacity of either labor unions or the state to provide for their economic and social welfare. Other major cities increasingly followed a similar pattern.

In a sense, Peru's modern internal migration represented the fulfillment of the long-envisioned thrust by the conquered *sierra* population into the *costa*. Channeling this demographic transformation toward a positive process of social and economic integration of the "two Perus," and away from a process of social disintegration in the form of the long-feared violent "revenge upon the conquerors" (an alternative made manifest by Sendero Luminoso), presented the Peruvian political system with what was probably its most formidable challenge among the many facing it during the transition to the new millennium.

NOTES

1. Henry F. Dobyns and Paul L. Doughty, *Peru: A Cultural History* (New York: Oxford University Press, 1976), p. 19.

2. Thomas M. Davies, Jr., *Indian Integration in Peru: A Half Century of Experience, 1900–1948* (Lincoln: University of Nebraska Press, 1974), p. 2.

3. Demographic data presented in this section are from República Peruana, Instituto Nacional de Estadística, *Resultos provisionales del censo del 12 de julio de 1981* (Lima: 1981); unpublished estimates by Kevin Kinsella, U. S. Bureau of the Census (Washington, 1985); Population Reference Bureau, *1985 World Population Data Sheet* (Washington, 1985); and Thomas G. Sanders, "Peru's Population in the 1980s," *UFSI Reports,* South America series, No. 27 (Hanover, N.H.: USFI, 1984). At the time of this writing (1990), the crisis-ridden Peruvian government had postponed its 1990 census until 1992.

4. Population Reference Bureau, *1985 World Population.*

5. Sanders, "Peru's Population," p. 8.

6. *Caretas,* May 23, 1987, p. 46.

7. A recent study that makes use of this analysis is by Peruvian anthropologist José Matos Mar, *Desborde popular y crisis del estado* (Lima: Instituto de Estudios Peruanos, 1985).

8. Richard C. Webb, "The Distribution of Income in Peru," pp. 11–25 in *Income Distribution in Latin America,* Alejandro Foxley, ed. (London: Cambridge University Press, 1976), p. 12.

9. See Richard C. Webb, *Government Policy and the Distribution of Income in Peru, 1963–1973* (Cambridge: Harvard University Press, 1977), and Alejandro Figueroa, "The Impact of Current Reforms on Income Distribution in Peru," pp. 163–78 in *Income Distribution in Latin America,* Alejandro Foxley, ed. (London: Cambridge University Press, 1976).

10. Michael Reid, *Peru: Paths to Poverty,* (London: Latin American Bureau, 1985), pp. 87–8. See also Carlos Malpica, *El poder económico en el Perú* (Lima: Mosca Azul Editores, 1989).

11. República Peruana, Instituto Nacional de Estadística, *Resultos provisionales,* p. 12.

12. Sanders, "Peru's Population," p. 5.

13. The extremes of this estimate are reflected in José María Salcedo, "Reportaje: El Perú informal," *Que Hacer* (Lima), October 1984, pp. 74–96, and Thomas G. Sanders, "Peru's Economy: Underemployment and the Informal Sector," *UFSI Reports,* South America series, No. 39 (Hanover, N.H.: USFI, 1984).

14. David P. Werlich, *Peru: A Short History* (Carbondale: Southern Illinois University Press, 1978), p. 23.

2

THE YEARS BEFORE 1919

THE PRE-HISPANIC PERIOD

The lack of a written language among pre-Hispanic inhabitants of Peru and the willful destruction of the cultural expressions of the native population by Spanish conquerors have added to the ravages of time to leave the period during which man occupied Peru before its discovery by Europeans shrouded in mystery. Nevertheless, archeologists have been able to obtain enough evidence, largely from comparatively well-preserved sites along the arid coastline, to indicate a long history of rich and diverse civilizations within the borders of the modern nation of Peru.

The Pre-Incan Period

The earliest evidence of human beings, found in caves near Ayacucho, dates from between 20,000 and 15,000 B.C. The earliest known large-scale regional culture, the Chavín, developed in about 1,400 B.C. Centered near the city of Huaráz, in the department of Ancash, Chavín culture spread throughout much of the central Peruvian *sierra* before declining around 400 B.C. Subsequent Peruvian cultures reflected the extraordinary religious and artistic accomplishments of the Chavín to a remarkable degree. A number of very important regional cultures rose and declined during the next 1,800 years in various areas of Peru.[1] The Moche, or Mochica, centered near Trujillo, emerged at the end of the Chavín period and endured for some 1,300 years. They are best known for their lifelike ceramic images and huge adobe temples in the valley of the Río Moche, where they also built vast irrigation networks that are used to this day. The Chimú, believed to have been descendants of the Mochica, conquered an area during the fourteenth century that extended for 1,000 kilometers along Peru's northern coast. The center of the Chimú (or Chimor) kingdom was at Chan Chan, a city near Trujillo that held between 50,000 and 100,000 inhabitants prior to the kingdom's subjugation by the Incas in 1477.

In the *sierra,* two important cultures—about which very little is known—coexisted between about 600 and 1,000 A.D. The Tiahuanaco was based south of Lake Titicaca and expanded northward into Peru's southern *altiplano,* reaching as far as the southern terminus of the Ayacucho-based Wari cultural area, which extended as far north as Cajamarca.

Inca Rule

The period of the Inca empire was short in comparison to many of its Peruvian predecessors. The rapid expansion of the Inca realm, known as Tawantinsuyu, began at the beginning of the reign of Pachacuti Inca Yupanqui around 1430, little more than a century before its subjugation by the Spanish. The territorial extent of Tawantinsuyu—reaching at one point from southern Colombia to central Chile—was unprecedented, however, and was a tribute to the superior political and military skills of the Cuzco-based conquerors. By the early sixteenth century, more than 70 different political entities had come under the centralized political and religious authority of the Inca ruler, the Sapa Inca, who was portrayed as a direct descendent of the deity of the sun. The forced relocation of many subject peoples and the imposition of the Quechua language throughout Tawantinsuyu gave the empire a certain cultural homogeneity as well, although distinct Quechua dialects in the *sierra* today testify to the cultural diversity that survived Inca imperial rule.

First-rate architects and builders, the Incas have been referred to as the Romans of the Americas. Furthermore, their extraordinary genius for administrative and organizational matters enabled them to incorporate the collective knowledge found within their far-flung empire. The *ayllu,* the basic agrarian social and productive unit found throughout most of pre-Incan Peru, was retained under the direction of a local patriarch, known in Inca times as a *curaca.* A pre-Incan tradition of taxation in the form of forced labor was expanded into a system known as the *mita,* in which Incan rulers required each subject to work for a prescribed time under the direction of the *curaca,* either in domestic service of local elites, in mines, or on such vast public work projects as terracing, irrigation systems, and roads. The vast system of roads built throughout the empire revolutionized communications and transportation in the Andes.

The empire reached its maximum extension under the eleventh Inca ruler, Huayna Capac. His sudden death in Quito in 1525, during an epidemic of what one Spanish chronicler described as "probably smallpox or measles" that had been brought from Panama by Spanish explorers, precipitated a venomous succession struggle between two sons. After more than a half decade of bloody warfare, Atahualpa, who had been born of Huayna Capac's wife in Quito, proved victorious over Huascar, born of another wife in Cuzco, capturing him on the very eve of the arrival of the conquistadores. By 1532, when Francisco Pizarro, a farmer from Trujillo in the rugged Spanish region of Extremadura, arrived at Tumbes, on Peru's extreme north coast, with 180 soldiers, the empire—at the height of its authority only a decade previously—had been devastated by civil war and by the newly introduced diseases that in short order were to kill millions of the inhabitants of Tawantinsuyu.

The Spanish Conquest

Atahualpa, resting near Cajamarca, in the *sierra* of northern Peru, following the capture of his half brother, had known of the arrival of foreign invaders for a number of months. It remains unclear why he did not order the obliteration of Pizarro's forces before their penetration into the heart of the empire. After a march of almost two months, Pizarro arrived in Cajamarca and summoned Atahualpa from the nearby thermal baths known today as the Baños del Inca. Accompanied by several thousand of his best troops, Atahualpa reluctantly went to Cajamarca's central plaza, where he was met not by the conquistadors, but by their chaplain, Fray Vicente de Valverde, who called on the Inca emperor to submit before the representatives of the Spanish Crown and the Christian God. Atahualpa replied contemptuously and threw a Christian prayer book to the ground, whereupon the hidden Spanish soldiers opened fire, killing thousands of Atahualpa's defenders and taking the Inca emperor captive. This slaughter, called "the decisive battle" in the conquest of Peru by historian Hubert Herring, took place on November 16, 1532.[2]

Huascar, who at this time was imprisoned in Cuzco by Atahualpa, was first summoned to Cajamarca and then ordered to be executed, along with hundreds of his nearest of kin, by a panic-stricken Atahualpa out of fear that Pizarro might be planning to depose him in favor of his rival brother. Thus continued the rapid annihilation, through a vicious civil war that now overlapped with the Spanish conquest, of the army and leadership of one of the great polities of modern history. Pizarro was not planning to depose Atahualpa but to execute him, as his mentor, Hernán Cortés, had recently done to the captured Aztec king in Mexico. First, however, Atahualpa filled his cell, once with gold, then twice with silver (estimated at 13,000 pounds of gold and 26,000 pounds of silver) as ransom for his release. He was then betrayed by his captors and decapitated on August 29, 1533, after a mock trial at which he was convicted of every charge that Pizarro could invent for the occasion. Having cut off the head of the Inca empire, Pizarro and Hernando de Soto moved south to

Cuzco—the heart of Tawantinsuyu—which they captured in November 1533.

Scattered resistance to the conquerors continued during the next four decades, but was no match for the superior weapons and military tactics of the Spanish. Disease continued to ravish the native population, which also suffered the loss of most of what remained of its legitimate national leaders as Pizarro captured every member of the Inca royal (Yupanqui) family he could find, killing some and using others to legitimize Spanish rule. The Peruvians were thus unable to mount a unified campaign against the invaders. The most serious Indian rebellion was led by Manco Inca, who, after laying seige to Spanish garrisons in Cuzco and Lima in 1536, established a neo-Inca state in the wilds of Vilcabamba, north of Cuzco. The Vilcabamba state's fourth leader and a descendant of Huayna Capac, Túpac Amaru, was finally captured and brought to Cuzco to be executed in 1572. Only then could the Spanish conquest be considered a certainty.

SPANISH COLONIAL RULE

During the early years of Spanish presence in Peru, the conquistadores also fought among themselves and against the authority of the Spanish Crown. A long-simmering feud between Pizarro and his partner in conquest, Diego de Almargro, led to a pitched battle in 1538 at which Almargro's forces were defeated and their leader was executed. Three years later, Pizarro was assassinated by Almargro partisans. The Crown, unhappy with the strife and its lack of control over its new colony, jailed Pizarro's brother Hernando when he returned to the Spanish court with Peruvian treasures. Francisco's other brother, Gonzalo, was executed in 1548 after he had rebelled against the local viceroy and declared himself governor of Peru. It was not until after the arrival of Viceroy Francisco Toledo in 1569 that the conquistadores were tamed and Peru was converted into an orderly component of the burgeoning Spanish empire.

On January 6, 1535, Pizarro founded the Spanish colonial capital in the valley of the Río Rímac, only a few kilometers from its mouth at the Pacific fishing village of Callao. Named "the city of kings" after the day of its founding, it soon became known as Lima, a corruption of Rímac. Lima was to remain the administrative capital of all of Spanish South America during most of the three centuries of colonial rule. All trade to and from the Viceroyalty of Peru was required to pass through Lima, where merchants who obtained concessions of the royal trade monopoly became a wealthy elite. During the eighteenth century, as part of the Crown's efforts to satisfy growing regional demands for autonomy from Lima and also to slow the growth of contraband trade, Peru was broken up into three separate viceroyalties. The Viceroyalty of Nueva Granada, established in

1717, had its capital in Bogotá, now the capital of Colombia; the Viceroyalty of the Río de la Plata, founded in 1776, had its capital in Buenos Aires, now the capital of Argentina. After that date, the boundaries of the Viceroyalty of Peru corresponded roughly to those of modern day Peru and Chile.

Spanish Colonial Administration

Colonial administrative institutions, highly bureaucratic and staffed with persons appointed by their superiors within the hierarchy, were designed to centralize authority in the Spanish Crown. Below the viceroy, who was the king's representative in Peru, were some 54 provincial authorities known as *corregidores.* These officials, who were the main contact between citizens and the system of colonial rule, were poorly paid and highly corrupt. The considerable autonomy granted local elites by *corregidores* in return for a variety of bribes to supplement their miserable incomes nonetheless became a key to the longevity of Spanish rule in America. Municipal administrative authority was granted to mayors and town councils, or *cabildos,* which consisted of prominent local citizens. *Audiencias* were given judicial and executive powers by the Crown to oversee the operation of the bureaucracy in Peru.

Another set of institutions was designed to control the Indian population and thus reap the benefits from their labors for the Crown. The earliest of these was the *encomienda,* under which Spanish colonists were given authority to collect tribute and exploit the labor of Indians in a specified area in return for responsibilities to protect and convert them to Christianity. Some 500 *encomiendas* were granted as rewards for military and civil services before widespread abuses led to a ban on further grants in 1542. As part of his effort to centralize royal authority in Peru and to stem the abuse of Indians by *encomenderos,* Viceroy Toledo then created several hundred reservations, known as *reducciones,* into which the Indian population was forced to settle. The Inca *mita* system was revived, and the *reducciones* proved to be convenient locations from which to press Indians into service in the colony's rich silver and mercury mines. Another institution, called the *repartimiento,* forced the native population to buy a variety of products that were distributed by royal officials. To facilitate its interactions with the indigenous population, the colonial administration maintained the Inca network of *curacas,* although it replaced many of these local Indian headmen with persons it could trust with such matters as the collection of tribute and recruitment for the *mita.* A small Indian elite was thus maintained, whose status depended on cooperation with the colonial power. As far as the native masses were concerned, the institutional framework set up by their Spanish conquerors was in many ways similar to that in existence during the prior reign of the conquering Incas. The Roman Catholic church initially played a relatively small role in colonial Peru, but it later came to wield enormous influence as a major property owner, a center of social and cultural activity, and the principal institutional ally of the Crown in Peru.

The Colonial Economy

Although the monarchy shared the church's goal of converting souls to Christianity as a means of social control, its overriding concern in its South American colony was the extraction of revenues. The head tax on the indigenous population and the various royal commercial monopolies were important sources of income for the Crown, but the great majority of its income in Peru came from mining activities. Gold and silver bullion from its American colonies brought vast economic power to Spain—if only temporarily—within the practice of mercantilism then prevailing in Europe. Only small deposits of gold were discovered in Peru, but Upper Peru (Bolivia) held a "mountain of silver" at Potosí, which was exploited throughout the colonial period. A second mine, the Santa Bárbara mercury mine in Huancavelica, was also of prime importance due to the need for mercury in the process then used to extract silver from low-grade ores. It was these two mines that made Peru Spain's most valuable territory in South America for more than two centuries.

The availability of a cheap labor supply in Peru was also vital, of course. Few volunteered to work in the mines, where conditions were appalling and thousands died annually from cave-ins, mercury poisoning, asphyxiation, and pneumonia. Nearly all Peruvian miners were Indians subject to the mining *mita,* which was the most onerous of several varieties of obligatory labor. Peru's native population was also subject to labor for the Crown as domestic servants, in agriculture and manufacturing, and on public works, among other activities. It has been estimated that the Indians spent as much as half their time fulfilling such forced labor obligations.[3]

Peru's agricultural development was, by and large, ignored in the Spanish colonial economy; many of the precolonial terraces and irrigation systems were allowed to deteriorate. Although Indian communities were theoretically allowed to keep their lands, in fact, much of the best land was usurped by colonists who supplied foodstuffs to Lima and to mining centers from vast haciendas that were thus created in both the *sierra* and the *costa.*

The Coming of Independence

By the mid-eighteenth century, Peru's rich mines were nearly exhausted, and the once wealthy colony fell into a protracted period of economic decline that was accentuated by the loss of its jurisdiction over Nueva Granada and La Plata. The final century of Spanish colonial rule also witnessed the outbreak of Indian rebellions on a scale not seen since the Vilcabamba revolt of the mid-sixteenth century. The first of these *curaca*-led uprisings took place in the 1730s; their culmination was the widespread revolt during the early 1780s under the leadership of José Gabriel Condorcanqui, a lineal descendant of the last Inca ruler of Vilcabamba who, as such, assumed the name Túpac Amaru II. After vainly petitioning Spanish authorities to reform a number of the most abusive of the colonial Indian policies, Túpac Amaru organized a (largely unarmed) army of 80,000 that quickly held sway from Cuzco south into Bolivia and even northern Argentina. The Spanish authorities wanted nothing of reform, however. In 1781, they captured Túpac Amaru and his family, killing his wife and sons before his eyes; then they publicly dismembered the Indian leader in Cuzco's central plaza by tying a horse to each of his arms and legs and having him drawn and quartered. Enraged by the brutal treatment of their leader, the rebellion quickened, with reprisals and counterreprisals that cost an estimated 80,000 lives on both sides engulfing the entire *altiplano* over the next two years. The rebellion's reformist goals were amplified, meantime, into a call for a complete break with the Spanish rulers.

While the Túpac Amaru II revolt has often been depicted as a precursor to Peru's independence struggle, the bloody uprising also planted an indelible fear within the *limeño* elite of the *sierra* Indian population, and thus contributed to Lima's support of Spain during the early nineteenth century in spite of economic hardship and the growing clamor for independence in the rest of Spanish America. Peru's liberation from colonial rule would come from outside.

The reluctance of Peruvians to confront Spain was also due to a realistic assessment of the presence of some 23,000 royalist troops, by far the largest Spanish military contingent on the continent. The leader of the Argentine independence struggle, José de San Martín, also realized that these troops had to be defeated if his victories in the south were to be secured. In 1820, three years after his heroic march over the Andes to liberate Chile, San Martín set sail with British ex-admiral Alfred Lord Cochrane to attack the Spanish stronghold at Lima. Before their arrival, however, the royalist troops retreated from Lima into the *sierra*. The Argentine general's declaration of Peruvian independence on July 21, 1821, before a public meeting of Lima's *cabildo*, came three years before there were decisive military victories by the patriotic forces.

The battles of Junín and Ayacucho, in Peru's central *sierra*, were the culmination of the struggle for independence—not just of Peru, but of all of Spanish South America. With the mercurial San Martín having quietly withdrawn from Peru after his celebrated July 1822 meeting with Simón

Bolívar in Guayaquil, these battles were fought under the leadership of two Venezuelans, Bolívar, the liberator of Gran Colombia (formerly Nueva Granada), and his protégé, Antonio José de Sucre. Peruvians did finally join in the struggle: they constituted some 4,000 of the patriot army of 10,000 soldiers. Although the December 1824 Battle of Ayacucho dealt Spanish America a fatal blow, diehard royalist forces held out in Callao until January 1826, when the last Spanish flag in Peru was lowered.

THE TURBULENT YOUNG REPUBLIC: 1826–1872

Early Leadership Struggles

Suffering from a power vacuum in the wake of the Spanish defeat and the sudden departure of Bolívar in 1826, the young republic fell into a period of struggle for supremacy among veterans of the war with Spain. Such war heros as Marshals José de la Mar from Ecuador and Andrés Santa Cruz from Bolivia, as well as regional caudillos from Arequipa, Cuzco, Lima, and Trujillo, fought continuously for control of Peru. The turbulence of Peru's early years of independence is evidenced by the rapid succession of presidents: one text on the period refers to over 30 Peruvian chief executives between 1826 and 1845; another alludes to seven presidents seated simultaneously at one point in 1837.[4] Near-anarchic political conditions were compounded by fluid postrevolutionary boundaries. Bolívar's dream of a Federation of the Andes to include Spanish South America as far south as Bolivia was to be short-lived, although subsequent caudillo presidents fought, albeit unsuccessfully, to incorporate Ecuador and Bolivia into Peruvian national territory.

Military prowess was the major political determinant of the day, although Peruvians were also divided over the philosophical underpinnings of the young republic, a division that was reflected in the numerous constitutions of the era. Conservatism in Peru was associated with San Martín's early efforts to establish a monarchy, and its proponents later sought an authoritarian presidential figure; liberals sought a more open political system. Conservative philosophy generally prevailed, although one law associated with liberal thought—Bolívar's 1824 declaration that Indians would be individual owners over their previously communally owned lands—came to have a profound, if unintended, impact on land tenure. Meant to recognize the rights of Indians as citizens and property holders, the law came to be used by unscrupulous rural bosses, known locally as *gamonales,* to coerce and defraud native Peruvians out of their landholdings. *Sierra* haciendas grew to the size of small states, and, given the weakness of central political authority, the *gamonales* acted as virtual dictators over their autonomous private realms.

The Guano Age

Peru's long-stagnant economy was left devastated by the independence struggle, with mines abandoned and the port of Callao in ruins. As early as 1822, Peru had to resort to external borrowing to finance its foreign trade deficit. It remained a backwater nation, poor in resources, until the 1840s, when it began to export a rich fertilizer made of bird dung, called guano, found in vast deposits on the Chincha Islands off its central Pacific coast. The lucrative guano trade was conducted under a monopoly held by the government, which negotiated contracts with (mostly British) firms to load, ship, and market the guano overseas. The government received a fixed share of the sales receipts, along with sizable loans, from the firms under the controversial consignment system that characterized the contracts. As the cash advances multiplied, Peru's prosperity came to be accompanied by a vast increase in its already sizable foreign public debt. The accumulation of this debt, and the general mismanagement of guano receipts, was to yield a government that was bankrupt at the end of the guano boom in the 1870s.

Before its denouement, however, a much-needed period of political stability accompanied the guano-induced economic prosperity. General Ramón Castilla, a veteran of both Junín and Ayacucho, ruled for all but three of the years between 1845 and 1862, a period in which the young republic saw significant gains in the process of nation building. Historian Fredrick Pike, making a connection between the prosperity and the political stability of the guano age, pointed out that the sudden increase in government revenues was used to maintain the first standing national army, to expand the state bureaucracy, to undertake job-producing public works projects, to foster public education, to end the payment of tribute by Indians, and to peacefully abolish slavery in 1854 through the compensation of slaveholders.[5]

The guano age also saw the incipient development of a Peruvian national bourgeoisie. This was partly due to the fact that guano receipts freed the government from the need to tax local commercial endeavors, but it was also attributable to the direct transfer of government earnings to the local elite during the interim presidency of José Rufino Echenique (1851–1854). After the government announced that it would pay domestic debts it had incurred during the three decades since independence, a vast number of fraudulent claims were filed by the president's elite associates and were paid directly from guano receipts. This massive case of corruption played an important role in the early accumulation of capital by the Lima-based coastal oligarchy.[6] By the early 1860s, this emergent Peru-

vian capitalist elite was powerful enough to take over—if only temporarily—the lucrative government guano contracts from European mer-
chant houses.

Spain, which had not yet recognized Peruvian independence, sought to
reassert its influence throughout much of South America during the
1860s. In Peru, it used the 1863 deaths of two Spanish colonists during a
nasty labor dispute on a hacienda in northern Peru as a pretext to demand
a sizable indemnity, then seized the guano-rich Chincha Islands to guar-
antee payment. Following Peru's capitulation and an ignoble treaty with
Spain, Colonel Mariano Ignacio Prado assumed the presidency in 1863
with a promise to avenge Peru's humiliation, and on May 2, 1866, he led
the successful defense against a Spanish naval fleet in Callao. Spain withdrew and shortly afterward finally acknowledged Peru's independent status. Although Peru's victory yielded a rare moment of national unity and
made Prado a national hero, it came at the cost of considerable additional
foreign borrowing to finance the war in the absence of guano receipts. By
the time that Prado's successor, Colonel José Balta, came to power in
1868, Peru's public coffers were nearly empty.[7]

Balta's youthful finance minister, Nicolás de Piérola, believed that self-
sustaining growth could be achieved through public investments financed
by even more borrowing. As only foreign firms held sufficient capital to
accomodate the government's new growth strategy, the guano contracts
with local capitalists were canceled in 1869 and a comprehensive financial arrangement was signed with Dreyfus and Company of France. In return for its monopoly on the European guano trade, Dreyfus agreed to
assume the servicing of Peru's foreign debt and to forward sizable new
loans. With Peru's financial house temporarily in order, Balta began to
spend lavishly on government salaries and a variety of public works. His
most ambitious project was in the construction of railroads designed to
link the nation's mines and southern haciendas with its coastal ports. Additional loans required to pay U.S. entrepreneur Henry Meiggs to build
these pioneering railways through the rugged Peruvian *sierra,* however,
proved ruinous. Public finances were in worse shape than ever when Balta
left office in 1872.

CIVILIANS, MILITARY, WAR, DISASTER: 1872–1895

The emerging civilian export oligarchy, unhappy with the near-mo-
nopoly on political power held by military figures since independence,
had cautiously begun to translate their growing economic muscle into political power. The Dreyfus contract and the spendthrift nature of the Balta
regime accelerated these efforts, and, in 1871, the nation's first political
party, the Partido Civil, was organized to challenge the military for the
presidency in 1872. It proved successful; the Peruvian presidency was

captured by Manuel Pardo, the aristocratic former mayor of Lima and leader of the *civilistas*—that is, members of the Civil Party.

Early Civilian Rule

The 1872 presidential contest, won by Pardo, inaugurated a period that David Scott Palmer has called the "limited liberal state," which lasted until 1919.[8] After a shaky beginning—which was interrupted by the disastrous 1879–1883 War of the Pacific, during which Peru had no fewer than seven presidents—the limited liberal state would evolve after 1895 into Peru's first extended period of stable, civilian rule.

Pardo's four-year term of office coincided with a worldwide recession that brought drastically reduced prices for guano and nitrates, also used in the production of fertilizer, which Peru had begun to export from its southernmost department of Tarapacá. With prices so low, Pardo's nationalization of the nitrate deposits did little to improve the bleak financial picture of the government, which was forced to undertake drastic austerity measures. The civilian bureaucracy was pared down, the size of the military was reduced by three-quarters, and military procurement was cut dramatically. The Dreyfus contract was cancelled in 1875, and the following year Pardo suspended payment on the foreign debt.

Peru's first elected civilian president also suffered a number of military uprisings, the most serious of which was inspired by the intemperate Nicolás de Piérola, who objected both to Pardo's mild anticlericalism and to criticism of his own tenure as finance minister under Balta. The conflict between the *civilistas* and Piérola (who later was to form his own political party and twice become president) was also a reflection of a wider struggle taking place between the emerging coastal export oligarchy and the old *sierra* landed interests. To mollify Pardo's many enemies within the military, in 1876 the *civilistas* named the popular retired colonel and former President Mariano Ignacio Prado to be their candidate. Two years later, former President Pardo was assassinated by an army sergeant, but *civilistas* laid the blame on Piérola's fiery anti-Pardo speeches. This fierce conflict between Piérola and the Partido Civil was not to be resolved until 1895, following the disastrous War of the Pacific and a decade of regression into military rule that came in its wake.

The War of the Pacific

Bolivia, also devastated by the world recession, decided in 1878 to raise taxes on the Chilean nationals who worked the nitrate operations in Antofagasta, its Pacific province bordering Chile. Chile occupied the long-disputed province the following year and, discovering the existence of a secret military alliance between Peru and Bolivia, declared war on

Peru as well in April 1879. Peru, with its military force much reduced and its civilian politicians fighting among themselves, tried unsuccessfully to avoid going to war with Chile, which had recently built up its own navy into a formidable fighting force. Despite the heroics of scores of martyrs, the most prominent of which was Admiral Miguel Grau, who remain highly honored in contemporary civic culture for having given their lives in the cause of the fatherland, the War of the Pacific was a one-sided contest. After Grau's valiant defense of Peru's coast was finally broken, Chilean military forces raided a number of coastal valleys virtually at will and then occupied Lima in January 1881. Its nearly three years of subjugation to Chilean rule were an utter disaster for Peru. While Chileans looted and destroyed its national treasures, commerce was totally disrupted, and the national debt soared.

The Treaty of Ancón finally put an end to the humiliating foreign occupation of Peru's capital city in October 1883. Under its terms, Peru lost its nitrate-rich, southernmost province of Tarapacá, and Chile was to occupy and administer Peru's two provinces to the north of Tarapacá, Arica and Tacna, for ten years. Thereafter, local plebiscites were to determine whether they would remain with Chile or revert to Peruvian sovereignty. No plebiscite ever took place, however, and the matter would not be legally settled.

The war gravely discredited Peru's civilian politicians, and its aftermath saw the return of old patterns of military *caudillismo.* General Andrés Cáceres, who repudiated the Treaty of Ancón and thus became one of the few national heros to come out of the War of the Pacific alive, was elected president in 1886. Initially a popular figure, Cáceres rapidly lost his appeal after inaugurating a series of austerity measures, including the taxation of exporters, that were designed to stabilize the fragile and inflationary postwar economy. His most controversial step was undertaken in order to satisfy Peru's foreign creditors. An 1889 agreement known as the Grace contract (after Michael Grace, the British negotiator) called for the cancellation of Peru's entire foreign debt. In return, British investors received long-term control over Peru's railway system, ownership over a huge tract of land in the *selva,* and all guano not used domestically, as well as 33 sizable annual payments to their newly formed Peruvian Corporation. The Grace contract, only reluctantly approved by Congress, would persist as the bane of Peruvian nationalists for years to come.

As Cáceres lost favor, he became increasingly dictatorial. Having organized the Partido Constitucionalista, the Constitutionalist Party, as a personalist vehicle, he engineered the election of his crony, General Remigio Morales Bermúdez, in 1890. Cáceres's claim to victory following obviously fraudulent elections in 1894 triggered an alliance between Nicolás de Piérola and his old *civilista* foes, who led a bloody popular revolt that ousted the caudillo in March 1895. Piérola's election to the presidency the following July was to usher in a lengthy period of stable civilian rule, something which had thus far eluded the hapless young republic.

THE ARISTOCRATIC REPUBLIC: 1895–1919

The period between 1895 and 1919 is commonly referred to as the Aristocratic Republic.[9] Although this period qualifies as Peru's first extended period of stable, civilian rule, the political reforms that one might term "democratic" initiated during the Aristocratic Republic were limited in scope. Elections, previously conducted within an electoral college, were opened to direct, popular participation. Suffrage, however, was limited to propertied, literate males, and the size of the electorate increased from a mere 4,539 in 1894 to 146,990 in 1904.[10] Furthermore, the absence of secret balloting led to widespread intimidation by local bosses at polling places. Political power was contested among four small parties—the Partido Civil, the weakened Partido Constitucionalista of former President Cáceres, Nicolás de Piérola's Partido Demócrata, and the Partido Liberal of Augusto Durand—that lacked any significant ideological distinction, and created and disbanded alliances among one another as it became useful in the electoral process.

By no means, then, did the Aristocratic Republic constitute a period of popular government: Peru's early civilian regimes were run by and for Peru's upper class. "The battles in which they engaged," notes Jack Child, "had little meaning for the vast majority of Peruvians, for in effect such contests settled only the question of the distribution of power and spoils at the pinnacle of the social structure."[11] The country's poverty-stricken rural masses were ignored, and when the urban poor came under the influence of anarcho-syndicalism during the early twentieth century, they were severely repressed.

The Economic Bases for Elite Rule

The period of the Aristocratic Republic has also been termed the "golden age of the oligarchy." Ruling in conjunction with the military, which began a program of modern professionalization conducted by a French military mission that was first invited by President de Piérola, representatives of the oligarchy (allegedly consisting of 44 powerful families) oversaw independent Peru's second period of economic prosperity. As in the guano age, Peru's wealth at the turn of the twentieth century was based on the exportation of raw materials. The nation's new export boom, however, was based on a variety of products, the most important of which were sugar, cotton, rubber, oil, copper and other minerals, and wool. International commodity prices remained high throughout most of the period, when Peru saw a rapid expansion in both the volume and value of its export trade.

The pinnacle of the export oligarchy consisted of the owners of coastal sugar and cotton plantations. By the 1920s, the north coast sugar industry became dominated by the huge irrigated plantations owned by the Gildemeisters and the Graces, immigrants from Germany and Ireland, respectively. Cotton plantations were generally smaller and were located in the southern *costa,* as well as in the north. While these coastal operations were mechanized agroindustries, wool was produced on feudal-like haciendas in the southern *sierra,* though it became an export commodity thanks to modern railway links. In the *selva,* a rubber boom from 1880 to 1915 created a small Iquitos-based oligarchy.[12]

Peru's major mineral concerns came under the control of foreign interests during the period. In 1901 a group of North American businessmen bought out a number of small copper mines in the central *sierra* and founded the Cerro de Pasco Corporation, which oversaw the tripling of Peru's copper production in a decade. Peru's early production of petroleum was centered in the rich La Brea y Pariñas field near Talara, in the extreme northern *costa.* In 1890 a Peruvian entrepreneur sold the field to a British firm that, in 1913, began negotiations for its sale to Standard Oil of New Jersey.

Commercial and industrial activity, particularly small textile and food and raw material processing plants, also grew in Lima during the golden age of the oligarchy, though not with the dynamism of the export trade. Much of this growth could also be attributed to foreigners: David Werlich reports that 451 of the 542 largest commercial and manufacturing firms in Lima were foreign owned by 1896.[13] The presence of United States firms was still minor, however, having a book value of only $6 million in 1897.

The Demise of the Limited Liberal State

For most of the period, the political domination of the oligarchy went unchallenged. Piérola's term in office (1895–1899) was followed by the orderly succession of four elected chiefs of state (Eduardo López de Romaña, Manuel Candamo, José Pardo, and Augusto B. Leguía) in and out of the presidency. The pattern was broken during the presidency of the millionaire businessman and fiery populist, Guillermo Billinghurst. Named by Congress in 1912 after a tumultuous election that was disrupted by Billinghurst's supporters, his 16 months in office saw the first widespread activity by organized labor in Lima. Using the incipient labor movement as a political base, Billinghurst oversaw the passage of the country's first laws to regulate labor relations. When stymied by opposition in Congress, he encouraged street demonstrations in support of his policies. Horrified by this breach of the monopoly on power by the aristocracy, the elite closed ranks against Billinghurst, who was ousted by troops under the command of Colonel Oscar R. Benavides in February 1914. The truncated Billinghurst regime was a precursor of future political patterns of popular resistance to elite rule and of military intervention on behalf of elites.

After an interim period of military rule, José Pardo, the son of the founder of the Partido Civil, was brought back for a second crack at the presidency in 1915. Pardo's second term in office was highlighted by growing unrest, both among the students of the University of San Marcos, whose demands included representation in governing the university (a right the Reform Movement at Argentina's University of Córdoba had gained in 1918), and by an increasingly militant labor movement, which in January 1919 organized Peru's first general strike in support of an eight-hour workday.

The 1919 elections were held in an atmosphere of economic decay, social disorder, and disarray within the Partido Civil. Former President Augusto B. Leguía, who in 1908 had run as a *civilista,* now ran as an independent. When the electoral board, which had long been packed with *civilista* partisans, made moves as if it were going to take an apparent victory from Leguía, the second coup d'état in half a decade, this one led by the venerable General Cáceres, placed Leguía back into the Pizarro Palace. It was to spell the end of the Aristocratic Republic and the beginning of an 11-year dictatorship (called the *oncenio*) that would mark a watershed in the evolution of the Peruvian political process. The demise of the political parties associated for a half century with the limited liberal state would be complemented during the Leguía *oncenio* by the birth of new, mass-based political organizations that had little in common with the elitist organizations of the past.

NOTES

1. A good discussion of the most important pre-Incan cultures is found in Henry F. Dobyns and Paul L. Doughty, *Peru: A Cultural History* (New York: Oxford University Press, 1976), pp. 26–45.

2. Hubert Herring, *A History of Latin America,* 3rd ed. (New York: Alfred A. Knopf, 1968), p. 139.

3. David P. Werlich, *Peru: A Short History* (Carbondale: Southern Illinois University Press, 1978), p. 45.

4. The first figure is from Werlich, *Peru,* p. 69; the second is from Jack Child, "Historical Setting," pp. 3–58 in *Peru: A Country Study,* ed. Richard F. Nyrop (Washington: U.S. Government Printing Office, 1981), p. 21.

5. Fredrick B. Pike, *The United States and the Andean Republics* (Cambridge: Harvard University Press, 1977), p. 85.

6. Thomas E. Skidmore and Peter H. Smith, *Modern Latin America* (New York: Oxford University Press, 1984), p. 193.

7. Dobyns and Doughty, *Peru,* pp. 178–81.

8. David Scott Palmer, *Peru: The Authoritarian Tradition* (New York: Praeger, 1980), pp. 58–62.

9. Palmer (ibid., p. 60, fn) attributes this term to Jorge Basadre, who is perhaps the most important Peruvian historian of the republican period.

10. Ibid., p. 59.

11. Child, "Historical Setting," p. 27.

12. See Michael Reid, *Peru: Paths to Poverty* (London: Latin American Bureau, 1985), pp. 25–7.

13. Werlich, "Peru," p. 127.

3

THE EVOLUTION OF THE MODERN POLITICAL SYSTEM: 1919–1968

THE LEGUÍA *ONCENIO* AND THE BIRTH OF THE MODERN POLITICAL PARTIES

The *oncenio* proved to be an important period of transition for the nation's political institutions. The elitist democracy of the Aristocratic Republic died as Leguía closed Congress, ended local elections, and promulgated a new constitution in 1920 to legitimize his seizure of power. The old political parties withered from irrelevance as Leguía perpetuated his dictatorship through periodic constitutional amendments, fraudulent elections, and the jailing or exiling of his opponents. The anarchist-oriented student and labor groups that had become quite active in the latter years of the Aristocratic Republic were harshly repressed by Leguía, but new organizations arose that would lay the bases for vital elements of Peru's modern labor and political party organizations. It was thus at a time when a personalistic dictatorship had undermined the institutional basis of the state that mass-based political organizations were able to challenge the long-held domination of the state apparatus by the elite.

Haya de la Torre and the Birth of APRA

Political dissent was most intense at the University of San Marcos in Lima, where a group of students from the northern city of Trujillo, led by Víctor Raúl Haya de la Torre, organized Peru's First National Congress of Students in 1920 and proved successful in extracting a number of government concessions based on the university reform agenda. The students also formed bonds with the working class, which witnessed gains during the early 1920s as well, although not without the loss of a number of lives at the hands of authorities. Hundreds of student activists were also sent to prison or into exile between 1919 and 1923. Haya de la Torre was exiled after leading a particularly vigorous anticlerical protest in May 1923 against a ceremony at which Leguía planned to dedicate Peru to the Sacred Heart of Jesus. He wound up in Mexico City, where in May 1924, he founded the Alianza Popular Revolucionaria Americana, or APRA.

Haya's early writings, reflecting his radical stance as a student leader and his upbringing in Trujillo, where foreign-controlled sugar interests had caused severe social dislocations, were stridently anti-imperialist and frankly Marxist.[1] His 1924 visit to the Soviet Union, however, convinced Haya that its revolutionary experience was not applicable to Latin America, where an entirely different set of historical and social circumstances prevailed. He then developed an elaborate theory of history, based on Einstein's theory of relativity and Toynbee's conception of the perspective of a historian, which was a variation on Marx's dialectical materialism. Called "historical time space," Haya's theory argued that each of the world's continental people had its own, unique, development process that was determined by its particular historical space and historical time. Latin America (which Haya called "Indo-America" to stress its Indian social character) would thus fail if it attempted a European political economic system, because neither capitalism, nor socialism, nor fascism was suitable to Indo-America's historical time space.

APRA, then, was conceived as a continent-wide movement. The party's early continental doctrine, called the Maximum Program, called for action against United States imperialism, the political unity of Latin America, the nationalization of lands and of industries and the "internationalization" of the Panama Canal, and solidarity with all oppressed peoples of the world. The Minimum Program, which would be put forth by the Peruvian Aprista Party in 1931 (when Haya foresaw each nation of Indo-America having its own *aprista* party) called for the organization of agricultural cooperatives, the decentralization of the Peruvian economy, and the institution of economic planning by a National Economic Congress composed of representatives from labor, management, professional organizations, and government. Haya's call for reforms to benefit the working class included ideas that were quite radical to Peru in the 1920s: APRA promoted trade union organization, minimum salaries, regulation of child labor and the length of the workday, and a program of social security. The enactment of the APRA program, according to Haya de la Torre, would constitute a revolution in which the Peruvian middle and lower classes, together with progressive intellectuals, would combat the oppression of the local landed oligarchy and their allies, the foreign imperialists. Haya de la Torre largely ignored any racial considerations in Peru's egregious social inequality.

Export-Led Growth

A more than doubling of the volume of exports during the 1919–1930 *oncenio* allowed Peru to maintain its current account balanced at a time of steadily declining prices for its export commodities. A rush of new foreign investment, particularly from the United States, responded to the political stability under Leguía and his regime's generous tax incentives to play an ever-larger role in the nation's export industries during the 1920s. By 1930, U.S. direct investment totaled no less than $200 million. British investment in Peru also reached its peak in 1925 at $125 million.[2]

In the words of Charles T. Goodsell: "The Oncenio was the original golden age for American business in Peru. . . . Speaking fluent English and at home with the American business mentality, Leguía developed personal friendships with all executives in Peru and actively encouraged them to expand their operations."[3]

The most significant U.S. inroad during the period was the acquisition from its British owners of the La Brea y Pariñas oil concession by the International Petroleum Company (IPC), a Canadian-based subsidiary of Standard Oil of New Jersey. Almost before the ink was dry on the purchase agreement, Leguía's critics accused the dictator of a shameful surrender of Peru's resources to the giant U.S. multinational, arguing that IPC had obtained the right to exploit far more territory than had been included in the British concession.

Unlike his predecessors in the Aristocratic Republic, Leguía viewed the state as performing an important function in the promotion of economic development. In addition to encouraging foreign investment, Leguía placed a major emphasis on public works programs. Vast sums were spent on major expansions of the nation's ports, highways, and railways, as well as on programs of urban beautification. Most of the funds were borrowed from overseas, with the result that Peru's foreign debt increased from $10 million to over $100 million during the *oncenio*. Borrowed funds, together with the expansion of raw material exports, gave the nation a sense of prosperity that would collapse along with the world financial and commodity markets in October 1929.

Mariátegui and the Birth of Peruvian Socialism

APRA, meanwhile, quickly gained a large following among Peru's workers and progressive intellectuals, including a young writer and journalist of humble origins named José Carlos Mariátegui. During the heady mid-1920s, both Haya and Mariátegui were steeped in the writings of Karl Marx, as well as those of Manuel González Prada, a Peruvian writer and political polemicist who, before his death in 1918, had become the nation's first major proponent of social revolution. In 1928, however, when each was 33 years old, an irreparable breach opened between Haya and Mariátegui, which was recorded in a series of letters. Mariátegui criticized Haya for transforming APRA from an "alliance" into a "party" without consulting "the members of the vanguard who work in Lima and the provinces," the failure of APRA to use the term "socialism," and its similarity to Italian fascism. Haya replied by extolling Mariátegui to

be realistic and try to take your discipline not from revolutionary Europe but from revolutionary America. You are doing a great deal of damage because of your lack of calm and your eagerness always to appear European within the terminology of Europe. . . . We shall accomplish the revolution without mentioning socialism, and by distributing land and fighting imperialism.[4]

Mariátegui's orientation toward European socialism was not the only source of their disagreement. He also felt that Peru's middle classes, which Haya saw as exploited and thus potential revolutionaries, had no place in a revolution that would come about from a socialist alliance between Peru's workers and campesinos.

In 1928, shortly after his break with APRA, Mariátegui and a small group of associates set up the first cell of the Socialist Party of Peru (PSP), which the following year brought a number of the country's major labor unions together into the General Confederation of Peruvian Workers (CGTP). Despite chronic medical problems, which necessitated the amputation of one of his legs, Mariátegui also continued to work tirelessly as a writer and social critic, and he is best remembered today for his *Seven Interpretive Essays on Peruvian Reality* and for having edited *Amauta* magazine. He died in 1930 at age 35. A month later, the PSP changed its name to the Peruvian Communist Party (PCP), which, together with the CGTP, was the original basis for the nation's Marxist political organizations. In the same year, in the wake of the fall of Leguía, the Peruvian Aprista Party was also legally constituted.

The End of the *Oncenio*

Long-postponed boundary treaties had been signed with Brazil and Bolivia in 1909, during Leguía's initial presidential term. Two more of Peru's modern boundaries were formally established during the *oncenio.* Peru's border with Chile, which had been left unsettled since the War of the Pacific, was finally settled by the June 1929 Treaty of Lima, which awarded Tacna to Peru and Arica to Chile. The two nations also agreed that neither could cede territory to any third nation (e.g., Bolivia, which lost Antofagasta and thus its access to the Pacific at the hands of the Chileans) without the consent of the other party to the treaty. Leguía also presided over the 1922 signing of the Salomón-Lozano Treaty that fixed the modern boundary with Colombia along the Putamayo River. While the Treaty of Lima was well received, it took years for the unpopular Salomón-Lozano Treaty to be ratified in the Peruvian legislature. It was no coincidence that one week after the territory, whose prize was the Amazon port of Leticia, was formally transferred to Colombia in August 1930, Leguía was ousted from power. In August 1930, a military revolt led by Colonel Luis M. Sánchez Cerro brought down the Leguía regime, whose externally oriented economic base had been shattered by the onset of the Great Depression. This coup also brought a 35-year period of minimal military interference in politics to a close. The overriding political dynamic of the next several decades would be the periodic intervention by the armed forces to prevent the rise to power of Peru's new mass-based political parties.

APRA VERSUS THE ARMED FORCES: 1930–1968

A few short weeks after having assumed power, the Sánchez Cerro regime crushed CGTP strikes in the petroleum and mining industries, and the leadership of the PCP was forced underground. These Marxist-oriented mass organizations would not play a significant role again until the 1970s. APRA, on the contrary, would burst quickly onto the political scene, then remain a vital political participant throughout those four decades. Its repeated efforts to gain power, through both legal and extralegal means, were nonetheless to prove fruitless.

The *Aprista* Revolt

APRA doctrine, although calling the party "revolutionary," did not prescribe a means of achieving power, and the party's attitude with respect to the democratic process has remained ambiguous ever since its founding in 1924. An outright revolutionary movement during its formative years under the Leguía dictatorship, APRA then competed in the October 1931 elections convoked by Sánchez Cerro to legitimize his seizure of power. The official results in that contest showed 155,378 for Sánchez Cerro to 106,551 for Haya; APRA has claimed ever since that 50,000 APRA votes were arbitrarily nullified, and nearly all historical accounts corroborate this allegation of Haya de la Torre's having lost the presidency in 1931 only on account of massive official fraud. Thus denied victory in the presidential balloting, APRA nevertheless gained 27 seats in the Chamber of Deputies. Fearing this opposition, Sánchez Cerro closed down APRA offices nationwide in December 1931, and soon thereafter he deported Haya, as well as all the APRA deputies.

The party's angry response consisted of an escalating cycle of violence that included the near-assassination of Sánchez Cerro and a failed mutiny by APRA partisans within the navy. The violent aftermath of the 1931 elections culminated in the tragic events of July 1932 in Trujillo, where armed *aprista* militants seized local offices of representatives of the central government, including police and military compounds. Government reinforcements sent to retake Trujillo arrived shortly after 60 military personnel had been murdered in their cells. Enraged, the military rounded up citizens of Trujillo and took them to the nearby pre-Incan ruins at Chan Chan, where they were summarily executed. Estimates of the dead in the Trujillo massacre range between several hundred and 5,000. The event poisoned relations between APRA and the armed forces for nearly a half century. This enmity was to play into the hands of the elites, who secured a powerful ally in their efforts to keep APRA out of the presidential palace. For 21 of the next 24 years, APRA was to remain officially outlawed, and the leadership of what remained Peru's principal political party was persecuted to varying degrees under different regimes.

A second *aprista* attempt in April 1933 to assassinate Sánchez Cerro proved successful, and Congress moved quickly to appoint General Oscar Benavides to serve the remainder of the presidential term. After Benavides appointed pro-fascist José de la Riva Agüero as prime minister, APRA was outlawed and its leadership was jailed and harassed. Haya de la Torre went into hiding, and *aprista* plots against the government continued to surface on occasion. Although proscribed from participation, APRA supported the independent candidacy of Luis A. Eguiguren in 1936. When it became apparent that APRA's man was going to win, the vote count was suspended and Benavides simply extended his presidential term for three more years.

Economic Reorientation and Political Reconciliation

The economy underwent a reorientation of sorts during the 1930s. The depression and the 1931 moratorium on servicing the debt accumulated by Leguía led to a pause in new foreign investments that would persist through World War II, and Peruvian entrepreneurs made inroads into export industries, particularly in mining, that had previously been under foreign control.[5] Export prices began to recover after 1933, while government interventionist policies promoted the textile industry, as well as other small manufacturing concerns. The steady growth of exports continued to promote a moderate economic growth into the early 1940s, when the government's participation in the economy would reach a new height in its vast scheme to transform the tiny coastal village of Chimbote into a major industrial complex capped by the nation's first steel mill.

After nearly a decade of military rule, the government's candidate in 1939 was Manuel Prado Ugarteche, a well-known member of the civilian oligarchy. With the nation's only organized political party still proscribed, he was an easy victor. APRA remained formally outlawed during Prado's six-year term of office, but it was allowed to function informally, and the persecution it had suffered under Benavides ceased. In recognition of the rising danger posed by European fascism, APRA took the first of several turns to the ideological right; it dropped much of its anti-U.S. rhetoric and assumed the name Partido del Pueblo in order to deemphasize its "revolutionary" activities of the past two decades.

The Communist Party also resurfaced after it was declared legal by Prado; a number of its leaders were appointed to government posts and others were elected to Congress. Jorge del Prado was able to organize the First Congress of the Communist Party of Peru, and the Party also established the Confederación de Trabajadores del Perú, or Confederation of Peruvian Workers (CTP), but APRA soon gained control of this largest of the nation's labor confederations.

Prado's reconciliation with the long-repressed mass-based political parties was due to a wide variety of factors, including APRA's ideological turn to the right and the cooperative spirit of the PCP that reflected the wartime alliance between the United States and the Soviet Union. Political reconciliation was also given a boost by the fact that APRA's principal political enemy, the armed forces, were not undertaking a direct role in governing. In 1941, instead, they were busy in the pursuit of their professional task of making war. The favorable outcome of this brief war with Ecuador also generated widespread nationalistic support for President Prado.

War with Ecuador

The war, like most armed conflicts among Latin American nations, was the product of an inadequate boundary definition at the dawn of the republican era. Nearly the entire length of their common border, involving the possession of some 170,000 square miles of territory, was left under dispute. For almost the entire colonial era, this territory had been a part of the Audiencia of Quito, a jurisdiction that corresponded roughly to postindependence Ecuador. Peru's claim, based on *uti possedetis,* stemmed from Spain's transfer of this Amazonian region to the Viceroyalty of Peru in 1802. Ecuador based its claim on an 1829 treaty between Peru and Gran Colombia that recognized the pre-1802 boundary as the basis for that between the two newly independent nations. Ever since Ecuador's declaration of independence from Gran Colombia in 1830, it has argued that it should properly assume the rights and obligations of this 1829 treaty.

The issue had smouldered ever since, during which two efforts at arbitration, one by Spain between 1887 and 1910 and another by the United

States beginning in 1924, had proceeded fruitlessly. The latter had yielded only diplomatic invective, followed by a series of scattered border clashes beginning in 1938 and then, in 1941, full-scale war. Each nation claimed the other fired the first shot, although, from the moment of the war's outbreak on July 5, the Peruvian forces were completely dominant on several fronts. By the time a cease-fire was called on July 31, Peru's troops were on the doorstep of Guayaquil, Ecuador's principal port city. In January 1942, Peru and Ecuador signed a Protocol of Peace, Friendship and Boundaries at a meeting of Foreign Ministers of the American Republics held in Rio de Janeiro. The United States, Argentina, Brazil, and Chile acted as mediators and, subsequently, as guarantors of the Protocol of Rio de Janeiro. Under intense pressure from the United States which, one month after the bombing of Pearl Harbor, was anxious to project an image of hemispheric solidarity, Ecuador surrendered some 5,000 square miles of territory to Peru and renounced its claim to about 80,000 additional square miles. Soon, however, Ecuador regretted having signed the protocol, calling it an "illegal imposition." In 1945, it protested by obstructing the demarcation of the final 78 kilometers of the new border. While Peru considered the Rio protocol to be definitive and binding, Ecuador continues to the present day to claim some 100,000 square miles in Peru's northern departments of Loreto, Amazonas, Cajamarca, Piura, and Tumbes, an area that appears as Ecuadoran territory on every map produced there. The majority of Ecuador's ongoing claim lies in a wedge-shaped region of Loreto between the Marañón and Napo rivers, an area that includes the city of Iquitos. Before long, this territorial dispute would again become the cause of armed clashes.

The *Trienio* of Bustamante

In 1945 the Partido del Pueblo was at last legalized, and Peru witnessed its first freely contested presidential election since 1931. Rather than running independently and thus inviting a coup, APRA joined a broad-based coalition called the National Democratic Front that elected José Luis Bustamante y Rivero, a popular jurist and intellectual, to the presidency by a wide margin. His term, a *trienio,* lasted for three years. Being the largest coalition partner, APRA anticipated a major governing role within the cabinet. When it received no ministerial posts, however, the party used its congressional representation (it had won 40 percent of the seats in Congress) and its numerous mayoral positions to press the party's agenda and obstruct the president's policy agenda.

The appointment of *apristas* to three cabinet posts in 1946 brought temporary peace between the executive and the legislature, but deeply disturbed the military and shifted the political battle to within the cabinet, where the new ministers disagreed with the president in a broad range of policy matters. Finally dismissing *aprista* cabinet officers in 1947, Bustamante accused APRA of "wanting to institute a single party dictatorship."[6] In order to prevent the passage of APRA's legislative program, non-*aprista* congressional delegations, on both the left and the right, boycotted the 1947 session of Congress. Legislation was issued that year by executive decree.

Meanwhile, Bustamante continued the interventionist economic policies pursued by his predecessor. Foreign currency exchange was rationed, and the rate of exchange between the dollar and the Peruvian sol was fixed. Import controls, heightened export taxes, and other measures designed to reduce the economy's dependence on foreign trade aroused the wrath of the export oligarchy, which waged an increasingly vigorous campaign against the government in the elite-owned press. Inflation soared along with government spending and wage settlements won by the APRA-controlled labor federation, the CTP.

While President Bustamante's efforts to institute a progressive domestic agenda were thwarted by unrelenting political and economic adversity, his 1947 decree giving Peru exclusive jurisdiction over the Pacific waters within 200 nautical miles of its coastline proved to be a lasting contribution in the arena of foreign affairs. Although it was to cause conflict with the United States for a quarter century, Peru's "200-mile thesis" was to be widely adopted by other maritime nations, even gaining the acceptance of the United States in 1977, and then became embodied in Peru's 1979 Constitution. As the president's popularity dwindled, he disassociated himself further from APRA in early 1948 by dismissing local governments that were under the party's control, and increasingly employed the military as both cabinet members and strikebreakers. The battered party became divided, and impatient "revolutionaries" began to plot the overthrow of the government. Their efforts culminated in a poorly coordinated revolt led by *aprista* naval officers in Callao in October 1948 that was quickly put down. Although APRA was immediately made illegal, and its members were rounded up and its offices were ransacked, the military accused the president of being "soft on APRA." Three weeks after the Callao mutiny, Bustamante was overthrown by his minister of government, General Manuel A. Odría, and sent into exile. It was an action that received the blessing of the disgruntled coastal elites.

The Odría Dictatorship

The installation of a military junta under the leadership of General Odría launched a dictatorship that was to last for eight years, an *ochenio*. The Odría rule occasioned the return of direct military rule, harsh repression of APRA, and an outward economic orientation in which Peru's export oligarchy and foreign capital investors were the major beneficiaries.

The junta ruled with full executive and legislative authority from 1948 to 1950, which it justified by the need to return order in the wake of three years of chaos under the failed Bustamante experiment in democracy. In 1950 Odría engineered sham elections in which he was the only presidential candidate and his supporters gained a wide majority in a Congress that was used to rubber-stamp the president's dictatorial rule during the next six years.

The Odría *ochenio* reversed Peru's postdepression economic orientation and inaugurated what Rosemary Thorp and Geoffrey Bertram called "a remarkable twenty-year period of total integration into the international system . . . in which the entry of foreign capital and the repatriation of profits were virtually unrestricted and in which government intervention and participation were kept to a minimum."[7] Payments were made on the foreign debt for the first time since the fall of Leguía, and investments and loans poured in from abroad.

A series of investment promotion laws, the most important of which concerned petroleum, electricity, and mining, also helped establish stable and profitable conditions for foreign capital. Investments by U.S. firms more than doubled during the period. The Marcona Mining Company and the Southern Peru Copper Company were among the larger firms to open operations in Peru during the *ochenio.* The IPC greatly expanded its operations, as did two of the oldest U.S. firms in Peru, Cerro de Pasco and Casa Grace. A 1954 study of W. R. Grace's oldest subsidiary found that "there is hardly a Peruvian participating in the money economy who does not eat, wear, or use something processed, manufactured, or imported by Casa Grace."[8]

Copper, which soared in price during the Korean war era of the early 1950s, led a major export boom. Currency devaluation and generous tax concessions also benefited local exporters, and fishmeal—ground up anchovies used as fertilizer—became a major export industry under the control of Peruvian entrepreneurs.

The persecution of APRA marked the entire *ochenio,* but it was especially fierce during its early months, when *aprista* militants were hunted down and jailed by the thousands. Haya de la Torre eluded capture, but was forced to spend more than five years in the Colombian embassy compound before being allowed to flee into exile in 1954. He was not to return to Peru until 1962. The APRA-controlled CTP was suppressed, and the Communist Party, although officially outlawed, was allowed to gain control over a number of *aprista* unions. Odría made concerted efforts to lessen the mass appeal of APRA through a variety of populist measures aimed at the working class. The social security system was broadened, wages were raised on various occasions, labor-intensive public works projects were undertaken, and squatters rights were granted to the residents of Lima's *barriadas.* The dictator's wife undertook well-publicized charity programs in an effort to emulate Evita Perón, her contemporary Argentine homologue. Female suffrage was granted in 1955 as part of a wide-ranging campaign to gain support among women.

Odría's popularity rested on the economic prosperity generated by the export boom, however, and suffered dramatically from the fall in prices following the end of the Korean conflict in 1953. Pressure for the dictator to step down built up within a wide spectrum of society, united within the National Coalition under the leadership of industrialist Pedro Rosselló, and led Odría to call elections in 1956. Wanting very much to determine the outcome, Odría supported conservative candidate Hernando de Lavalle. This "official" candidate faced the opposition of another conservative, former President Manuel Prado, and, on the left, a fast-rising newcomer from Arequipa, Fernando Belaúnde Terry, then the dean of the school of architecture at the University of San Marcos. APRA was not allowed to field a candidate, but shortly before the election, its leaders met with Prado and Odría to forge a pact designed to scuttle the anticipated victory of Belaúnde. Under the terms of the so-called Monterrico Pact, Odría switched his support to Prado, apparently in return for an agreement not to investigate corruption during the *ochenio,* while APRA was promised legal recognition in exchange for its endorsement. This last-minute deal, denounced by anti-*apristas* and many of APRA's idealistic militants as well, brought Prado a 110,000 vote margin of victory over Belaúnde.

Whether due to a growing conservatism accompanying the aging process or a belief that victory through the electoral process was imminent, the APRA party that reentered the legal political ring in 1956 had lost its revolutionary fervor. Official *aprista* doctrine now emphasized anti-Communism, while downplaying its revolutionary and anti-U.S. aspects. Between 1956 and 1962 and again from 1963 until 1968, APRA's congressional delegations would ally themselves with Peru's most conservative political parties. Military coups d'état in 1962 and 1968, nevertheless, were to continue to deny Haya de la Torre the electoral path to the presidency.

Prado and the 1962 Coup d'Etat

Following the 1956 elections, then, *aprista* congressmen cooperated with Prado in passing conservative legislation, while the party's labor leaders restrained the strike activities of the CTP. In return, Prado dismantled the repressive apparatus of the Odría dictatorship, granted APRA a general amnesty, and retained the party's legal status. APRA's *convivencia* ("living together") with Prado caused a crisis within the party: most of its youth wing left the party and formed APRA Rebelde, which a few years later would take up armed struggle in the *sierra.* While

APRA's second period of cooperation with Prado thus came at the high cost of its hard-earned revolutionary legitimacy, it also brought the party to the brink of earning the presidency in 1962.

Prado's second term in office was plagued by economic problems. Odría's emphasis on exports and foreign investments was retained, unwisely, at a time of recession in the United States, and thus sowed fiscal and balance of payments crises that were compounded by a series of natural disasters. Obligatory austerity measures bred widespread discontent, which escalated in 1959, when IPC was granted a gasoline price hike following a decade of aggressive lobbying by the multinational oil giant. Outbursts against IPC had been commonplace during the decades since 1922, when the Leguía regime had first granted it the controversial drilling concession in Peru's northern oil fields. During the 1960s, however, this long-standing conflict would finally come to a head.

By 1962 the Peruvian electorate sought an alternative to the conservative approaches of the previous 14 years. The election offered two: Belaúnde, who had transformed his Arequipa-based Frente Nacional de Juventudes Democráticas (FNJD) into the nationally organized political party, Acción Popular (AP), and Haya de la Torre, who returned to Peru to run for the presidency for the first time since 1931. Odría, who organized the personalistic Unión Nacional Odriísta (UNO) out of his old populist coalition of elites plus the well-orchestrated political machines in poor communities, offered himself as the candidate of the conservatives. Belaúnde had broadened his appeal since his 1956 defeat through a nationwide campaign that attracted a variety of new followers, including disaffected *apristas,* and was confident of victory. The election results, nevertheless, showed Haya with 558,237 (32.98 percent), Belaúnde with 543,828 (32.13 percent), and Odría with 481,404 (28.44 percent).

The election law stated that if no candidate received 33.34 percent of the popular vote, the victor was to be decided in Congress. Political maneuverings quickly grew to a level even more intense than those in 1956: Belaúnde raised charges of fraud engineered by the government on behalf of APRA, while Haya became convinced that the military was not going to allow him to assume the presidency and so cut a deal to support his former archenemy, Odría. Instead of raising APRA's image with the military, however, this ploy served to discredit Odría among his former colleagues. A month after the election, amid mounting tensions and demands by Belaúnde that the election be annulled, the armed forces obliged by overthrowing Prado and pledging to hold new elections the following year.

The July 1962 coup represented a new kind of military intervention into Peruvian politics. Although largely motivated by *antiaprismo,* as in 1948, this was the first coup undertaken on behalf of the military as an institution—which ruled for a year through a four-man junta consisting of its top commanders—rather than in the name of a particular leader. The interim military regime was also of a different ideological cast from those preceding it. While civil and political rights were generally respected, measures were undertaken in economic planning and agrarian reform that foreshadowed the nationalistic and reformist policies of the post-1968 military regime.

The Promise of Belaúnde

The June 1963 elections, conducted without allegations of major fraud, brought a narrow victory to Belaúnde, now aligned with the Christian Democratic Party (PDC) and also receiving a considerable number of votes from the anti-*aprista* Marxist left, which gained 36.2 percent against Haya's 34.4 percent and 25.5 percent for Odría's UNO. In congressional elections, however, APRA gained more seats than AP in the Chamber of Deputies, and in the Senate AP won only two seats more than APRA. Seeing this, together with the respectable showing of the *odriistas*, APRA revived its 1962 agreement with Odría, strengthening it into a congressional alliance that, having a majority in both houses of Congress, was able to control the legislative process.

This *superconvivencia* between APRA, which did not want Belaúnde to receive credit for a reform program similar to the one it had unsuccessfully sought for more than three decades, and the conservative UNO, which wanted nothing of reform, served until the waning months of Belaúnde's five years in office to block much of the president's legislative agenda.[9] Capping 12 years of APRA's open collaboration with the oligarchy, the alliance also furthered the party's loss of its legitimacy as a mass-based revolutionary force and led to added disillusionment within its membership. The cynicism of the *superconvivencia* also aggravated *antiaprismo* within the military, particularly among a growing reformist wing, which grew increasingly skeptical of the possibility of social reform being achieved within the confines of a stalemated constitutional political process.

Belaúnde was born in Lima into an aristocratic family in 1912. His father was a diplomat who, in 1945, became prime minister under President Bustamante y Rivero. Fernando's secondary schooling was in Paris; he then studied architecture at the University of Texas. His political career had begun in 1945, when he was elected to the Chamber of Deputies as a member of Bustamante's coalition. During these early years of his career, Belaúnde also authored a number of books, the best known of which is *The Conquest of Peru by the Peruvians,* outlining economic and fiscal reforms and a wide variety of public works projects that he was later to introduce when he was president. An inveterate campaigner, he had traveled to remote regions of the nation to rally audiences in 1962 and 1963, in classic populist style that included personal charm, dazzling oratory, and a charisma that earned him renown among his countrymen as "the last caudillo."

AP ideology was deliberately vague, and changed over the years. It claimed to be populist, although it was widely identified with the middle classes, whose interests it has favored in practice. In the 1960s AP was commonly described as center-leftist. Party manifestos called for state planning and the incorporation of Peru's eastern jungle region into the nation through highway building and other public works, including thousands of small self-help projects that Belaúnde dubbed *cooperación popular.* During his successful 1963 campaign, Belaúnde promised a "revolution without bullets" and the development of the nation's full potential through such programs as agrarian reform and opening the Peruvian interior to modern development. If such ideas could be incorporated into an ideology, it might have been described as developmentalist and technocratic: above all, Belaúnde believed that pragmatic planning would lead to solutions, achieved through the application of technical expertise, to Peru's development problems.

In his successful electoral campaign, Belaúnde had promised a government that would build on the incipient reformism of the interim military regime. His vision for Peru was also profoundly nationalistic, seeking to recapture the greatness achieved by the Incas and to integrate the *sierra* and the *selva* into national life. Belaúnde's political vision was sincerely democratic, and he promoted that vision in 1963 by presiding over the first municipal elections held in Peru since 1923. The state's role in the economy was increased, but, on the whole, economic reform was minimal and export performance continued to be the key to growth as in the past.

The centerpiece of Belaúnde's early legislative efforts, agrarian reform, was far from a radical proposal, and by the time the APRA-UNO congressional delegation had its input, there was almost nothing of substance left. In the end, its major effect was to legalize the land seizures by several thousand families that had taken place prior to the legislation's implementation in 1964. Almost no land was actually transferred under the new law.

Rural Rebellion and Colonization

The failure of the agrarian reform program of the Belaúnde government took place amid a severe crisis in the agrarian-based socioeconomic system in the *sierra,* which had been suffering a decline ever since the rise of the dominant position of the coastal export oligarchy in the early twentieth century. Land distribution had become even more unequal over generations as campesinos subdivided their small shares among their heirs, and by the late 1950s desperate groups of peasant farmers had begun seizing lands within the *sierra*'s huge, increasingly underutilized haciendas. The most successful of these efforts was in La Convención Valley, north of Cuzco, and had been led by a Quechua-speaking Trotskyite named Hugo Blanco.

Although his capture and imprisonment by the military government in 1963 brought this episode to a close, Hugo Blanco, together with the Cuban Revolution and the *foco* guerrilla war strategy of Ché Guevara and Regis Debray, who believed that small guerrilla bands could mushroom into armies as they gained the support of the local campesino population, were to inspire other youthful radicals to take up his cause in 1965. Luis de la Puente led the Movement of the Revolutionary Left (MIR), formerly APRA Rebelde, which opened one *foco* in La Convención and another in the high jungle of the central department of Junín. A third *foco* in northern Ayacucho department was opened by the National Liberation Army (ELN), led by a disaffected PCP leader, Héctor Béjar. Poor preparation, however, together with a lack of coordination between the two groups and an almost total failure to gain the sympathies (or even learn the language) of the local population, doomed their efforts. By January 1966, de la Puente had been killed, Béjar imprisoned, and the guerrilla threat from the *sierra* neutralized.

Despite the military's victory, the brief and bloody war had a profound effect on the reformist element within the armed forces, which became convinced that the threat of a much wider conflict persisted as long as the structural inequalities that caused campesino unrest were not addressed by the government. The perception of this threat, especially within the army, was to play a major role in the justification of the coup d'état in 1968.

Another effort by Belaúnde to tackle the problems associated with land scarcity was a wide-ranging scheme to colonize the *ceja de la selva* in Peru's vast eastern jungle. In this vision of "Peru's own conquest," the colonization of the *selva* would untap new sources of natural resources and increase agricultural production at the same time that it would stem the historical concentration of population and economic resources in Lima and serve a geopolitical purpose by populating this massive, empty region that bordered Brazil. Transportation links were vital to the effort, and the construction of the so-called marginal highway, which spanned the country from north to south through the *ceja de la selva,* became a personal obsession for *el arquitecto,* as Belaúnde was commonly known. Ironically, his efforts proved to be less successful than those being pursued at the same time on the other side of the border in Brazil. "By the early 1970s," according to Stephen Gorman, "many Peruvians had become convinced of Brazilian expansionist tendencies, or at a minimum were concerned with the longstanding pattern of Brazilian political, economic and even demographic penetration of neighboring countries in an almost osmotic fashion."[10]

Economic and Political Headaches

Belaúnde's difficulties in financing his massive public works projects were compounded by the United States' withholding of development loans as part of an effort to pressure Peru for a settlement of the long-simmering controversy over the IPC concession. Belaúnde's own vacillation and procrastination during the protracted contract negotiations, meanwhile, added fuel to the spreading fire of Peruvian nationalism building throughout the 1960s. Thus, largely denied low-interest loans available through the Alliance for Progress, he was forced to borrow from relatively expensive private foreign bank sources. The quadrupling of Peru's external debt during Belaúnde's five years in office, to $750 million by 1968, contributed heavily to mounting economic difficulties.

Budget deficits that averaged no less than 17 percent over the five years added to inflationary pressures, and in September 1967, in a move that aroused widespread opposition, the sol was devalued by 40 percent against the dollar. Efforts to raise taxes were blocked by the APRA-UNO congressional opposition. To make matters worse still, the country's fishmeal industry, which in a short space of time had become the world's largest, was devastated in 1965 by the sudden disappearance of anchovies from Peruvian waters, and an international recession in 1966–1967 yielded still lower export revenues.

As pressing fiscal problems mounted during his last two years in office, *el arquitecto* lost interest in their solution and retreated instead into an even greater obsession with his public works agenda.[11] Likewise, he was apparently oblivious to the growth of corruption in the awarding of public works contracts and of a major smuggling operation being directed by civilian and military officials in his government. By 1968, Belaúnde's regime had become tainted by a number of such scandals.

Mounting economic and political difficulties caused both parties within the governing coalition to suffer major factionalizations. In December 1966, conservatives within the Christian Democrats, led by Luis Bedoya Reyes, who were opposed to government policies that they felt inhibited private enterprise, left the party to form the Popular Christian Party (PPC). The suddenly liberalized PDC left the governing coalition shortly afterward. Then, in September 1968, the liberal wing of AP, led by Edgardo Seoane, who had been the architect of the government's original agrarian reform program and was slated to be AP's presidential candidate in 1969, announced his break with Belaúnde in a nasty dispute that featured a public brawl between the party's two factions over physical control of the party's headquarters on Lima's Paseo Colón.

The rift within AP, as well as the ouster of *el arquitecto* by the military a month later, were sparked by the August 1968 Act of Talara, an agreement signed with IPC after five years of difficult negotiations. Controversy over the Act of Talara's allegedly favorable terms for IPC turned to scandal in September, when the politically ambitious head of the Peruvian state petroleum corporation, who had acted as one of the treaty's chief negotiators, publicly charged that the government had suppressed a secret page of the document in which favorable concessions were granted to IPC in its purchase of crude oil from the company he headed. Although it was never conclusively determined that the missing "page 11" really existed, a storm of protest erupted over Belaúnde's alleged surrender of the national patrimony to foreign interests that sent the already weakened government back on its heels. On the morning of October 3, it fell in a bloodless coup led by army commander Juan Velasco Alvarado.

The 1968 Coup d'Etat

The reasons for the coup were complex and went well beyond the "page 11" scandal. The internal security concerns of the reform-minded segment of the military that was to play a major role in the early years of the military regime have already been mentioned. Another motive often cited by observers was a desire to quash anticipated investigations of corruption by military officers. A fourth motivating factor was the military's anticipation of an *aprista* victory in the elections scheduled for June 1969. The disarray within APRA's primary electoral opponents, AP and the Christian Democrats, while APRA itself had been able to retain a sizable and loyal following despite its many political gyrations over the years, left little doubt as to the validity of this prognosis.

APRA's cynical use of alliances with other political forces, regardless of their ideological beliefs, in order to achieve its own goals, also had a profound affect within the military. As if APRA's alliance with the UNO had not been bad enough, in early 1968 it suddenly dropped this alliance and, apparently aiming to shore up the faltering government so that it would not succumb to a coup before the 1969 elections, dropped its opposition to Belaúnde. The military officers who masterminded the coup that brought down the Belaúnde government had thus become convinced that the political party system had become both dysfunctional and inimical to Peru's progress.

The persistence of *antiaprismo* within the military, then, was one of a number of factors motivating the October 1968 coup. A myopic analyst might view it simply as another in a long line of episodes since 1931 in which the military exercised a veto over the assumption of power by APRA. The military regime that assumed power in 1968, however, was to be unlike any other in Peru's long history of governments by military men. Many givens in the nature of Peruvian political dynamics— including the military's refusal to allow APRA into the presidential

Peru

palace—were soon to fall by the wayside, as the country was about to embark on an era of profound change.

NOTES

1. Peter F. Klarén, *Modernization, Dislocation, and Aprismo: Origins of the Peruvian Aprista Party* (Austin: University of Texas Press, 1973) is an excellent study of the conditions in northern Peru that influenced Haya's early thought.

2. Figures on the book value of foreign investment are from Frederick B. Pike, *The United States and the Andean Republics* (Cambridge: Harvard University Press, 1977), p. 193.

3. Charles T. Goodsell, *American Corporations and Peruvian Politics* (Cambridge: Harvard University Press, 1974), pp. 39–40.

4. Quoted by Jorge Basadre in his "Introduction" to José Carlos Mariátegui, *Seven Interpretive Essays on Peruvian Reality,* Marjory Urquidi, trans. (Austin: University of Texas Press, 1971), pp. xxii–xxiii.

5. Rosemary Thorp and Geoffrey Bertram, *Peru, 1890–1977: Growth and Policy in an Open Economy* (New York: Columbia University Press, 1978), pp. 147–8.

6. Alvaro Rojas Samanez, *Partidos Políticos en el Perú,* 3d. ed. (Lima: Centro Documentación Andina, n.d.), p. 126.

7. Cited in Thorp and Bertram, *Peru, 1890–1977,* p. 205.

8. Cited in Goodsell, *American Corporations,* p. 52.

9. The term *superconvivencia* is used by Jane S. Jaquette in her excellect overview of Belaúnde's first term, *The Politics of Development in Peru* (Ithaca, N.Y.: Latin American Studies Program, Cornell University, 1971).

10. Stephen M. Gorman, "Geopolitics and Peruvian Foreign Policy," *Inter-American Economic Affairs,* Vol. 36, No. 2 (Autumn 1982), p. 73.

11. Pedro-Pablo Kuczynski, *Peruvian Democracy under Economic Stress: An Account of the Belaúnde Administration, 1963–1968* (Princeton, N.J.: Princeton University Press, 1977), p. 282. Also see David P. Werlich, *Peru: A Short History* (Carbondale: Southern Illinois University Press, 1978), p. 288.

4

MILITARY REFORMISM: 1968–1980

THE NEW GOVERNMENT

The coup d'état destined to launch 12 years of military rule, like its predecessor in 1962, was no *cuartelazo* (barracks uprising) in favor of a particular military leader but, instead, was made in the name of the armed forces as an institution. Positions of authority within the Revolutionary Government of the Armed Forces (as the new government dubbed itself) were thus allocated strictly according to military rank and seniority.

Institutional Basis

Division General Juan Velasco Alvarado, who was both general commander (comandante general) of the army and chairman of the joint military command at the time of the coup, was named president of the republic immediately after the Revolutionary Junta assumed control of the government. The junta, in turn, was composed of the (new) general commander of the army, Division General Ernesto Montagne Sánchez, plus the general commanders of the navy, Vice Admiral Raul Ríos Pardo de Zela, and the air force, Lieutenant General Alberto López Causillas. The president's cabinet was headed by General Montagne, and the ministries were each led by senior generals or admirals. Although the 1933 Constitution was never formally abrogated, the junta issued a Revolutionary Statute of Government immediately upon assuming office that disbanded Congress and all popularly elected municipal governments, and outlined a system of military rule by decree under which Peru was to be governed during the next 12 years.[1] The military made an effort to transform the judicial branch of government as well. In a belief that the judiciary had been corrupted under the influence of dishonest civilian politicians, hundreds of the most notorious judges were forced into retirement. Little structural reform ensued, however, and before long the judges installed by the military were no less corrupt than those whom they had replaced.

Ideological Basis

The October 3 coup was not planned and executed by the entire military institution, of course, but by a handful of progressive-minded generals and colonels who sought to impose a "revolution" that would end what they viewed as the historical predominance of foreign economic interests and the local oligarchy in the political and economic life of the nation. On the day of the coup, the new regime issued a manifesto in which it promised to reverse the "unjust social and economic order which places . . . the national wealth solely within the reach of the privileged, while the majority suffer the consequences of a marginalization injurious to human dignity."[2] In addition to being progress-minded, the government's early communiqués reflected a high degree of nationalism, proclaiming a desire to end the dependency of the Peruvian economy on factors under the control of foreigners and to pursue an autonomous developmental process within a framework that was "neither capitalist nor communist, but Peruvian."[3]

The need to preserve the institutional integrity of the armed forces proved to be a major constraining factor on the Revolutionary Government of the Armed Forces.[4] The fact that President Velasco, who led the coup d'état and later acted as a moderating force among various ideological factions, was the military's highest ranking officer contributed greatly to the regime's remarkable success in this effort. Promotion schedules were strictly observed, and cabinet posts and other top administrative positions were distributed according to seniority and in a manner that gave representation to ideological moderates and conservatives (found primarily in the air force and, especially, the navy) in addition to the radicals, most of whom were found in the army.

The radicals retained their predominating influence throughout the early years of the regime through their majority within the Council of Presidential Advisors (COAP). Consisting of 15 high-ranking military officers whose head was granted ministerial status, COAP screened all proposals for decree laws submitted by the ministries, then revised them before being presented to the full cabinet and President Velasco for final action. COAP was to remain a vitally important body throughout the military *docenio,* or 12-year reign, spearheading some of the most profound political and economic transformations ever to impact the Peruvian landscape.

MILITARY NATIONALISM

Widespread public skepticism over the progressive intentions announced by the military regime at the time of the 1968 coup was quieted on October 9, when Velasco annulled Belaúnde's agreement with IPC and ordered troops to occupy the company's oil field and refinery complex at Talara. The sudden IPC expropriation, an action that decisively resolved a problem that had been a cause célèbre of Peruvian nationalists since the 1920s, brought a great burst of public support for the new regime. This reserve of popular backing was to be an important element in creating the political space that enabled the Velasco government to pursue its far-reaching reform agenda over the next half decade.

The Role of Foreign Investment

The IPC was only the tip of the iceberg in a growing political controversy over the role of foreign investments in Peru. Part of the problem was their historical association with the two most durable dictatorships of the twentieth century, the Leguía and Odría regimes, when the vast majority of new foreign investment took place. In larger part, the problem stemmed from a growing willingness of the government of the United States to take an active stance as an advocate of U.S. business interests in Peru, and thus threatening Peru's sovereignty over its own economic decision making. This had been clearly illustrated in the IPC case. A third problem was the sheer magnitude of the presence of multinational—particularly U.S.-based—firms in Peru. By 1970, more than 300 U.S. firms operated in Peru, accounting for some $700 million, or two-thirds of the total direct foreign investment in Peru. U.S. firms mined nearly all of Peru's minerals and marketed much of its cotton and sugar output. Foreigners controlled most of the modern manufacturing industries and railroads in Peru, more than 80 percent of the oil industry, its major telephone and electricity firms, and a considerable portion of the banking system.[5] Peruvian entrepreneurs justifiably complained that the nation's most profitable business concerns were monopolized by foreigners, thus leaving little for themselves.

The Velasco regime made an unprecedented raid on foreign-based private business concerns in Peru, taking over more than a dozen companies—which were owned by some of the largest U.S.-based multinational firms—and engaging in a wide variety of economic activities. Expropriations were designed to limit or remove foreign participation in certain strategic aspects of the economy, such as agriculture, banking, telecommunications, and the marketing of petroleum and minerals.

Compensation, for the most part, was generous. Standard Oil, which the Peruvian government claimed owed some $700 million in unpaid back taxes, was never directly compensated for its loss of IPC, however, nor was W. R. Grace compensated for the loss of its Peruvian properties. Eleven other expropriated U.S. firms, including subsidiaries of International Telephone and Telegraph, Chase Manhattan Bank, Anderson Clayton, and Cerro de Pasco, received generous compensation from the Peruvian government, thanks to an agreement reached with the United States in 1974. Marcona Mining Company, whose Peruvian assets were taken over in 1975, was also compensated for its loss with a mutually agreeable sum of money.

At the same time, the Velasco regime sought to encourage foreign investments in other areas of the economy, particularly manufacturing, within its strict new foreign investment guidelines. Not surprisingly, these efforts had a limited amount of success, although a number of significant new investments were forthcoming. Most notable was Occidental Petroleum Company's 1971 entry into oil exploration in the northern jungle region. Another U.S. giant, the Southern Peru Copper Company, dramatically increased its investments in Peru during those years. In sum, net direct foreign investment (that is, after subtracting the considerable sums paid as compensation to the expropriated firms) totaled no less than $400 million between 1968 and 1975.[6]

Independent Foreign Policy

The restructuring of Peru's relationship with foreign-owned business enterprises under Velasco was mirrored in the regime's pursuit of an "independent" foreign policy, free of Peru's historical ties of dependency, especially with the United States. While the expropriation of IPC served to legitimize the military regime within Peru, its high profile within the United Nations, the Nonaligned Movement, and various multilateral regional organizations brought it considerable international prestige as a champion of Third World nonalignment. Peru was especially active within the United Nations Conference on Trade and Development (UNCTAD), which during the early 1970s was making a bold effort to forge a "New International Economic Order" in order to improve the benefits attained by the Third World's participation in the international economy. Peru's new activism was rewarded in 1971 by being elected to a two-year term on the U.N. Security Council.

The Velasco government was also outspoken in its criticism of the dominant position of the United States within inter-American multilateral organizations. It sought unsuccessfully to have the headquarters of the Organization of American States (OAS) moved from Washington to Latin America and to have Cuba's full membership rights in the OAS reinstated. The 1975 inauguration of the Latin American Economic System (Sistema Económico Latinoamericana, or SELA)—a Caracas-based body with 23 Latin American nations as founding members, and excluding the United States—was, in large measure, a response to the criticisms of the OAS voiced by Peru and others during the early 1970s. The Velasco government also sought, without success, the modification of the 1947 Rio treaty on collective hemispheric security in order to reduce the legal authority of the United States to intervene in the hemisphere, as well as a reorganization of the Inter-American Development Bank aimed at reducing U.S. power there. Emphasis was also given to regional integration efforts. While the unwieldy Latin American Free Trade Association (LAFTA, which in 1980 would become the Asociación Latinoamericana de Integración, or ALADI) languished during the 1970s as a testament to the diversity of its 11 member nations, Peru concentrated its efforts at regional integration on the more homogeneous, six-member Andean Common Market (Ancom), which was founded in 1969 and headquartered in Lima. Peru played a leading role during the Velasco years in Ancom's establishment of trade liberalization among member nations, common external tariffs, joint industrial planning, and common treatment of foreign capital. Peru reaped considerable benefits from its participation in Ancom in the early 1970s, including a sizable increase in its nontraditional exports to fellow members and regional support, through Ancom's Decision 24, for its own restrictive stance toward foreign capital. These benefits were not shared equally by all Ancom participants, however, and by mid-decade a growing ideological diversity in the region that resulted in varying responses to the onset of the economic crisis throughout the region brought about a gradual loss of influence of the once-promising Andean Common Market.[7]

The 200-Mile Territorial Sea

It was the Velasco regime's advocacy of Peru's 200-mile territorial sea, however, that crowned its patronage of so-called Third World issues. The concern was not new to the military government, of course, but dated back to President Bustamante y Rivero's unilateral declaration of 1947 (see Chapter 3 in this volume). Five years hence, Peru had joined Chile and Ecuador in signing the Declaration of Santiago, in which they proclaimed exclusive jurisdiction over waters up to 200 nautical miles off their contiguous Pacific coastlines. Peru subsequently encouraged other coastal nations to support its "200-mile thesis," while it engaged in on-again, off-again "tuna wars" with the Western Hemisphere's strongest fishing power, the United States. In 1954, Peru had begun seizing foreign fishing boats that lacked permits to operate within 200 miles of its coast. On repeated occasions, fishermen (who were encouraged to test the Peruvian thesis by the United States, which upheld a 3-mile concept of territorial sea until the mid-1960s, when its own fishing industry successfully lobbied for a 12-mile zone off the U.S. coast) were towed into Callao or Chimbote and forced to pay fines and/or purchase proper licensing.

In 1970, a year after the Velasco government inaugurated a new round of seizures of U.S. ships, Peru and eight other Latin American nations raised the stakes by asserting a 200–nautical mile territorial sea in the Declaration of Montevideo. The "tuna wars" reached a climax in January 1973, when seizures of California-based boats escalated, adding to existing bilateral tensions over negotiations for compensation for expropriated U.S. business interests and the growing Soviet presence in Peru to nearly cause a rupture in diplomatic relations. A reopening of discussions cooled tempers, however, and the inauguration of the U.N. Conference on the Law of the Sea later that year brought the dispute, which had gained ever-widening interest over the years, into a global forum. The final adoption of a universal 12-mile territorial sea and a 188-mile exclusive economic zone by the Third Conference on the Law of the Sea in 1982 would vindicate Peru's position over the previous 35 years.

Foreign Military Relations

Persistent tensions between the United States and Peru, stemming from the "tuna wars" and from prolonged negotiations over the IPC concession, then compensation for expropriated U.S. firms, had a profound effect on bilateral military relations. This was especially evident with respect to military procurement by Peru's armed forces, in which the United States had held a virtual monopoly until 1967. In that year the Peruvian air force, which had grown sensitive about the approval process associated with United States aid programs after having economic aid through the Alliance for Progress withheld between 1963 and 1965 pending a settlement of the IPC case, lost patience with the sluggish U.S. government procedure to approve their purchase request for F-5 jet fighters, cancelled the order and purchased the first of a number of Mirage jets from France. In 1969, after Peru's seizure of several U.S. fishing boats, the United States banned all arms sales to Peru. Given Peru's almost complete reliance on imports for its military hardware, the Velasco administration moved quickly to find new suppliers. Britain, West Germany, and Italy quickly joined France as major arms suppliers of Peru during the 1970s. Beginning in 1973, the Soviet Union became Peru's most important arms supplier, however. During the next 12 years, the Soviets sold no less than $1.6 billion worth of military equipment, including Su-22 jet fighters, to Peru. Most of the sales were on concessionary terms.[8]

U.S. military sales to Peru resumed on a small scale in 1973, following the resumption of discussions to resolve the "tuna wars" dispute and compensation claims of U.S. companies whose properties had been expropriated. Annual military aid, in the form of Foreign Military Sales credits on the order of $10 million (used primarily to purchase spare parts for old U.S. equipment) and International Military Education and Training grants of about $800,000, continued throughout the remainder of the military regime.[9]

ECONOMIC REFORM: FROM A MIXED ECONOMY TO STATE CAPITALISM

The Mixed Economy

The initial goal of the military reformers was to create a mixed economy, in which a "socially responsible" private sector would coexist with an expanded public sector, and a so-called social property sector. The latter, modeled after the collective, worker-managed enterprises in Yugoslavia, was envisioned as eventually becoming the major form of ownership in Peru. Although this plan was relatively successful in Yugoslavia, Peru's "social property" sector received neither public support nor necessary financial backing from the government, and so the mixed economy was never instituted on a large scale in Peru.

Another innovation in labor-management relations, known as the industrial community, was much more successful. Under the provisions of a 1970 law, each private firm was to create an industrial community, through which workers were given gradually increasing participation in the company's management and an increasing share, up to 50 percent, of its ownership. Although hostile owners pursued a variety of means to evade this legislation, by 1975 there were some 3,500 industrial communities with a total of about 200,000 members, or fully 38 percent of the industrial labor force, which held an average of 13 percent of their company's ownership shares.[10]

Government incentives for the private sector to move its capital from agriculture into industry were key to its efforts to promote industrialization and to encourage private investment. Other factors, including the industrial community law and an employment stability law that made it extremely difficult to fire workers after they had been on the job for three months, as well as the general environment of increased state intervention in the working of the economy, however, only contributed further to a reluctance of Peru's private sector to invest that had persisted since the 1950s.[11]

It was the expanded public sector that witnessed truly impressive growth under the military governors. By the mid-1970s, the public sector accounted for 45 percent of total investments and no less than 21 percent of the economy's output. The latter figure was twice the level of the state's participation in the economy in 1968, leading some analysts to conclude that the most salient result of the economic reforms of the Revolutionary Government of the Armed Forces was the development of a system of state capitalism.[12] Numerous laws decreed the increase in state participation in particular sectors of the economy such as fishing, mining, and finance. The most far-reaching legislation was the 1970 General Law on Industries, which gave the state a monopoly in a number of industries, including steel and nonferrous metals, chemicals, cement, and paper, and which also limited the participation of foreign capital within local industrial firms.

Growth of the State

Prior to the Velasco regime, the Peruvian government had been extremely limited in the scope of its activities. Until the 1960s, for example, the economic activities of the Peruvian government had been limited to state monopolies in the exploitation of guano and in the marketing of salt and coca, as well as a handful of state banking, steel, and energy enterprises established to provide low-cost inputs to the fledgling private industrial sector. Public services in health, education, and social security had remained among the least developed in the hemisphere.

During the 1960s the government began to take a more active interest in social and economic management. The founding of the National Planning Institute in 1962 signaled the first attempt by the government to engage in comprehensive economic planning. It was not until the creation of the Banco de la Nación in 1964 that the central government began collecting its own taxes; before that time, this vital fiscal function had been carried out by a consortium of private banks that gained a handsome commission for providing this service to the state. The government's budget for education also increased dramatically during the first Belaúnde presidency, when a national housing agency was also created and other social measures were undertaken that, although modest in scope by modern standards, represented a marked increase in the social responsibility historically assumed by Peru's public sector.

It was during the Velasco regime, however, that the government witnessed its greatest period of expansion. This growth was linked less to an expansion of the social programs initiated by Belaúnde than to the rapid increase in the government's direct participation in the economy, largely through its acquisition of assets from the local and foreign-owned private sectors. One source placed the growth in the number of minority- and majority-owned state enterprises from 18 in 1968 to 174 in 1976.[13] Another source placed government employment in 1977 at 500,000—not counting 85,000 in the armed forces and about 140,000 in the state enterprises.[14]

By 1975, publicly owned state enterprises accounted for fully 20 percent of all industrial production, two-thirds of the banking system, and over half of all output from mining. In addition, the state held a monopoly on the refining and marketing of oil, controlled the marketing of all agricultural products and of most export products, and ran the nation's electrical and telephone systems, as well as its ports, airports, railways, and one of its two major airlines.[15] According to E. V. K. Fitzgerald, "In 1975, in round figures, the public sector handle[d] nine-tenths of exports and half of all imports on the one hand and [was] responsible for about two-fifths of employment and one-third of output in the modern sector on the other."[16] In all, more than one-half of Peru's total capital formation was in the hands of the public sector by the mid-1970s. The largest of the state enterprises in 1976 are listed in Table 4.1.

The acquisition of state enterprises during the late 1960s and the early 1970s was conducted in a rather haphazard manner. The military governors lacked an overall plan—whether to promote economic development through the expansion of state capitalism, to generate income for the government from profitable concerns, or to control particular strategic industries. Nationalism was clearly one motivating factor, as some of the largest of the acquisitions were made from foreign firms. Most of the new government enterprises were created from assets acquired from domestic interests, however; the sources of many—most notably the fishing enterprises—were bankrupt local firms that, continuing to operate at a loss under public ownership, would become major contributors to the state's increasing fiscal burdens.[17] The growth of the government's economic role during the 1970s also took the form of an increase in state regulation of the private economy. Well-intentioned efforts with such aims as upholding the welfare of company workers and ensuring the proper collection of taxes were foiled, however, by the government's inability to enforce its own regulations. Administrative incompetence and corruption, a prolonged economic crisis that dawned in the mid-1970s, and the vast increase in the growth rate of Lima's population were all to blame for the failure of the government to fulfill its regulatory functions.

As the legal red tape involved in opening and operating a business grew more burdensome, the vast majority of new private ventures ignored the regulations and operated outside the legal framework. This so-called informal or illegal sector soon came to account for the vast majority of activity in a large number of sectors of the economy, including transportation, retailing, and construction, employing well over half of the labor force. Many thousands of small and medium-sized businesses, therefore, paid no taxes, ignored labor regulations, and confounded official statistical and planning efforts. Thus, ironically, at the same time that the governmental role in the economy increased significantly, its perusal over a vast portion of the economy, and hence the effectiveness of its macroeconomic policies, weakened to a considerable degree.[18]

Table 4.1
Major State Enterprises, 1976

NAME (product)	PREVIOUS OWNER (if acquired)	DATE OF FOUNDING OR ACQUISITION (if known)
Mining		
Petroperú (oil)	International Petroleum Co.	1969
Centromín (copper)	Cerro de Pasco	1973
Hierroperú (iron ore)	Marcona Mining	1975
Mineroperú (exports)		1970
Minpeco (marketing minerals)		
Agriculture and Fishing		
Pescaperú (fishing and fishmeal)		1973
Epsep (fishing services)		
Simaperú (dockyards and shipbuilding)		1972
Ecasa (rice marketing)		1970
Enci (food marketing)		1970
Manufacturing		
Siderperú (steel)		
Indumilperú (military industries)		
Transportation and Tourism		
Aeroperú (airline)		1972
Compañía Peruana de Vapores (shipping)		
Enafer (railways)	The Peruvian Corporation	1972
Enatruperú (municipal bus service)		
Enturperú (state hotels)		
Foptur (tourism promotion)		
Corpac (airport authority)		
Communications and Utilities		
RTP (Radio, television, cinema)		
Compañía Peruana de Teléfonos (telephone)	ITT	1973
Entelperú (telecommunications)	ITT	1973
Electroperú (electrical supply)		
Electrolima (electrical supply)		
Sedapal (water and sewerage)		
Banking		
Banco Continental (commercial)	Chase Manhattan Bank	1969
Banco de la Nación (import and export financing)		1964
Banco Agrario del Perú (agriculture)		1931
Banco Industrial del Perú (industry)		1936
Banco Minero del Perú (mines)		1942
Banco Central Hipotecario (housing)		1929

Source: Compiled by author from various sources.

AGRARIAN AND POLITICAL REFORM

Agrarian Reform

A centerpiece of the military government's reform program lay in the agrarian sector, where production had long been stagnant and violent unrest among campesinos during the 1960s had prompted the military to seek reform as a measure to safeguard the national security.[19] The June 1969 Agrarian Reform Law thus decreed what was to be one of the more sweeping agrarian reform programs—along with those of Cuba, Mexico, and Bolivia—in the modern history of Latin America. Although not as large in scope as originally projected, some 8.5 million hectares (almost 40 percent of all agricultural lands) and about 375,000 farm families (about one-fourth of the total) were eventually affected by the reform. By 1976, all private latifundia (defined under the Agrarian Reform Law as properties larger than 50 hectares in the *costa* or 30 hectares in the *sierra*) had been eliminated, along with the last vestiges of the once-powerful landed oligarchy. Compensation to former owners was primarily in the form of long-term bonds that could be redeemed for cash if the money were invested in state-approved industrial projects.

The first targets of expropriation were the eight largest and most efficient coastal sugar plantations, including those of the Gildemeisters and W. R. Grace. Smaller coastal properties and *sierra* haciendas were confiscated gradually over a period of several years, giving many owners time to cut their losses by decapitalizing and dividing their estates among family members. The government distributed a small percentage of the properties as private, family plots, but the vast majority was turned into cooperatives—more than 600 in all—that were owned and operated by those who had previously worked the land. In the *sierra,* a multiplicity of land disputes between *hacendados* and neighboring campesino communities led to the adoption of a different kind of cooperative, called an agrarian social interest society, or SAIS.

The estate laborers, who now became full cooperative members, had previously earned relatively high incomes, and thus had been somewhat of an elite in rural Peru. Under the SAIS structure, inhabitants of the impoverished nearby campesino communities were made associate members of the cooperatives, and they were to share in the profits of the SAIS, though not in the use of its lands. Profits proved to be scarce, however, and, as a result, few within the campesino communities (some 40 percent of the total agricultural work force) were to be satisfied with the effects of the agrarian reform. Rather, the reform exasperated a long-standing conflict of interest between the *comuneros* (members of the campesino communities) and the estate laborers that in the 1980s would be exploited by Sendero Luminoso in its campaigns to build support in the central and southern *sierra.*

The major problem of the reform, then, was its failure to address the needs of the poor rural majority: the landless *minifundistas* (small land-owners), and the estimated 4 million people living in some 5,600 campesino communities. Another problem was the government's failure to supply credits and technical support to the new cooperatives. Those supplying domestic markets were additionally hurt by policies designed to keep food prices low for the benefit of urban consumers. Despite these difficulties, the vast political and social changes wrought by the agrarian reform made it the most significant and durable of the military government's reform measures.

Representative and Participatory Organizations

The Velasco regime's reforms in the political arena proved to be less momentous. The agrarian reform earned it the enmity of the political right, of course, and the dissolution of the major representative organization of the landed elite, the National Agrarian Society (SNA), marked a definitive end to its once politically dominant position. The Velasco administration was less decisive, however, in its dealings with the mass organizations of the center and left, whose members were seen as the regime's natural constituency. The government saw no place in "revolutionary" Peru for political parties or for traditional labor and peasant organizations, which it considered as corrupt and ineffective vehicles designed to promote the ambitions of their leaders rather than the well-being of their followers. Reluctant to risk the popular reaction that might result from direct confrontation, however, in 1971 the regime opted for an alternative of creating a corporatist structure of representative organizations under its own aegis in hopes that the traditional mass-based organizations would wither away.

None of the political parties, then, was officially banned by the Revolutionary Government of the Armed Forces. The parties themselves varied greatly in their stances toward the military government. On the day of the coup, APRA vehemently denounced the new government on radio and in its newspaper, *La Tribuna*. It was rewarded by having the paper closed down and a ban placed on outdoor rallies. The APRA leadership subsequently toned down its public criticism, though it continued to chide the Velasco regime for adopting APRA's reform program without giving the party credit. Many of the Velasco reforms were, in fact, clearly designed to undercut the political muscle of APRA. The regime's labor policies, for example, sought to build up alternatives to the APRA-controlled CTP, and the agrarian reform especially benefited the north coast sugar plantation workers, long a foundation of APRA strength, in an effort to reduce the party's political hold on the *norte sólido*. While the party's aging leadership subsequently assumed a passive stance toward the dictatorship, militant APRA youth were to play a leading role in the outbreak of violent antiregime disturbances in Lima at the time of a police strike in February 1975.

The Christian Democrats and AP each continued to be fractionalized with respect to their views of the military regime. The left wing of each, headed by Héctor Cornejo Chávez and Edgardo Seoane, respectively, supported the regime in its early years. Cornejo Chávez was even named chief justice of a reorganized Supreme Court. The political fortunes of these factions fell as a result, however, and neither survived the 1970s as viable political entities. The conservative wings of these parties by and large ceased to function. With Belaúnde in exile in the United States, AP was virtually silent until July 1974, when the government expropriated the only six Lima daily newspapers that had escaped the military's previous mass media expropriations. AP then organized protest demonstrations, and its principal leaders not as yet in exile were arrested and deported.

Shortly after the coup, the Moscow-line Peruvian Communist Party–Unity, or PCP–U ("U" for *Unidad,* after the party's newspaper, and the name used after 1964 to distinguish PCP–U from other Communist party factions), threw its support behind the military government. The government's reciprocal backing of the PCP labor confederation, the General Confederation of Peruvian Workers (CGTP), revitalized the party and cast it into a stronger position than at any time since its founding four decades earlier. The decision to back the military government was controversial among party militants, nevertheless, and caused further schisms, including the loss of its peasant organization, the Confederation of Peruvian Campesinos (CCP), and the powerful teachers' union, the National Union of Peruvian Education Workers (SUTEP).

The first alternative to the traditional parties to be set up were Cuban-style Committees for the Defense of the Revolution, organized by leftist supporters of the military-led "revolution." They were quickly disbanded, however, by officers who feared communist infiltration or any popular mobilization that was not under the control of the military. It was not until June 1971 that the regime finally created its own National System for the Support of Social Mobilization (SINAMOS) to act as a transmission belt between the government and the citizenry in order to channel popular participation in an orderly fashion. Other objectives of SINAMOS included the "training, orientation, and organization of the national population; the development of social interest entities; and the communication and particularly dialogue between the government and the national population."[20] SINAMOS also acted as an umbrella for numerous corporatist-style organizations that were designed to represent various sectors of society.

The rise and fall of two of its largest participant bodies, the National Agrarian Confederation (CNA), which was to represent all agrarian interests, and the National Confederation of Industrial Communities (CONACI), representing both management and labor, provide an indication of the problems encountered by SINAMOS.

Shortly after being initiated, CONACI was disbanded by the government when it became apparent that representatives of the PCP's newly strengthened CGTP were dominant among its membership. The regime-supported Workers' Confederation of the Peruvian Revolution (CTRP), created outside the SINAMOS framework, was poorly organized in comparison to its communist-affiliated rival. The CNA, which was founded in 1972, initially acted according to plan—as a counterweight to the communist CCP. As the agrarian reform slowed down, however, the CNA joined the CCP in opposition to the government, and in 1978 it, too, was officially disbanded.

The fact that the military regime was unwilling to support any organization in which it could not retain political control pointed to the government's essentially authoritarian character and to the contradiction inherent in its attempt to foster "mobilization from below" within a "revolution from above." SINAMOS quickly lost its participatory function and began, instead, to look more like an instrument for a government that, after 1973, grew increasingly unpopular. Local SINAMOS offices frequently became scenes of protest demonstrations, and the organization's Lima headquarters was burned down in February 1975 riots. Shortly afterward, the decision was made to let SINAMOS gradually die.

Economic Difficulties and Another Coup

The strong showing of the economy during the early years of Velasco's rule (the gross national product grew at an average of 6.5 percent between 1970 and 1973, while inflation averaged less than 7 percent) began to falter in 1974 due to increasingly unmanageable fiscal and balance of payments deficits. Exports suffered from a steep decline in the fishing catch and in the price of copper (down from $1.50 a pound in 1973 to $0.55 in 1976), but most damaging was the failure of huge investments in the oil and copper industries to produce the significant increase in export revenues that had been anticipated. Inflation grew to 17 percent in 1974 as the regime, unwilling to raise taxes or to curb spending on either development projects or military hardware, resorted to the printing press and heavy foreign borrowing. The public foreign debt quadrupled under Velasco to reach $3 billion in 1975, when annual service payments totaled $500 million. Thus, instead of achieving the regime's goal of ending Peru's dependency on foreign-controlled economic activity, Velasco substituted one kind of dependency for another. The periodic need to refinance this debt would invoke huge political, economic, and social costs during the next decade and a half.[21]

The economic problems that beset the regime after 1973 undermined the institutional balancing act, in which Velasco had been able to play a moderating role among the various military factions, that had served as the regime's political foundation since 1968. Military unity became increasingly tenuous as both the economic and political situations deteriorated over the next two years.

A strike by the Civil Guard (police) in Lima in February 1975 was occasioned by severe rioting, allegedly spearheaded by militant *aprista* youth, that cost 100 lives. Austerity measures imposed the following July brought a sharp public reaction, particularly among labor unions, which scheduled a general strike for late August. Concerns over the possibility of a breakdown in public order similar to that in February further weakened the regime on the heels of its first major corruption scandal, in which 100 officials were arrested and two ministers dismissed, and the continuing outcry over the press expropriations. Furthermore, President Velasco's capacity to govern, lessened considerably since the onset of debilitating circulatory problems in 1973, was devastated in February 1975 by a severe attack, believed to have been a stroke. Little public protest was voiced when, on August 29, while Peru was hosting a meeting of foreign ministers of the Nonaligned Movement, a politically and physically enfeebled Velasco was removed in a bloodless coup that brought Francisco Morales Bermúdez Cerrutti to power, initiating what Peru's new military president would dub Phase Two of the Revolutionary Government of the Armed Forces.

PHASE TWO AND THE TRANSITION TO CIVILIAN RULE

Morales Bermúdez, whose grandfather had been president of the republic between 1890 and 1894 and whose father, also an army officer, had been assassinated in Trujillo by *aprista* gunmen in 1939, had himself served as finance minister under Belaúnde for several months during 1968, then again under Velasco between 1969 and 1974, when he had earned credit, both at home and abroad, for much of the regime's early economic success. His coup, like Velasco's in 1968, came with the full backing of the armed forces hierarchy, and thus could claim "institutional" legitimacy. Morales Bermúdez's recent appointment as Velasco's prime minister added to his claim of institutional continuity, as did his reactivation of the Revolutionary Junta, which had become largely ceremonial as Velasco ruled in an increasingly arbitrary manner, as the maximum governing authority.

Morales Bermúdez's initial cabinet broke the Velasco tradition of being exclusively military; although it consisted largely of military technocrats, also included were an officer from the Civil Guard and a civilian. The retention of two radical officers seemed to confirm the new president's initial promise of continuity with his predecessor. Phase Two of the Revolutionary Government of the Armed Forces, he pledged, was to consolidate the gains made under Velasco, to rectify previous mistakes, and to "institutionalize the revolutionary process." As the new regime came to grips with pressing economic problems during its first year in office, however, it took on a more conservative profile. In July 1976, the month following the first in a series of economic stabilization packages undertaken during Phase Two, the last of the military radicals would be purged from office.[22]

The Conservative Response to Economic Adversity

The conservative nature of Phase Two was evident in the termination of a number of the radical programs of the Velasco era, including the agrarian reform, the faltering experiment in "social property," and corporatist political participation through SINAMOS. Other Velasco-initiated reforms were altered to become far more moderate. The job security law, for example, was changed to require workers to be on the job three years, rather than only three months as the law had originally been designed, before their tenure was secure; and workers' management and ownership of their workplaces, through the industrial communities, was reduced to a simple profit sharing scheme. Regulations on profit remittances by foreign-owned firms were also eased as part of a neoliberal economic program designed to regain the favor of the international financial community that was necessary to seek loans in support of Peru's faltering balance of payments.

The June 1976 stabilization package, implemented under pressure from a consortium of U.S. banks that Morales Bermúdez had approached with the belief that it would have been less strident than the International Monetary Fund (IMF), cut severely into real wages as the sol was devalued by 44 percent and consumer subsidies for oil, food, utilities, and transportation were slashed, while wages were increased only modestly. Noisy street demonstrations against the measures led the government to implement a nationwide state of emergency—suspending a number of legal guarantees, including the right of public assembly and the right to strike, and imposing a curfew in Lima and Callao—that was to last for over a year. Further austerity packages (designed by the IMF, as the banks were unwilling to continue supporting Peru's balance of payments without the endorsement of the IMF) were introduced in June 1977 and May 1978 as the regime continued its efforts to meet foreign creditors' conditions to receive new loans. A standby agreement was finally signed with the IMF in September 1978 after two years of on-again, off-again negotiations.

Political Tensions at Home and Abroad

Government austerity and an inflation rate that rose precipitously as price controls were abandoned extracted a heavy toll on the national standard of living, especially among the poor. By the end of 1978, real wages were half of what they had been in 1974. Employment statistics, showing less than half the population fully employed by 1977, were equally grim. Successive announcements of price increases were each met by angry protests and calls for strikes by increasingly militant labor unions. No less than five general strikes were staged in Lima between July 1977 and June 1979. Spearheading this unprecedented burst of labor protest was the Maoist-led teachers' union, SUTEP, whose lengthy and violent nationwide strikes in May 1978 and June 1979 were highly political, in part because the government was the employer of the vast majority of teachers.[23]

In addition to these mounting political tensions, the September 1973 coup that brought Augusto Pinochet to power in Chile triggered international tensions with Peru. Initially based on ideological rivalry between the ultraconservative Pinochet and "revolutionary" Velasco regimes, they were to intensify to alarming levels before the end of the decade. Concern was raised among Peru's military rulers in 1974, when Chile resumed diplomatic relations with Bolivia after a 13-year hiatus, and the two entered into negotiations over Bolivia's long-deferred demand for access to the Pacific. Chile soon offered Bolivia a corridor through Arica in exchange for an equal amount of inland Bolivian territory. Peru, granted veto power over any such agreement between Bolivia and Chile in the Treaty of Lima, and painfully aware of its loss of Arica and Tarapacá as the 1979 centennial of the War of the Pacific approached, made a counteroffer that was designed to be unacceptable to Chile. Peru's proposal called for the creation of a zone of joint Peruvian-Bolivian-Chilean sovereignty in Arica, with Bolivia granted a corridor and a port well south of the Peruvian frontier. Although Bolivia was tempted by both proposals, each was unacceptable to the other signatory of the 1929 treaty, and discussions broke down in 1976. "What remained," noted Stephen Gorman, "was a renewed level of tension between Peru and Chile over formerly dormant Peruvian geopolitical interests."[24]

Strain between Peru and Chile was reflected in an ominous arms race during the years leading up to the centennial of the War of the Pacific. Peru's defense expenditures rose throughout the decade of military rule, but the rate was particularly alarming between 1975 and 1977, when they reached a staggering 7.3 percent of the GDP.[25] Such unprecedented levels of military expenditures, although contributing significantly to the government's destabilizing fiscal deficit, were felt by the regime to be necessary in order to strengthen its political base within the military during this volatile period of street demonstrations, strikes, and growing demands for the return of civilian rule.[26]

The jitters intensified as the 1979 centennial became imminent. In December 1978, Peru expelled a number of Chilean diplomatic and military personnel for alleged spying activities. Shortly afterward, a retired Peruvian air force sergeant was executed after being convicted of spying for Chile, and, in January, Peru recalled its ambassador from Santiago and declared Chile's ambassador in Lima persona non grata. This diplomatic bravado, thankfully, proved to be the culmination of this episode; Peru's relations with its southern neighbor improved as quickly as the anniversary of the War of the Pacific passed and its own political climate cooled off.

Plan Túpac Amaru and the Constituent Assembly

In February 1977 the Morales Bermúdez government had belatedly issued its strategy to "consolidate the gains made during Phase One of the revolution and to correct its errors," in what it entitled the Plan Túpac Amaru. Its political component included a plan to get the military back into the barracks: elections for a Constituent Assembly, which was to draft a new constitution, were to be held in June 1978, and an elected, civilian government would take office in 1980.[27]

No less than 12 political parties presented lists of candidates for the Constituent Assembly elections, the first elections to be held in Peru since 1966. The campaign was undertaken amid near-chaotic conditions of government repression and public protests, with a number of the candidates of the four participating Marxist coalitions either jailed or in exile. The government did little to hide its support of APRA. Morales Bermúdez had personally initiated a process of reconciliation between the armed forces and APRA shortly after having assumed power by promoting a series of private talks between leaders of these two historic enemies. This process had come to light in an extraordinary speech by the president in Trujillo in April 1976, when he publicly called for an end to the bitter feud initiated in Trujillo 44 years earlier.[28] APRA was thus able to garner 37 of the 100 seats in the Constituent Assembly, and Haya de la Torre was named president of the body (see Table 4.2).

Acción Popular, despite having been the first party to petition the National Elections Tribunal for recognition, did not present candidates for the 1978 election. Whether or not this decision was made for the reason stated by Belaúnde—that he saw the military's limitation of the role of the Constituent Assembly to simply writing the constitution as unacceptable—it did prove to be a brilliant tactical move. As a presidential candidate two years later, Belaúnde would be able to claim the most steadfast credentials in opposition to the unpopular military regime.

APRA worked closely in the Constituent Assembly with the PPC

Table 4.2

**National Elections: Constituent Assembly (1978) and Presidential (1980)
(percentage of valid votes)**

		1978	1980
RIGHT (total)		27.65	56.92
	PPC	23.79	9.57
	AP	*	45.37
	FRENATRACA	3.86	1.98
APRA		35.34	27.40
LEFT (total)		29.43	13.86
	PRT		3.90
	UNIR		3.26
	UI		2.83
	UDP	4.58	2.39
	FOCEP	12.32	1.48
	PSR	6.62	
	PCP	5.91	
OTHER		7.58	1.82

Note: If space is blank, then either that party did not exist at the time or its
candidate ran under a coalition such as UI or UNIR.

PRESIDENTIAL CANDIDATES (1980)

RIGHT

PPC:	Luis Bedoya Reyes
AP:	Fernando Belaúnde Terry **
FRENATRACA:	Roger Cáceres Velásquez

APRA   Armando Villanueva del Campo

LEFT

PRT:	Hugo Blanco Galdós
UNIR:	Horacio Zevallos Gámez
UI:	Leonardo Rodríguez Figueroa
UDP:	Carlos Malpica Silva Santistevan
FOCEP:	Genaro Ledesma Izquieta

* Chose not to participate
** Victor

KEY TO PARTY NAMES

AP	Acción Popular
APRA	Partido Aprista Peruano
FOCEP	Frente Obrero, Campesino, Estudiantil y Popular
FRENATRACA	Frente Nacional de Trabajadores y Campesinos
PPC	Partido Popular Cristiano
PRT	Partido Revolucionario de los Trabajadores
UDP	Unidad Democrático Popular
UI	Unidad Izquierda
UNIR	Unión de Izquierda Revolucionaria

Source: Fernando Tuesta Soldevilla, *Perú Político en Cifras* (Lima: Fundación Friedrich
Ebert, 1987), pp. 223, 231.

which, gaining much of the AP vote, was able to win 25 seats, in writing the constitution that was ratified on July 12, 1979. The four lists representing the Marxist left gained a total of nearly 30 percent of the vote, giving them 28 Assembly seats. After failing in an attempt to convert the Constituent Assembly into a deliberative body, the leftist assemblymen used the Constituent Assembly as a forum to denounce the Morales Bermúdez government. As a result, they had little input into the 1979 Constitution.

The 1980 Elections

Favorable world prices for Peru's traditional export crops, an abundant harvest of anchovies, exported as fishmeal, the coming on stream of new oil and copper production as a result of substantial investments made earlier in the decade, and an impressive growth in nontraditional exports fostered by Minister of Economy and Finance Javier Silva Ruete all contributed to an impressive turnaround in Peru's balance of payments during 1979, when it registered an astounding $1.6 billion surplus. Little of this foreign exchange windfall was used to reactivate the crisis-ridden local economy, however; instead it went largely in payments on the nation's mounting foreign debt, which at that time totaled just under $10 billion. It nevertheless contributed to the sense of optimism that pervaded the presidential and congressional elections of May 1980.

APRA's cooperation in the Constituent Assembly earned it the praise of the military government and brought an end to the military's long-held veto on APRA's assumption of power. The death of the 84-year-old Haya de la Torre on August 2, three weeks after he had signed the new constitution into law in July 1979 and less than a year before the election in which he was the odds-on favorite to capture the presidency at long last, threw the future of APRA into doubt, however. A bitter struggle for control of APRA between the conservative Andrés Townsend, Haya's close collaborator in his later years, and Armando Villanueva del Campo, who wanted the party to return to the revolutionary spirit of Haya's early years, culminated with an armed Villanueva forcefully taking the party's headquarters in Lima's Avenida Alfonso Ugarte. Shortly thereafter, Villanueva emerged as the party's candidate for the 1980 presidential election. His candidacy remained tainted by this sordid beginning, however, which only confirmed his reputation outside the party as a roughneck (*búfalo*).

Villanueva's primary opponent was the very man who had been overthrown by the military 12 years earlier, Fernando Belaúnde Terry. In an energetic campaign that belied his age, the 67-year-old former president promised to create a million jobs during his five years in office, to "expand the agricultural frontier" into the jungle region, and, true to his party's symbol—a shovel—to build roads, housing, and other public works.

Figure 4.1
Evolution of the Electoral Left, 1978–1990

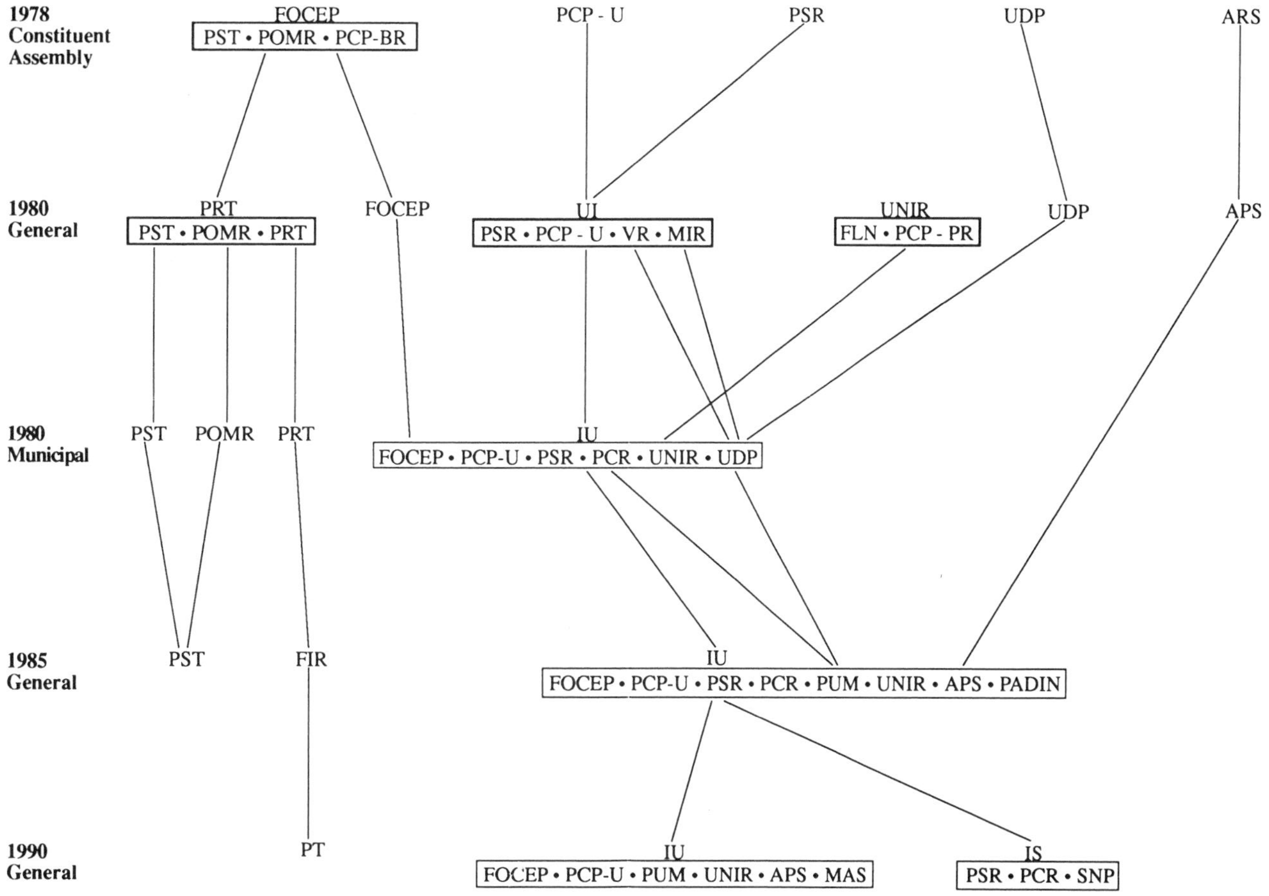

Early hopes that the Marxist left would be able to consolidate its forces into an even larger coalition than it had managed in 1978 were dashed by the persistence of ideological and personal incompatibility among its numerous parties (see Figure 4.1). In the end, the left emerged even more divided, and as a result, its five presidential candidates gained among them less than half the left's percentage of 1978.

The left and, to a lesser extent, APRA paid a high price in 1980 for the public quarreling among their members. The poor showing of the PPC, relative to its vote of two years earlier, was no surprise, as much of its 1978 vote had come from *populistas*, whose party did not participate. The magnitude of the AP victory, with Belaúnde garnering more than 45 percent of the presidential total and his party winning a clear majority of the seats in the Chamber of Deputies and falling just five seats short of a majority in the Senate, was startling nevertheless. Belaúnde's triumph was attributed to a variety of factors, including the unity of AP behind a well-known and charismatic figure. Perhaps most importantly, his having been overthrown in 1968 and his boycott of the Constituent Assembly elections brought him sympathy among the voters as the most antimilitary candidate at a time when, after a half-decade of social and economic crisis under military rule, antimilitarism was the most powerful political sentiment among Peru's voting public. Belaúnde was viewed as an experienced leader and as a pragmatist who was "antimilitary but not irresponsible." His victory was hailed as signaling the triumphant return of Peruvian democracy.

Political and economic failure, together with the need to preserve the institutional integrity of the armed forces, first put an end to the regime's progressive and nationalistic reform program in 1975, then five years later caused it to give up the reins of power entirely. Peru's experiment in military-led "revolution" had, however, by no means been an unconditional failure. The agrarian reform, which capped the long decline of Peru's traditional rural oligarchy, together with a widening perception (though it would soon prove somewhat inaccurate) of the growing political power of the masses, and the vast growth of the economic power of the state, all added up to a profound transformation of Peru's social and economic landscape. President Belaúnde was soon to discover that governing Peru in the 1980s was quite a different matter from what it had been prior to the military *docenio*.

NOTES

1. The Revolutionary Statute of Government is reproduced in *El Comercio* (Lima), October 4, 1968, p. 1.

2. Quoted in Thomas E. Skidmore and Peter H. Smith, *Modern Latin America* (New York: Oxford University Press, 1984), pp. 216–17. This manifesto,

dated October 2, 1968, is also reproduced in *El Comercio,* October 4, 1968, p. 4.

3. See Jack Child, "Historical Setting," pp. 3–58 in *Peru: A Country Study,* Richard F. Nyrop, ed. (Washington, D.C.: U.S. Government Printing Office, 1981), p. 39.

4. David Scott Palmer, *Peru: The Authoritarian Tradition,* (New York: Praeger, 1980), pp. 104–6.

5. Werlich, *Peru: A Short History,* (Carbondale: Southern Illinois University Press, 1978), pp. 25–6.

6. John Weeks, *Limits to Capitalist Development: the Industrialization of Peru, 1950–1980,* (Boulder, Colo.: Westview Press, 1985), p. 232.

7. Ancom is also known as the Andean Pact and by the name of its founding document, the Cartagena Accord. Worthwhile studies of Peru's participation in Ancom during the 1970s include Scott Horton, "Peru and ANCOM: A Study in the Disintegration of a Common Market," *Texas International Law Journal,* Vol. 17, No. 1 (Winter 1982), pp. 39–61, and William P. Avery, "The Politics of Crisis and Cooperation in the Andean Group," *Journal of Developing Areas,* Vol. 17, No. 2 (January 1983), pp. 155–84.

8. U.S. Arms Control and Disarmament Agency, *World Military Expenditures and Arms Transfers, 1973–1983* (Washington, D.C.: 1985). See also Rubén Berríos, "Relaciones Perú—países socialistas: comercio, asistencia, y flujos de tecnología," *Socialismo y Participación* (Lima), No. 22 (June 1983), pp. 55–65.

9. Figures on U.S. military aid are from the annual *The Military Balance* (London: International Institute for Strategic Studies).

10. E. V. K. Fitzgerald, *The State and Economic Development: Peru since 1968* (Cambridge: Cambridge University Press, 1976), p. 73. See also Skidmore and Smith, *Modern Latin America,* p. 219.

11. See Daniel M. Schydlowsky and Juan J. Wicht, "The Anatomy of an Economic Failure," pp. 94–143 in *The Peruvian Experiment Reconsidered,* Cynthia McClintock and Abraham F. Lowenthal, eds. (Princeton, N.J.: Princeton University Press, 1983), p. 116.

12. See, for example, E.V.K. Fitzgerald, "State Capitalism in Peru: A Model of Economic Development and its Limitations," pp. 65–93 in McClintock and Lowenthal, *The Peruvian Experiment Reconsidered.*

13. Luis E. García Barreto and Guillermo Fernández Maldonado C., "Empresas públicas: un debate nacional," *Que Hacer,* No. 25 (November 1983), p. 54.

14. Pedro-Pablo Kuczynski, "The Peruvian External Debt, Problem and Prospects," *Journal of Inter-American Studies and World Affairs,* Vol. 23, No. 1 (February 1981), pp. 8–9.

15. Michael Reid, *Peru: Paths to Poverty* (London: Latin American Bureau, 1985), p. 45.

16. Fitzgerald, *The State and Economic Development,* p. 41.

17. A valuable discussion of the historic growth of the economic role of the government can be found in E.V.K. Fitzgerald, *The Political Economy of Peru, 1956–1978: Economic Development and the Restructuring of Capital* (Cambridge: Cambridge University Press, 1979), pp. 184–99. For those who read Spanish, see

also Fernando Sánchez Albavera, "Política de desarrollo y empresas públicas en el Perú: 1970–80," *Socialismo y Participación* (Lima), No. 26 (June 1984), pp. 31–65.

18. Hernando de Soto, *The Other Path: The Invisible Revolution in the Third World* (New York: Harper and Row, 1989) is a detailed study of Lima's informal economy. José Matos Mar, *Desborde popular y crisis del estado* (Lima: Instituto de Estudios Peruanos, 1985) is an essay, more accessible than de Soto's rather turgid work, that eloquently presents a case for the correlation between the growth of Lima and the inability of the government to adequately perform a modern role.

19. Howard Handelman, "Peasants, Landlords, and Bureaucrats: The Politics of Agrarian Reform in Peru," *American Universities Field Staff Reports,* South America series, No. 1, 1981, p. 6.

20. Palmer, *Peru,* p. 113.

21. See Kuczynski, "The Peruvian External Debt," for an excellent account of the growth of the external debt during the 1970s.

22. A valuable account of the tenure of the radical officers is found in George D. E. Philip, *The Rise and Fall of the Peruvian Military Radicals, 1968–1976* (London: Athlone Press, 1978).

23. Reid, *Peru,* pp. 65–78, provides a good overview of the turbulent labor panorama during the Morales Bermúdez regime.

24. Stephen M. Gorman, "Geopolitics and Peruvian Foreign Policy," *Inter-American Economic Affairs,* Vol. 36, No. 2 (Autumn 1982), p. 70.

25. For further discussion of Peru's military buildup during the 1970s, see Jennie K. Lincoln, "Peruvian Foreign Policy Since the Return to Democratic Rule," in *The Dynamics of Latin American Foreign Policies: Challenges for the 1980s,* Jennie K. Lincoln and Elizabeth G. Ferris, eds. (Boulder, Colo.: Westview Press, 1984), pp. 141–5.

26. Reid, *Peru,* p. 68.

27. An English translation of the Plan Tupác Amaru was published by the U.S. Joint Publications Research Service (JPRS) in *Translations on Latin America,* 24 February 1977, pp. 15–61.

28. This historical reconciliation is detailed by Carol L. Graham in *APRA 1968–1988: From Evolution to Government—The Elusive Search for Political Integration* (D. Phil. thesis, Oxford University, January 1989), pp. 111–15.

President Alan García during one of the many speeches, popularly known as *balconazos*, that he delivered from the balcony of the Presidential Palace. In this 1985 *balconazo*, García outlined his government's position on the external debt and roundly criticized the IMF. *Photo by Alejandro Balaguer.*

Rondas campesinas, armed with machetes and homemade spears, being trained by the Naval Marines in the province of Hunata, near Ayacucho. *Photo by Alejandro Balaguer.*

Rondas campesinas parading with their weapons in the central plaza of a village in the department of Ayacucho. *Photo by Vera A. Lentz.*

Military, with a captured *senderista* flag, patrolling a village in the *sierra. Photo by Vera A. Lentz.*

Campesino harvesting coca leaves near Aucayacu, in the heart of the Upper Huallaga Valley. *Photo by Alejandro Balaguer.*

Money changers aggressively pursue their trade in the midst of traffic in downtown Lima. *Photo by Vera A. Lentz.*

One of many communally operated kitchens organized by the women in the *barriadas* of Lima in order to feed their families more economically. *Photo by Vera A. Lentz.*

Women making artisanry in order to help fund their communally operated soup kitchen. *Photo by Vera A. Lentz.*

Entire family participating in the construction of their home in a *pueblo jóven* in Lima. *Photo by Vera A. Lentz.*

5

THE BELAÚNDE REPRISE: 1980–1985

Fernando Belaúnde Terry's resumption of the presidency on July 28, 1980, was accompanied by a great wave of popular optimism. The wide margin of his electoral victory and the corresponding failure of both the Marxist and *aprista* opposition provided President Belaúnde with breathing space like he had never enjoyed during his first term. A further source of political space for Belaúnde in 1980 lay in the fact that the military had been so discredited as political actors in the public eye that a repeat of its 1968 intervention was almost inconceivable. A number of economic factors also augured well for the new democratic regime. Peru had recently become a substantial petroleum exporter at a time when oil prices were increasing markedly, and prices for copper, its second most valuable export, had also risen substantially. Finally, Peru's nearly $10 billion external debt had recently been renegotiated, and a number of officials in the new government also enjoyed close friendships with key figures within the vital international lending community.

Peru's return to civilian rule, furthermore, was part of a continent-wide transition to democratic political structures that took place between 1979 and 1984, following more than a decade during which nearly every nation of Latin America had been under the dictatorial rule of the military. The promise among Peruvians of personal liberty as well as of prosperity, thanks to a friendlier international environment and a more competent civilian administration, was fortified each time another country in the region joined Peru in returning to government under democratic political structures.

THE 1979 CONSTITUTION

The system of government set up by the 1979 Constitution was, in most respects, similar to that outlined in the constitution ratified in 1933. In a number of areas, however, the 1978 Constituent Assemblymen had attempted to improve on the previous governing statute in order to strengthen the institutions associated with democracy that had so often succumbed in the past. Most significantly in this respect, the executive branch was strengthened markedly vis-à-vis the legislature. The new constitution also created a new body, a nine-member Court of Constitutional Guarantees, to be situated in Arequipa, in order to judge the constitutionality of laws. Other important changes in the constitution included the abolition of the death penalty, except in time of war and, in a right that had been exercised during the recent elections for the first time in the nation's history, the granting of voting privileges to Peru's sizable population of illiterates.

Peru's new supreme law consisted of 307 articles; Article 79 defines the state as an independent, sovereign, and democratic republic. The national territory is defined as the soil and subsoil within the national boundaries and the 200-mile territorial sea off its Pacific coastline, as well as the airspace above these areas. Spanish is recognized as the official language, although the official use of Quechua and Aymara, which had been promoted by the Velasco regime, continued to be sanctioned under certain circumstances. The 1979 Constitution recognizes the Roman Catholic church as an "important element in the historical, cultural, and moral formation of Peru," but stops short of declaring Catholicism the official religion.

The primary obligations of the state are described as the defense of the national territory and "guaranteeing the basic human rights of its citizens, while promoting their well-being and eliminating all forms of exploitation." Venturing further yet into the realm of idealistic objectives, the state is mandated to eradicate illiteracy and to "promote social and economic conditions under which poverty will be eliminated and all citizens will have useful occupations." An enlarged role of the state in the social and economic life of the nation is also reflected in a number of other provisions, such as that which calls upon the government to periodically adjust minimum wages.

Amending the constitution requires approval by a majority of each legislative body and ratification by the same procedures in the subsequent session of Congress. Under these difficult requirements, no amendments were passed during the first decade in which the new constitution was in force.

Political and governmental authority is concentrated in the president who, as chief executive, is the head of government. The constitution also designates him as head of state and commander in chief of the armed forces, and states that he "personifies the nation." He is empowered to appoint members of the cabinet (formally known as the Council of Ministers), including the prime minister, as well as Supreme Court judges; to submit draft legislation; to review (but not veto) laws drafted by Congress; and, under certain circumstances described below, to enact laws by decree. The president's power to suspend constitutional guarantees for a renewable period of 60 days under a state of emergency was invoked continuously after 1982 in the areas affected by *senderista* violence (see "The Challenge of Sendero Luminoso," this chapter).

James M. Malloy calls Peru's governmental system a "modified presidential system similar to Fifth Republic France in which a prime minister acts as the head of the president's governmental team and represents him before the legislature."[1] However, the prime minister (also known as the president of the Council of Ministers) has no power independent of the president, who appoints and dismisses him at will, as he does with the rest of the cabinet.

As is commonly the case with Latin American legislative bodies, the Peruvian Congress has little real power within a governmental system that is dominated by the president. This had not always been the case: under the 1933 Constitution, a political opposition with a majority in Congress had the power to seriously impede the legislative program of the executive, and it was also extremely easy to bring a motion to censure a cabinet official to the floor of Congress. Recalling President Belaúnde's tremendous difficulties at the hands of the congressional *aprista-odriista* majority during the 1960s, the Constituent Assembly that delineated the 1979 Constitution purposely weakened the power of Congress. Thereafter, it took 45 deputies (rather than one, as had previously been the case) to bring a motion of censorship before the Chamber of Deputies.

Also anticipating legislative stalemates such as those of the 1960s caused by an opposition-controlled Congress, the framers of the 1979 supreme law gave the president substantial power to rule by decree. Article 199, for example, denies Congress any role in increasing or decreasing government expenditures during the budget process, thus giving the executive almost complete legal control over the management of the economy. Furthermore, the executive is empowered by Article 211, Section 20, to legislate "extraordinary economic measures" by decree-law whenever the president considers it to be "in the national interest." As a result, less than half the laws that came into force between 1980 and 1989 had ever seen the light of day in Congress; most laws were drafted within the ministries and approved by the Council of Ministers.[2] Moreover, the executive branch expedited nearly all legislation of major importance. All too often, Congress was left to legislate insignificant matters, such as the declaration of a city as the capital of a typical folk dance or as "the cradle of the patriotic struggle during the War of the Pacific."[3]

The 1979 Constitution contains a number of innovations designed to rectify long-standing problems within the judiciary and to make it more efficient and a truly independent third branch of government. The much-

heralded provision of the new constitution that at least 2 percent of the
annual government budget be devoted to the judiciary was envisioned as
maintaining the judiciary with a level of resources sufficient to operate efficiently and to insulate it from the many corrupting influences to which
it had been exposed in the past. Furthermore, all supreme and superior
court judges were now to be chosen by the president, not arbitrarily as before, but rather from a list of qualified candidates presented by an independent, six-member National Justice Council headed by the attorney
general of the republic. These judges were then to be subject to the approval of the Senate. Local justice councils named lower level judges. Another innovation of the new constitution was that judges no longer had a
fixed term of office; they were now appointed permanently, barring mal-
feasance in office, but were required to retire at age 70.

CONSERVATIVE POPULISM: ECONOMIC LIBERALISM AND ECONOMIC DECAY

In the classic style of Peruvian populism, Belaúnde had been elected on
image rather than substance; his campaign had produced little in the way
of concrete policy initiatives. Electoral analyses revealed that a large
number of his votes came from people who remembered his image as a
center-leftist during his previous term in the presidency. A postelectoral
announcement that the AP would form an alliance with the conservative
PPC offered the first indication of Belaúnde's new ideological leaning.
PPC was given two cabinet portfolios, the Ministries of Justice and Industry, in return for a legislative alliance that would give the new president a
majority in both congressional bodies. The legislative prospect hence contrasted favorably with Belaúnde's first term, when an opposition majority
coalition had presented the president with insurmountable legislative
obstacles.

The Dynamo

The conservatism of Belaúnde's second term also arose as a result of
factionalization within his own political party. The most progressive wing
of AP, led by Manuel Seoane, had left the party at the end of Belaúnde's
first term. A bitter rivalry subsequently developed within the second rung
of party leadership between the pragmatic party boss, Javier Alva
Orlandini, and conservative millionaire businessman, Manuel Ulloa
Elías, while Belaúnde tried to remain above the fray as the neutral mod-
erator between the *alvista* and *ulloista* wings of the party.

Tapped by the president in July 1980 to be his prime minister and minister of economy and finance, Ulloa contributed most to the conservative

ideological color of Belaúnde's second term. Born in Lima in 1922 and trained as a lawyer, Ulloa was widely known for his technical expertise in economics, for his financial business dealings, and for being a millionaire and international jet-setter (as a sexagenarian he married a European princess). He was the owner of controlling interest in Lima's daily newspaper *Expreso* and was closely associated with Channel 5, Peru's largest television station. His association with AP dated from 1960, and in 1968 he had briefly held the post of minister of economy and finance.

Ulloa led Belaúnde's economic team, consisting of bankers and technocrats, that became known as "the Dynamo." Like Belaúnde, most of the Dynamo had spent the years of military rule in the United States. Two of its best-known associates were Richard Webb, associated with the World Bank and Princeton University, who was named to head the Central Bank, and Pedro-Pablo Kuczynski, an associate of various U.S. business and financial firms who became minister of energy and mines.

Belaúnde's economic team brought an enthusiasm for neoliberal economic policies—stressing free-market strategies and export-led growth based on integration into global markets—that were being practiced with some success at the time by Margaret Thatcher in Britain and Augusto Pinochet in Chile. Ulloa's neoliberal agenda emphasized, first of all, a reduction of the state's role in the economy and a concurrent strengthening of the private sector. It also pursued policies aimed at "getting [Peru's] prices right," such as lowering government subsidies of public consumption and lowering tariffs on imports in order to open the economy to the international market and thus emphasize Peru's traditional primary product export sector. Also designed to increase Peru's export volume were monetary policies such as high interest rates and frequent minidevaluations of the Peruvian currency.[4]

Ulloa's neoliberal economic agenda was received with great enthusiasm within international financial agencies and the U.S. government, where it was viewed as a furthering of the much needed reversal, initiated under Morales Bermúdez, of the harmful state interventionist policies of the Velasco government. Heartened by what looked at the time like a turnaround in Peru's economic picture under the direction of responsible management, the international banking community made some $1.8 billion in new loans during 1981. In 1982, however, Peru's commercial creditors insisted once again, as they had in 1977, on an agreement with the IMF before they would consider any further loan activity. In June, Ulloa signed a letter of intent with the IMF, permitting Peru to draw over $200 million in IMF funds, then renegotiate its debt with the banks as well as the Paris Club and the socialist nations.[5] In return, it promised the IMF that it would refrain from seeking external financing for a number of development projects deemed unproductive, to limit its 1982 short-term borrowing to $1.1 billion, and, most importantly, to hold its fiscal deficit to 4.2 percent of the GDP and to finance that, not through low taxes, but through foreign borrowing.[6]

Multinational business concerns also took heart at the welcome mat that the Dynamo set out for foreign investors. Belaúnde's economic team pledged to lift the restrictive ceiling on profit remittances mandated under the Andean Pact's Decision 24, and to liberalize still further the constraining labor legislation governing Peru's industrial communities. The 1982 industrial law and the 1981 mining code, which ended the state monopoly on the marketing of copper and granted generous tax rebates to firms conducting oil exploration, were both designed, furthermore, to attract foreign investment capital. Indeed, a brief spurt of new investments brought direct investment in Peru by the United States to $2,236 million by the end of 1982. A large majority of these investments, however, remained within the traditional export sectors of mining and petroleum.[7]

Political Opposition

Ulloa's pursuit of neoliberal economic policies was never as popular in Peru as it was overseas, however. AP's own coalition partner, the PPC, and its Peruvian business community constituency vigorously protested the deep cuts in external tariffs, by an average of about two-thirds between 1980 and 1982, and the lowering of subsidies for exporters. The resulting flood of imports contributed to an unprecedented number of bankruptcies among Peruvian businesses and a sharp slowdown in the operations of others. Manufacturing output fell by some 20 percent in a period of two years, while automobile assembly declined 50 percent between 1980 and 1983.[8] From a respectable 4.2 percent in 1980, growth in the GDP declined to a mere 0.7 percent in 1982.[9]

Not surprisingly, the neoliberal road pursued under Ulloa's direction was decried even louder by the government's opposition on the left. It abhorred the government's opening the economy to foreigners on principle, accusing the prime minister and his globalist colleagues within the Dynamo of engaging in a process of *entreguismo*—of surrendering the national patrimony to foreign interests. It also condemned the fate of the working people under neoliberal economics. Between 1980 and 1984, the deep economic recession that had been brought on, in part, by austerity measures undertaken to comply with foreign creditors led to the riffing of a fifth of the country's industrial workers and a 40 percent decline in real incomes. By 1984, official unemployment stood at 10.8 percent, while some 60 percent of the total labor force was considered underemployed.[10]

Opposition to the Dynamo's policy orientation also came from within the government itself, thus generating economic policies that were inconsistent in their methods as well as their goals. President Belaúnde's strong developmentalist orientation, for example, was an important factor acting against the conservative fiscal orientation of his own economic team. Seeing himself within a Peruvian tradition of builder presidents, Belaúnde initiated or followed through on a number of massive irrigation, energy, and highway projects. Several of these, most notably the $2 billion Majes irrigation project in the department of Arequipa, came at costs well above their projected returns.[11] Foreign financing for many of these projects contributed substantially to the nearly 50 percent increase in Peru's external debt, to some $13.7 billion, during Belaúnde's term in office.

Another goal of the Ulloa-led economic team, the reduction of the state's role in the economy, met the resistance of well-entrenched managers of state-run agencies and corporations who put political pressure to bear in order to protect their vested interests. State monopolies in a number of basic industries were abolished, but only a handful of the 60-odd state enterprises, of which the Dynamo had proposed divestiture, were actually sold.

Economic Decay

Government budget deficits, which increased from 1.5 percent of the GDP in 1979 to 8.8 percent in 1982, then to an incredible 11.9 percent in 1983 (the year for which the IMF had demanded a fiscal deficit not above 4.2 percent), were only partially due to Belaúnde's seeming obsession with construction projects. A decline in the government's tax receipts from 17 percent of the GDP in 1980 to 12.4 percent in 1984 was due to both lower prices for Peru's export products (some 40 percent of Peru's tax revenues come from the foreign trade sector) and to inflation that swelled from 60 percent in 1980 to 125 percent in 1983, precipitating a corresponding decline in real tax revenue.[12] The extraordinary fiscal demands of the military, which consumed between one-fourth and one-third of the government's budget annually, were damaging as well. Ignoring the growing fiscal as well as foreign debt crisis, the air force signed an $870 million agreement to purchase 26 ultramodern Mirage 2000 jet fighters in December 1982.[13]

Such policy inconsistencies were only partially to blame for the economic disaster that evolved during Belaúnde's second term in office. Government officials blamed the dramatic decline—most estimates were in the neighborhood of 50 percent—in Peru's terms of trade during the early 1980s. Indeed, the worldwide recession of 1981–1983 saw the prices of Peru's two major exports—petroleum and copper—fall precipitously, while interest rates (capital loans being Peru's major import at the time) leaped to all-time highs. Thus, international factors beyond the control of Peruvian policymakers could justifiably be cited.

Equally outside the regime's control was the climatic disaster of 1983 triggered by a particularly forceful occurrance of El Niño, the periodic reversal of the dominant south-to-north Humboldt Current that dominates the weather system throughout the west coast of South America. Severe drought in the south devastated its agricultural activity, while torrential rains in the north destroyed crops, inundated mines and oil fields, and wiped out residential areas in the normally arid coast. The fishing industry suffered the most, but manufacturing, particularly in textiles, was also severely affected by the loss of agricultural raw materials. Largely as a result of El Niño, 1983 was an unmitigated economic disaster for Peru, with the GDP falling no less than 11.8 percent.

Although it could do nothing to change either international economic conditions or the weather, the Peruvian electorate could express its displeasure with the decaying state of the economy in the November 1983 municipal elections. Predictably, the contest was devastating for Acción Popular, which gained only 17.2 percent of the national vote total. This debacle sent off alarm signals within the party machine, headed by Javier Alva Orlandini, who was seeing his presidential hopes in the upcoming elections rapidly fading (see "Party Politics and the 1985 Electoral Campaign," this chapter).

The following March, the party forced the resignation of Minister of the Economy and Finance Carlos Rodríguez Pastor (whom Ulloa had designated as his successor at the ministry with his resignation in December 1982), and thus spelled a symbolic end to the regime's neoliberal economic approach. Belaúnde's effort to improve the government's image by naming author Mario Vargas Llosa to the prime ministership was blocked by the *alvista* party faithful; instead Sandro Mariátegui, son of José Carlos and longtime AP militant, was named prime minister while José Benavides, an engineer with little knowledge of economics, was moved from the Ministry of Energy and Mines into the Economy and Finance portfolio in March 1984. At the same time, the PPC also saw the writing on the wall for the 1985 electoral contest, and ended its nearly four-year alliance with AP.

Policy reversals, including the erection of new tariff barriers to protect local industry and a slowdown in payments on the foreign debt (debt service payments in 1983 were fully 62 percent of Peru's export earnings), had already been made, however, partly in response to political pressures. Few further alterations in policy would be forthcoming from the new cabinet members during the last year of the AP government. In April 1984, the new economic team signed an agreement with the IMF for a $260 million standby loan that had been negotiated by Rodríguez Pastor. But the program—which called for tax increases, further reductions in consumer subsidies, and cuts in wages as well as in military spending—proved politically unacceptable, and the government fell out of compliance within a few short months.[14]

FOREIGN DIVERSIONS

Ecuador Again

Barely six months into Belaúnde's second presidency, tensions that had been building ever since the bitter 1941 war between Peru and Ecuador erupted into renewed conflict along the 78 kilometers of their border left undemarcated. While the 1942 Protocol of Rio de Janeiro had essentially recognized Peru's long-standing territorial claims, virtually every succeeding president of Ecuador had called for a renegotiation of this treaty, claiming it to be nonbinding, as it had been imposed by force (see "APRA versus the Armed Forces," Chapter 3 in this volume). Tensions grew perceptibly throughout the 1970s, when both nations were under military rule and Peru's accelerated military buildup had been a concern to its smaller northern neighbor and had blocked advancement of regional integration projects on a number of occasions. Fighting erupted briefly in January 1978.

In each subsequent year, nervousness mounted among the soldiers stationed along the undemarcated zone as the January 29 anniversary of the signing of the Rio protocol approached. Border skirmishes were renewed in January 1981, January 1983, and January 1984. The fighting in 1981, which each side claimed to have been precipitated by the other, raged for five days before a formal cease-fire took effect. Almost ritualistic celebrations of the treaty that was so resented by Ecuador, these brief conflicts also reflected the internal political and economic actuality in both countries. In Ecuador as well as in Peru, a newly installed civilian regime was suffering considerable distress, from which these annual bursts of nationalistic fervor served as convenient distractions. Also in both nations, they provided a much-needed boost in the public's image of military establishments that had been dealt severe blows as a result of their enormous unpopularity during the final years of the recently concluded military regimes.[15]

The Falkland/Malvinas Islands

When Latin American sovereignty was perceived to be under threat from an outside power, on the other hand, Peru did not hesitate to express solidarity with its regional neighbors. During the 1970s, for example, both the Morales Bermúdez and Velasco governments had contributed Peru's diplomatic muscle to Panama's bid for control over the Panama Canal. When, in April 1982, the Argentine armed forces occupied the Falkland/Malvinas Islands, the widespread perception within Peru was that Argentina was taking possession of territory that, as an anachronism from the colonial era, was rightfully Latin American.

Following the failure of the U.S. effort to mediate a cease-fire between Argentina and Britain, nevertheless, President Belaúnde launched his own diplomatic initiative in search of a cease-fire. Reportedly based on the establishment of a tripartite administration of the islands, with the participation of the United States, to be followed by negotiations over the islands' future sovereignty, the initiative sank on May 2, along with the Argentine cruiser *General Belgrano.*[16]

Peru quickly became an unabashed partisan of the Argentine position during the ensuing South Atlantic war. Belaúnde's stance went well beyond the verbal support for Argentina expressed by most Latin American governments, as he provided Argentina with substantial military assistance, including the reported transferral of a squadron of Peru's jet fighters to an air base in northwest Argentina for contingency purposes. The open support of the United States for the British position during that conflict led to strains that marred an otherwise cordial period in U.S.–Peruvian relations.

THE CHALLENGE OF SENDERO LUMINOSO

In addition to its economic woes, Belaúnde's second term was also plagued by the outbreak of what was quickly to become Peru's most serious peasant rebellion since that led by Túpac Amaru during the late eighteenth century. Sendero Luminoso launched the violent phase of its guerrilla war on the very day that Belaúnde had been elected, May 18, 1980, when it burned the ballot boxes in Chuschi, a market town in Cangallo province, in the southern part of the department of Ayacucho. This action brought little notice at the time from a nation that was in a state of euphoria over the end of 12 years of military rule.

The Setting: Ayacucho

The south-central Andean region around Ayacucho was used to being ignored. Since its heyday during the colonial era, when it was an important stopping-off point between the Spanish capital at Lima and the old Inca capital at Cuzco, Ayacucho and its environs had been consistently bypassed by the central government and allowed to deteriorate. Cynthia McClintock reports that Ayacucho, with 3 percent of the nation's population, received only 1 percent of the central government's expenditures between 1968 and 1982.[17]

The deterioration of the *ayacuchanos'* standard of living, moreover, had been especially marked during the 1970s. The Velasco government's agrarian reform had benefited only 15 to 20 percent of the needy peasant families in the region—a proportion much lower than that for Peru as a whole. The 1981 census revealed that fully 54 percent of Ayacucho's population was illiterate, while the department of Ayacucho's half-million inhabitants had a total of only 30 doctors, 366 hospital beds, 827 telephones, and 44 kilometers of paved roads (see "Population Dynamics," Chapter 1 in this volume).[18] Per capita income within Ayacucho's peasant communities was estimated to have fallen below $50 a year, a level closer to the poorest African nations of the so-called fourth world than to Peru's coastal communities.[19] During his 1980 election campaign, Belaúnde had promised a renewal of government investment in the agricultural regions of the *sierra,* but the years following the end of military rule saw a continuation of the secular decline in the region's economic indicators.[20]

The Early Development of Sendero

The leadership of Sendero Luminoso was well aware of the long history of neglect of Ayacucho by the Lima-based central government. Abimael Guzmán Reynoso arrived at Ayacucho's National University of San Cristóbal de Huamanga from Arequipa in 1963. From his position as a philosophy professor in the university's education program, Guzmán recruited students for a variety of activities, including trips to Cuba and extension programs in literacy, farming, health, and nutrition in the Ayacucho countryside, and he also hosted myriad small-group political discussions in his home. In 1966, following the Sino-Soviet split, Guzmán and the several scores of students and faculty who regularly engaged in these activities joined the Maoist Peruvian Communist Party–Red Flag, or PCP–BR, but by 1970 they had left this Lima-based organization and adopted the name Peruvian Communist Party–Sendero Luminoso (Shining Path, from José Carlos Mariátegui's assertion that "Marxism-Leninism will open the shining path to revolution").

From its birth until 1973, Sendero Luminoso was the leading political force at the university, having a decisive influence in the selection of students, teachers, and course content, as well as the extension program. Throughout the 1970s, *senderista* militants (i.e., those who espoused the policies of Sendero Luminoso) who graduated from the education program assumed teaching positions throughout the department of Ayacucho, when they learned Quechua, if necessary, and often married into local families. Sendero thus gained widespread political influence among the region's youth; by 1980, the number of *senderista* militants was estimated at between 250 and 500.[21]

Early Government Response

Ongoing activities by Sendero, which included widespread theft of dynamite from the area's many small mining centers, attacks on local government offices and other "symbols of the bourgeois state" (including the blowing up of numerous electrical pylons), and the dissemination of revolutionary graffiti throughout the Ayacucho region, were initially dismissed by the government as the work of "isolated criminal delinquents" and "agents of hostile foreign powers." Belaúnde's reluctance to call on the armed forces to meet this challenge was due both to this cavalier attitude, which emanated from a lack of good intelligence data on Sendero or a serious attitude on the threat it might impose, and to the widespread concern that enlisting the military against a subversive enemy could result in a coup d'état, as it had in Argentina and Uruguay less than a decade before.

The government's most drastic early measure was the adoption, in March 1981, of a sweeping antiterrorist law that made a broad range of crimes punishable as acts of terrorism. Several of its provisions—especially those that provided for the detention of suspected terrorists, without charges, for 15 days, and that made it a crime punishable by up to 25 years in prison to "speak out publicly in favor of a terrorist"—were widely condemned as measures that could be used to unjustly punish the government's legitimate opposition on the left. Thousands of opposition figures, particularly among IU militants and peasant and labor union leaders, were in fact detained under the law's provisions during subsequent years.[22]

Sendero Luminoso's first attack on a police post, at Tambo in Ayacucho's La Mar province, the following October, made the government sit up and take notice, however. Along with four other Ayacucho provinces, La Mar was placed under a state of emergency, thus suspending a number of constitutional guarantees, including the right to public assembly, and allowing police to search homes and make arrests without a warrant. Members of the Civil Guard's elite Sinchi (meaning "those who can do anything" in Quechua) battalion were also sent to Ayacucho for the first time. They proved, however, to be "effective recruiting sergeants for Sendero, [as they] raped and killed indiscriminately, and failed to prevent further attacks on police posts."[23]

Escalation under a State of Emergency

Indeed, *senderista* activity in Ayacucho increased dramatically during 1982. In addition to the types of activities described above, guerrillas began to close down local markets in an (unpopular) effort to force peasants to cease all capitalist activity and produce exclusively for subsistence purposes. More ominous, Sendero began a murder campaign against mayors and other government officials, local landowners and shopkeepers whom Sendero determined to be "enemies of the people," and peasants who refused to cooperate with them, who were termed "traitors." These activities invited, at the time, Sendero's comparison to the Khmer

Rouge of Pol Pot in Cambodia. In March and again in August 1982, Lima was blacked out by the simultaneous dynamiting of numerous electrical pylons, which were followed by a number of explosions under cover of darkness that brought the terror to Peru's capital city. Two events in the city of Ayacucho were even more worrisome, however. The assault on the Ayacucho prison in March 1982, when 247 persons were freed, including many of Sendero's top leaders, made it clear to all that Sendero was a well-organized and formidable opponent. The attendance of between 10,000 and 30,000 persons at the Ayacucho funeral of 19-year-old slain *senderista* Edith Lagos the following September demonstrated, furthermore, that the insurgents had gained the backing of considerable numbers of the local population. This conclusion was supported by numerous estimates at the time by journalists, scholars, and even the police chief of Ayacucho that Sendero had gained the allegiance, whether through admiration or fear, of a large majority of the citizens of Ayacucho, particularly among its youth.[24]

The escalation of Sendero's assassination campaign during mid-December, which included the gunning down of Ayacucho's deputy mayor in front of his wife and children, at last led the government to call the armed forces into the counterinsurgency campaign. Army and naval marine units were called in to reinforce the police forces, which had clearly been losing an escalating war with Sendero, and the state of emergency was extended to four more provinces, to make a total of nine. A Politico-Military Command, headquartered in the city of Ayacucho, was also created, and political-military chiefs (either army or navy officers) assumed responsibility for governing at the departmental, provincial, and district levels throughout the emergency zone. In July 1984, following reports of an upsurge in violence that was associated with a growing rift between the military and Civil Guard units in the emergency zone, the zone was extended to include a total of 13 provinces in the departments of Ayacucho, Huancavelica, and Apurímac, and command over the joint counterinsurgency campaign was passed to the army. Thereafter, the armed forces controlled all antisubversive activities nationwide.[25]

Rather than bringing about the anticipated pacification, however, the deployment of the armed forces in January 1983 intensified the conflict in the emergency zone. The number of deaths attributed to the war against Sendero, including military, *senderistas,* and civilians, jumped from 170 in 1982 to 2,807 in 1983, and 4,319 in 1984.[26] The widening scope of the war, furthermore, was accompanied by a growing list of allegations against government troops in their conduct of the war. Although military units (particularly the marines) were believed most responsible for the significant increase in the numbers of civilian casualties, pinning blame for such atrocities was often difficult, as Sendero itself became increasingly violent, murdering not only individuals but also entire villages that it suspected of collaborating with authorities. Fearful campesinos, caught in the middle, then undertook violence as a self-protective measure in a situation in which they were being forced to take sides.

The horror of the escalating war in the Andes was brought to the world's attention in January 1983 by the brutal murder of eight journalists by campesinos in Uchuraccay (Huanta province, Ayacucho). The eight were on their way to the village of Huaychao to investigate reports by military authorities that local residents there had killed a band of *senderistas.* Before reaching their destination, however, the unfortunate journalists were apparently mistaken for *senderistas* at Uchuraccay. The murders were never solved, and virtually every witness to the crime "disappeared" over the course of the next few years, while Uchuraccay was transformed into a ghost town. In the course of a government investigation of the incident and two inconclusive trials, however, it became evident that local campesinos, terrorized by both Sendero and the government authorities, were being engaged in the struggle against Sendero by military authorities.[27] Subsequently, it became clear that security forces, as a matter of policy, were actively promoting paramilitary civil defense patrols, known as *montoneros* or *rondas campesinas,* within local communities in the emergency zone.

The Political Ramifications

The escalating war in the *sierra* had profound political ramifications in a number of areas. The November 1983 municipal elections were, predictably, a disaster for Belaúnde's AP party (see "Party Politics and the 1985 Electoral Campaigning" this chapter). In Ayacucho, elections were held only in the central province of Huamanga, and there, fully 56 percent of those who voted either knowingly or unwittingly followed Sendero's instructions by submitting a blank or spoiled ballot. A majority of the eligible voters in Huamanga, moreover, simply abstained.[28]

Government (i.e., military) policy in the emergency zone was also an area of acute political concern. Within the officer corps itself, this was reflected in the existence of two schools of thought on how to best combat the insurgency: one that saw the solution as a purely military one, and another that saw political and developmental aspects to the successful campaign against Sendero Luminoso.[29] The first commander of the Ayacucho-based emergency zone, General Clemente Noel Moral, was from the first school, while the second, General Adrián Huamán Centeno, who replaced Noel in January 1984, was of the second school. General Huamán, himself a native of Apurímac, publicly declared that a solution to the threat posed by Sendero necessitated government funding of development projects that would begin to reverse the secular process of social and economic decay in the region surrounding Ayacucho. In August

1984, amid a series of embarrassing revelations in the Lima press regarding a growing number of atrocities perpetrated by the marine units in control of the province of Huanta, General Huamán was relieved of his command—after stating in an interview in the Lima daily *La República* that "the solution for Ayacucho is not military, but the reversal of 160 years of abandonment," then adding that "a change of attitude in Peruvian society is needed, so that the exploitation of the people in the rural areas does not continue and Lima does not keep collecting all the money of Peru."[30]

The Dispersal of Sendero and the Appearance of MRTA

The response of Sendero to the increased military presence in the emergency zone after December 1982 was to disperse from its Ayacucho stronghold into other regions of the country. Guerrilla activity moved northward during 1983, into the mining region around Cerro de Pasco and the coca-growing region of the *ceja de la selva* between Tingo María and Tarapoto, in the departments of Huánuco and San Martín, where *senderistas* were able to capitalize on the growing hostility of local peasants to the government's mounting U.S.–supported anti-coca campaign (see "Armed Adversaries," Chapter 6 in this volume). In mid-1984, this latter region became the site of the second emergency zone created in the government's counterinsurgency campaign.

Bombings and other *senderista* activities became increasingly commonplace in Lima as well. Two of the most spectacular *senderista* actions of 1983 took place in May, when several large Lima business establishments, including a multimillion-dollar Bayer chemical factory, were destroyed by incendiary devices under cover of darkness caused by Sendero's sabotage of a large number of electrical pylons, and in July, when *senderista* gunmen attacked AP party headquarters, killing two people and injuring scores of others.

In June 1984, a second guerrilla organization, the Movimiento Revolucionario Túpac Amaru, or MRTA (named after the Cuzco-based leader of the eighteenth-century Indian rebellion against the Spanish) began its own bombing and assassination campaign in Lima. Led by former *aprista* (and friend of Alan García) Víctor Polay Campos, and containing many youthful ex-militants from the United Left (IU) as well as APRA who had become disillusioned with the post-1980 democratic process, the MRTA was a much more traditional, romantic, and "heroic" guerrilla organization than was the secretive and enigmatic Sendero Luminoso. It targeted leaders and properties of foreign companies, state agencies and enterprises, and local banks, and it also engaged in Robin Hood–style robberies of food that was later distributed in poor neighborhoods. Unlike Sendero, which shunned publicity, the MRTA employed a great publicity apparatus, often issuing "revolutionary manifestos" on radio and television stations that it had seized or blackmailed.

By early 1985, the death toll from nearly five years of guerrilla warfare exceeded 7,000. The majority of the fatalities were campesinos, victims of a conflict beyond their own control. This "dirty war" in the central Andes placed an ugly scar on the return to democratic rule in Peru and begat the major irony to befall the second period of Belaúnde's rule. The fact that democratic rule brought with it violations of human rights that were far beyond those experienced during the 12 years of military rule tragically helped Sendero Luminoso achieve considerable success in attaining its goal of discrediting the government as being repressive, weak, and with little control over its military forces—that is, democratic in name only. From Sendero Luminoso's distorted point of view, the Belaúnde government was, like the military government before it, simply "fascist."

Military coup plots were indeed uncovered on numerous occasions during Belaúnde's second term. The fact that none unfolded successfully, and the president was thereby able to complete his term in office, wound up being one of the few positive accomplishments (along with the holding of scheduled municipal elections in 1980 and 1983 and the return of a free and open press) in an otherwise dismal period for the Peruvian nation. By the time the campaign for the April 1985 election of Belaúnde's successor got under way, there was a widespread sense among the electorate that the president had abdicated his authority over the deteriorating situations with respect to both Sendero Luminoso and the economic crisis and, as a result, the nation was hopelessly adrift.

PARTY POLITICS AND THE 1985 ELECTORAL CAMPAIGN

The Right

The magnitude of the failure of the Belaúnde administration, reflected in the miserable showing of AP in the 1983 municipal contests, also doomed Javier Alva Orlandini's presidential bid from the outset of his hapless campaign. His efforts to distance himself from the unpopular government served to rankle the AP party chief, but did nothing to save Alva from his unhappy electoral fate. Born in Cajamarca in 1927, Alva had organized Belaúnde's first presidential campaign in 1956, then in 1963 he was named minister of interior, a position he used to gain control over the party organization through his appointment of local government officials. Managing to retain his control over the party machinery throughout the next two decades, Alva also became Belaúnde's second vice president and the leading AP party figure in the Senate between 1980 and 1985.

Maintaining his persona as a consummate party boss and pragmatist during his presidential campaign, Alva expressed little to distinguish himself ideologically other than his opposition to the neoliberal economic policies associated with Ulloa. Unable to shake his association with a government that by now was widely ridiculed for its incompetence, however, Alva could not attract more than an embarrassing 7 percent of the vote total, fully 10 percent below his party's sorry 1983 tally. AP's former partner on the right, the PPC, allied itself this time with conservative ex-Aprista Andrés Townsend Ezcurra's Movimiento de Bases Hayistas, and managed to gain almost 12 percent of the total for the candidacy of Luis Bedoya Reyes. The 1985 election, simply put, was little short of a disaster for the Peruvian right (see Table 5.1).

The Left

The Marxist left, however, had dramatically improved its situation since 1980, when not one of its five presidential candidates had gained a respectable vote count. Coming so soon after having demonstrated the wide electoral appeal of the left in the 1978 Constituent Assembly elections, the left's 1980 electoral failure had made it clear that a concerted effort at cooperation among the diverse factions of the Marxist left was essential if they were to be successful in future electoral endeavors.

This lesson, together with the similarity of the vote totals of the five Marxist presidential candidates in 1980, had laid the basis for a renewed effort—this time successful—at coalition building in order to compete in the November 1980 municipal elections. In September, IU was formed as an electoral front that brought together three recently created coalitions of Marxist parties (the UNIR, UI, and UDP), together with the FOCEP and a group of "non-party militants." Of all the electoral parties on the left, only the Trotskyite PRT did not join IU (see Figure 4.1 in this volume). This cooperative effort yielded immediate rewards: IU gained 23.3 percent of the national vote total in November 1980, winning the mayorality of Arequipa, the nation's second city, and finishing second in Lima, eight percentage points behind the victorious AP candidate. IU's candidate for mayor of Lima had been Alfonso Barrantes Lingán, a non-party militant who was a principal proponent of the creation of IU and was to serve as its president from its inception until 1987. Barrantes, an intelligent and likable native of Cajamarca, was born in 1928, was active as a student leader at the University of San Marcos in Lima, and was an Aprista militant before joining the Communist Party in 1959. He came down on the Maoist side of the Sino-Soviet split, but dropped his affiliation with the Maoist UDP before the creation of IU. During the 1980s, in

Table 5.1
National Presidential Elections: 1985 and 1990 (percentage of valid votes)

	1985	1990 *
RIGHT (total)	21.39	33.78
FREDEMO		32.62
CODE	11.88	
(PPC and MBH)		
AP	7.26	
FRENATRACA	1.41	1.16
FDUN	0.84	
APRA	53.11	22.64
CAMBIO 90		29.09
LEFT (total)	24.68	13.05
IU	24.68	8.24
IS		4.81
OTHER	0.82	1.45

Note: If space is blank, then either that party did not exist at the time or its candidate ran under a coalition such as IU or FREDEMO.

PRESIDENTIAL CANDIDATES

RIGHT

FREDEMO:	1990 -- Mario Vargas Llosa
CODE:	1985 -- Luis Bedoya Reyes
AP:	1985 -- Javier Alva Orlandini
FRENATRACA:	1990 -- Roger Cáceres Velásquez
	1985 -- Roger Cáceres Velásquez
FDUN:	1985 -- Francisco Morales Bermúdez
APRA	1990 -- Luis Alva Castro
	1985 -- Alan García Pérez **
CAMBIO 90	1990 -- Alberto Fujimori Fujimori **

LEFT

IU:	1990 -- Henry Pease García
	1985 -- Alfonso Barrantes Lingán
IS:	1990 -- Alfonso Barrantes Lingán

* First-round election. Second-round, runoff election results were as follows: CAMBIO 90--62.50 percent; FREDEMO--37.50 percent
** Victor

KEY TO PARTY NAMES

AP	Acción Popular
APRA	Partido Aprista Peruano
CODE	Convergencia Democrática
CAMBIO 90	Cambio 90
FDUN	Frente Democrático de Unidad Nacional
FREDEMO	Frente Democrático
FRENATRACA	Frente Nacional de Trabajadores y Campesinos
IS	Izquierda Socialista
IU	Izquierda Unida
MBH	Movimiento de Bases Hayistas
PPC	Partido Popular Cristiano

Sources: Fernando Tuesta Soldevilla, *Perú político en cifras* (Lima: Fundación Friedrich Ebert, 1987), p. 199; *El Comercio*, May 17, 1990, p. A8; *El Comercio*, July 4, 1990, p. A5.

openly expressing his predilection for democratic socialism, Barrantes found himself one of the most moderate among the leadership in IU.

On the basis of its electoral success in the 1980 municipal contest, the IU's participants decided to maintain the electoral coalition in anticipation of future elections. Its success in the 1983 municipal elections, in which IU captured 29.5 percent of the national vote and Barrantes was elected mayor of Lima, surpassed even its own expectations. In only three years, the IU had become no less than the strongest Marxist electoral force to appear in Latin America since Salvador Allende's Popular Unity Coalition, which had ruled Chile more than a decade before.

Barrantes proved to be a popular and successful mayor of Lima. He ran up against some difficulties, for example, in the perennial problem area of garbage collection. For the most part, however, the capital city was administered efficiently during his three-year term, and several highly successful programs, most notably the "glass of milk" program for poor children of the *barriadas,* were initiated. Many considered Barrantes's mayoral term a successful test of the IU's ability to govern.

During his 1985 presidential campaign, Barrantes attempted to capitalize on this image as a moderate, a representative of the so-called "responsible" left, in an effort to broaden his appeal beyond the IU's normal constituency among the poor in the southern *sierra* and the *pueblos jóvenes* that surround Lima and Peru's other coastal cities. The program to which he committed himself—which included the nationalization of both the Southern Peru Copper Company and the Banco de Crédito, a moratorium on repayment of Peru's debt to foreign commercial banks, and a revision of oil exploration contracts with foreign firms—was less moderate than this public image, however. As a result of these, as well as other, radical positions maintained by some factions within the IU, which included lifting the Ayacucho state of emergency, neither the armed forces nor the middle classes ever overcame their distrust of Barrantes's candidacy.[31]

In the end, Barrantes managed to gain only 24.7 percent of the total valid vote, some five percentage points below IU's nationwide average in 1983. The major problem of his campaign had not been of his own making, but was due, rather, to the extraordinary strength of the candidacy of his *aprista* opponent.

APRA and the Rise of García

Party insiders already knew of the extraordinary political talents of Alan García Pérez, who had managed to bridge the enormous crevice created by the death of Haya de la Torre, the crushing defeat of Villanueva in the 1980 presidential contest, and the subsequent defection of Andrés Townsend, the party's other principal post-Haya leader. With the help of such key allies among the *aprista* old guard as Luis Alberto Sánchez, Luis Felipe de las Casas, and Jorge Torres Vallejo, García had been able to edge out Carlos Enrique Melgar for the top party position of secretary general at the October 1982 party congress.[32] From his position of party secretary general, García had then easily defeated Javier Valle Riestra in 1984 internal party elections to become APRA's candidate for the 1985 presidential elections.

García's party credentials were impeccable. Both his parents were *aprista* militants; his father had been imprisoned for party activity during the first five years of Alan's life. He was born and raised in Lima, where at age 11, he joined the APRA youth and later attended San Marcos and the Catholic universities. In 1972, he went to Europe to continue his studies, earning a doctorate of law at the University of Madrid and also studying for a time with François Borricaud at the Sorbonne before returning to Peru in 1977. He was elected to the Constituent Assembly in 1978, named APRA's national organization secretary (the same post that his father had held when he was imprisoned) the following year, then elected to the Chamber of Deputies in 1980.

Under García's leadership of the party, there was an acceleration of the renovation of APRA's public image, begun during the 1970s, in order to present the party as politically moderate and unequivocally in favor of a democratic electoral process. This process culminated in García's presidential campaign, during which APRA was fashioned in the mold of a European-style social democratic party. García's campaign slogan, "My promise is to all Peruvians," was purposely fashioned by García's image makers to contrast with APRA's age-old slogan, "Only APRA can save Peru," in order to temper public concern over the sectarian character of the APRA party.

García's position in public opinion polls remained so strong throughout his campaign that he saw little need to publicly debate any of his opponents, or even to define his political program beyond a promise to reactivate the moribund economy. The April 14 election saw García take an astounding 53 percent of the valid vote total. A recently enacted law, however, stipulated that null and blank ballots were to be included in the calculation of whether a candidate receives the absolute majority required by the constitution if he/she is to avoid a second-round election. Thus defined, García's vote reached only 45.7 percent of the total (valid plus invalid) votes, consequently forcing him into a second-round election against the runner-up, Alfonso Barrantes. Shortly afterward, however, acknowledging that his first-round vote total (less than half of that of García) left him no chance to win, Barrantes declined to participate in a second round. The National Electoral Jury accepted this concession, and in June it named García president-elect. One of García's most cogent campaign slogans had been "Peru has hope." Indeed, for many of the independent voters who gave APRA its first presidential victory in its 60-year history as Peru's most important political party, Alan García was seen as the only salvation at a time of extraordinary national distress. García's inauguration on July 28, 1985, marked the first transition from one freely elected Peruvian president to another since 1919. Along with this milestone in the consolidation of Peruvian democracy came the realization that solutions to the urgent problems of economic development and social equity would have to be found if this welcome respite in Peru's authoritarian political history was to endure.

NOTES

1. James M. Malloy, "Peru's Troubled Return to Democratic Government," *UFSI Reports,* South America Series, No. 15 (Hanover, N.H.: UFSI, 1982), p. 5.

2. Of a total of 3,965 laws expedited between July 28, 1980, and June 26, 1989, the executive expedited 2,114, while the Congress expedited for only 1,851. See "La primera década de la Constitución," *Debate* (Lima), Vol. XI, No. 56 (July/August 1989), p. 62.

3. Ibid., p. 63.

4. See Michael Reid, *Peru: Paths to Poverty* (London: Latin American Bureau, 1985), pp. 81–92. Also useful on the political economy of Belaúnde's second term is Thomas G. Sanders, "Economics and the Peruvian Political Process," *UFSI Reports,* South America series, No. 28 (Hanover, N.H.: UFSI, 1984), pp. 6–9.

5. Sanders, "Economics," p. 7.

6. David Scott Palmer, "Peru," in *Latin American and Caribbean Contemporary Record, Vol. I, 1981–1982,* Jack W. Hopkins, ed. (New York: Holmes and Meier, 1983), p. 351.

7. U.S. Department of Commerce, "Marketing in Peru," *Overseas Business Reports* (June 1984), p. 17. Net foreign investment figures published by the Banco del Crédito in its English-language *Peruvian Quarterly Report* confirm a positive flow of foreign investment until 1984, when it turned negative.

8. Reid, *Peru,* p. 85; Thomas G. Sanders, "Peru between Democracy and Sendero Luminoso," *UFSI Reports,* South America series, No. 21 (Hanover, N.H.: UFSI, 1984), p. 3.

9. Sanders, "Peru," p. 2.

10. Carol Wise, "Democratization, Crisis, and APRA's Modernization Project in Peru," in *Debt and Democracy in Latin America,* Barbara Stallings and Robert Kaufman, eds. (Boulder, Colo.: Westview Press, 1989), p. 169.

11. *The Andean Report* (Lima), June 1983, pp. 109–112.

12. World Bank report, December 17, 1985.

13. *The Andean Report* (Lima), October 1983, p. 183. This extraordinary report on Peru's defense contracting states that Peru's defense budget is considered a state secret. The Stockholm International Peace Research Institute, *World Armaments and Disarmament: SIPRI Yearbook, 1984,* pp. 129–131, however, shows

Peru's defense spending rising from 5.7 percent of the GDP in 1980 to 8.2 percent in 1984.

14. U.S. Department of State, *Background Notes: Peru,* February 1985, pp. 5–6. Also see *The Andean Report* (Lima), April 1984, p. 61.

15. William P. Avery, "Origins and Consequences of the Border Dispute between Ecuador and Peru," *Inter-American Economic Affairs,* Vol. 38, No. 1 (Summer 1984), pp. 69–72.

16. David Scott Palmer, "Peru," pp. 393–411 in *Latin America and Caribbean Contemporary Record, Vol. II: 1982–1983,* Jack W. Hopkins, ed. (New York: Holmes and Meier, 1983), p. 401.

17. Cynthia McClintock, "Democracies and Guerrillas: The Peruvian Experience," *International Policy Report* (Washington, D.C.: Center for International Policy, 1983), p. 4.

18. These figures are reported by David Scott Palmer, "Rebellion in Rural Peru: The Origins and Evolution of Sendero Luminoso," *Comparative Politics,* Vol. 18, No. 2 (January 1986).

19. Cynthia McClintock, "Why Peasants Rebel: The Case of Peru's Sendero Luminoso," *World Politics,* Vol. 37, No. 2 (October 1984), pp. 59–61. For the percentage of agrarian reform beneficiaries, see Palmer, "Rebellion in Rural Peru," p. 22.

20. See Reid, *Peru,* pp. 99–102, and Cynthia McClintock, "The Performance of the New Andean Democracies: A Preliminary Effort at Comparison for Peru and Ecuador" (Paper presented to the Latin American Studies Association meeting in Albuquerque, New Mexico, April 18–20, 1985), pp. 14–21.

21. Cynthia McClintock, "Sendero Luminoso: Peru's Maoist Guerrillas," *Problems of Communism,* September–October, 1983, p. 20. On the growth of Sendero during the 1960s and 1970s, see also Palmer, "Rebellion in Rural Peru," and Colin Harding, "Antonio Díaz Martínez and the Ideology of Sendero Luminoso," *Bulletin of Latin American Research* (London), Vol. 7, No. 1 (1988), pp. 65–74.

22. America's Watch Committee, *Abdicating Democratic Authority: Human Rights in Peru* (New York, October 1984), pp. 32–36.

23. Reid, *Peru,* p. 111.

24. McClintock, "Why Peasants Rebel," p. 54.

25. "Army Now Controls Anti-Sendero Action," *Latin America Weekly Report,* July 27, 1984, p. 9. Also see Americas Watch Committee, *Abdicating Democratic Authority,* p. 81.

26. República Peruana. Comisión Especial del Senado sobre las Causas de la Violencia y Alternativas de Pacificación en el Perú, *Violencia y Pacificación* (Lima: DESCO y la Comisión Andina de Juristas, 1989), p. 375.

27. The controversial results of the government investigation can be found in Mario Vargas Llosa, "Inquest in the Andes: A Latin American Writer Explores the Political Lessons of a Peruvian Massacre," *The New York Times Magazine* (July 31, 1983), pp. 18–56.

28. McClintock, "Why Peasants Rebel," pp. 56–7, and Palmer, "Rebellion in Rural Peru," p. 6.

29. Philip Mauceri, *Militares: insurgencia y democratización en el Perú, 1980–1988* (Lima: Instituto de Estudios Peruanos, 1989), pp. 41–50.

30. Quoted in America's Watch Committee, *Abdicating Democratic Authority,* p. 3. Also see Reid, *Peru,* pp. 118–20.

31. *The Andean Report* (Lima), February 1985, pp. 4–8, 13.

32. Carol L. Graham, "APRA 1968–1988: From Evolution to Government—The Elusive Search for Political Integration in Peru" (D. Phil. thesis, Oxford University, January 1989), pp. 142–50.

6

ALAN GARCÍA PÉREZ AT THE HEIGHT OF HIS POWER: 1985-1987

ILLUSIONS OF GRANDEUR

Not unlike his predecessor, then, Alan García took office on a crest of public optimism. Hope stemmed from the departure of President Belaúnde, who had widely been perceived as having been incapable of governing effectively since the economic debacle of 1983, as well as from the advent of a youthful new president who brought with him fresh ideas and enthusiasm to attack Peru's long-standing economic quandaries of poverty and underdevelopment.

Indeed, the dreadful recent performance of the economy had left plenty of room for improvement. The per capita GDP, after plunging some 15 percent in 1983 and recovering less than 2 percent during 1984, was left at a level 12.3 percent below that of 1980. A 1985 World Bank study that measured a 19 percent decline in average real household income between 1972 and 1983 also found that the highest income groups had been far more successful in protecting their incomes than had the poor, and thus income distribution had deteriorated substantially during the interim. The extent of the economic recession was evidenced by the prevalence of unutilized capacity, measured by some as high as 55 percent of the total, of Peru's industrial sector. Inflation, 112 percent in 1984 and headed for more than 200 percent in 1985, was perceived to be out of control. Employment figures were equally grim: open urban unemployment was at 16 percent, up from 11 percent in 1980, while underemployment had grown from 51 to 57 percent in the same five-year interval. To top off the economic morass, by mid-1985 Peru was more than $2 billion in arrears on its external debt payments.[1]

García entered the presidency with a pledge to attack inflation and to stimulate an economic reactivation. Citing Peru's unused industrial capacity as evidence, García and his team of economic advisors, putting into practice what became known as heterodox economic theories, rejected the standard diagnosis of inflation as being caused by excess demand; they saw cost-push factors, instead, as being the primary culprits. The new government's anti-inflation program, announced less than a week after assuming power, accordingly consisted of a freeze in exchange rates, a freeze in the prices of a wide spectrum of goods and services, and a lowering of interest rates. Policies aimed at reactivation were enacted gradually over the next several months, and included generous wage increases to stimulate consumer demand, along with severe restrictions on the importation of goods competing with products made in Peru. To stimulate employment, García created a temporary work program, the Support Program for Temporary Income, known by its Spanish acronym PAIT, which paid minimum wage to some 50,000 to 75,000 workers who engaged in public works programs.

The 10 Percent Solution

These early measures were of great interest to the people of Peru, who were grateful for having an alternative way out of their economic straits. García came to the attention of the rest of the world, however, as a result of his dramatic inaugural address announcement that his government would bypass the International Monetary Fund in its foreign debt negotiations and would unilaterally limit its debt service payments during the next 12 months to an amount equal to 10 percent of Peru's export earnings. Full debt service payment in mid-1985 would have amounted to approximately 60 percent of Peru's $3 billion annual export earnings; if unpaid prior sums were included in the calculation, the figure would have swollen to over 100 percent.[2] On the question of which creditors would be paid, García pledged to pay in full, first of all, any new debt contracted. Next, multilateral lending agencies were to receive payment up to the amount of new money flowing into Peru. Then came government creditors and, lastly, private banks.

The world took notice not because the new Peruvian government decided to limit its debt payments; that had been the *de facto* policy of the Belaúnde regime since 1983, and during the first half of 1985, it had paid virtually nothing on Peru's debt. García's innovation was, rather, political: restricting debt payments now became official government policy. His highly vocal public criticism of the international financial system presented a challenge to Peru's creditors as well as to fellow debtor nations to seek innovative solutions to a problem that had become of increasing concern to both since Mexico had triggered the Latin American debt crisis in 1982.

Peru's creditors, not surprisingly, were antagonistic toward García's debt stance, especially fearful that he would spur larger debtor nations into assuming similar postures. The U.S. government took early action, pronouncing Peru's debt "value impaired" in October, which required private banks to increase their capital backing for their Peruvian loans, and temporarily halting new military assistance as well as loans through the Agency for International Development when Peru fell more than a year behind in its payments. Peruvian government officials displayed little concern at their "value impaired" status, even though it meant that Peru was unlikely to receive further U.S. private bank loans. "We don't need fresh money," Central Bank President Richard Webb was quoted as saying at the time, "we're better off without it for the next five or ten years."[3]

In April 1986, the IMF demanded payment of the $70 million in arrears that Peru had accumulated or risk being declared ineligible for new loans, a status that would virtually assure Peru's isolation from Western financial circles. The last-minute payment of about half the sum elicited a postponement of Peru's reckoning with the IMF until the following August when, according to the timetable presented in his July 28, 1985, inaugural speech, García's "10 percent solution" was scheduled for revision.

Meantime, the new Peruvian government sought to widen the scope of new foreign borrowing and was successful in obtaining development assistance loans from West Germany, Italy, and Canada. A sizable amount of Peru's multibillion-dollar debt with Soviet bloc nations, most of which had been accrued in the purchase of weapons, was renegotiated to be repaid in nontraditional exports in lieu of hard currencies. The new government hoped to promote other such barter arrangements in the future.

Multilateral Foreign Policy Initiatives

García's efforts to mobilize his fellow Latin American debtors began auspiciously, with 7 Latin American presidents and 13 foreign ministers attending García's inauguration and signing the so-called Lima Declaration, which called for international financial reform measures, including increased flexibility on the part of creditors. García immediately boosted Peru's participation in the Cartagena Group, an organization of 11 of Latin America's major debtor nations that had been formed in June 1984 to address their common problem. Peru's debt stance received an early endorsement from the U.N. Group of 77 developing nations, and, at a September 1985 meeting of the Nonaligned Movement in Angola, a Peruvian resolution was introduced that called for placing a limit on debt service payments.

García expressed a belief that the United States was the main beneficiary, if not the arbiter, of the prevailing international financial system. In a major speech before the U.N. General Assembly in September, García compared the IMF letters of intent to "letters of colonial submission to the prevailing unfair economic conditions. Moreover," he continued, "the IMF calls for austerity only in poor countries, while favoring the most powerful nation on earth. Ever since the U.S. dollar was taken off the gold standard in 1971, the United States has been the only country that can issue currency indefinitely to cover its own deficit."[4] The U.S. fiscal deficit was also a common object of García's criticism as a cause of the extraordinarily high interest rates that prevailed during the early 1980s.

Such tough talk accompanying García's debt stance was a key ingredient in his government's effort to renew Peru's position of leadership among the nonaligned nations that it had held under Velasco. García clearly took these ambitions personally, and the politics of multilateral solidarity among the poor nations also coincided with long-standing APRA ideology that saw the party in a vanguard position in the promotion of regional integration and anti-imperialism. The populist appeal of multilateralism, as an expression of Latin American and Third World nationalism, appealed to APRA's opposition on the left, at home, and helped garner support abroad for Peru in its anticipated clashes with the United States over the foreign debt.

The invigoration of the sagging process of Latin American economic integration was, accordingly, given priority among the new government's foreign policy goals. Increased Peruvian activism in both the Latin American Economic System (Sistema Económico Latinoamericana, or SELA) and the Latin American Integration Association (Asociación Latinoamericana de Integración, or ALADI, formerly LAFTA) was pledged, but the major concern was the reactivation of the Andean Common Market (Ancom, also known as the Cartagena Accord). It was an uphill battle; neither SELA nor ALADI had ever been especially effective, while Ancom had suffered a series of reversals since its heyday in the early 1970s. By the mid-1980s, Chile had long ago left the Common Market, Bolivia was a member in name only, and Venezuela and Ecuador were both on the verge of leaving Ancom over long-held differences with respect to the organization's restrictive trade and foreign investment regulations.

The García administration also sought to diversify Peru's patterns of trade, in which the United States had traditionally weighed heavily, due both to the persistence of extensive protectionist sentiment in the United States, which had recently manifested itself in restrictions on Peruvian textile imports, as well as to anticipated adverse U.S. actions in response to García's debt stance. The nations of the Middle East and the East Asian shore of the Pacific Basin were singled out in this effort as especially promising future trading partners. Increased trade was also sought with the nations of Latin America, particularly Argentina, Brazil, and Peru's Andean neighbors.

The energetic foreign ministry under Allen Wagner pursued a number of additional international initiatives during the early months of the García administration's tenure in office. In December 1985 the U.N. General Assembly approved a Peruvian proposal calling for Latin American disarmament. Arguing that the impoverished Latin American nations could no longer afford to continue their arms-buying spree of recent decades, García's regional disarmament campaign had been launched by his inaugural address announcement of his government's reduction in Peru's previously planned purchase of 26 Mirage 2000 jet fighters from France. Bilateral talks with Chile and Ecuador on mutual disarmament were subsequently undertaken, although García's stated goal was a multilateral agreement to reduce Latin American arms expenditures and to freeze the purchase of new weaponry within the entire region.

Unilateral action, on the other hand, taken by the Reagan administration to destabilize the Sandinista regime in Nicaragua, was viewed as a threat to the sovereignty not just of Nicaragua, but of all Latin America. In his U.N. speech, García expressed his belief that "the future of Latin America is now at stake in that [Central American] region," and that the crisis wracking Central American was a Latin American problem requiring a Latin American solution.[5]

In July 1985, following García's inaugural address call for the democratic nations of Latin America to join Peru in a front to support the Contadora nations in seeking a peaceful solution to the Central American crisis, the Contadora Support Group was organized. Joined by Argentina, Brazil, and Uruguay in addition to Peru, the Support Group held a number of formal meetings with the foreign ministers of the four Contadora nations. In February 1986 the foreign ministers met with Secretary of State George Shultz in Washington, urging the United States to pursue its Central American policies through diplomatic, rather than military channels. A month later, with a view toward his government's professed role in the vanguard against imperialism, García announced that Peru would break diplomatic relations with the United States should it invade Nicaragua.[6]

At the same time that the García government advocated a multilateral foreign policy strategy, particularly when it championed the concerns of the developing nations, it was also critical of the established multilateral bodies. The Nonaligned Movement was criticized as having become discredited by its increasingly close association with the Soviet bloc. Peru's debt proposal at the 1985 Angola meeting was part of a promised effort to redirect the Nonaligned Movement from East–West to North–South issues. The OAS was criticized for its domination by the United States and its irrelevance with respect to the important issues facing the hemisphere. In late 1985, the Peruvian foreign minister proposed the creation of an informal mechanism within the OAS in which the Latin American nations could consult on such issues without U.S. participation. García also called on the United Nations to become more active in promoting a just distribution of the world's wealth and challenged the compatibility of the veto authority held by five world powers within the Security Council with the U.N. principle of the equality of nations.

The Stance toward Multinational Firms

In the same populist spirit of rectifying the accounts between the developed and developing nations, García called the foreign multinational corporations operating in Peru to task. Only days after assuming office, García cancelled the oil exploration contracts, containing controversial tax rebates, that in 1982 had been granted to the three U.S.-based firms operating in Peru. The following December, two of the firms reached new agreements that included an increase in their tax burdens, the payment of back taxes, and higher levels of profit reinvestment. The third, the U.S.-based Belco Petroleum Company (Peru's second largest foreign producer, operating offshore of Peru's north coast since 1960, with investments estimated at $58 million), decided not to negotiate, however. In an action applauded by García's opposition on the left and decried on the right, the assets of Belco were swiftly taken over and transferred to a new state-owned enterprise, Petromar. Parallels were promptly drawn to Velasco's takeover of the International Petroleum Company, also over a dispute involving back taxes, during the early days of his rule. Others noted, however, that the Belco takeover was aimed at the policies of the Belaúnde government, which had been considered overly eager to attract new oil exploration, rather than at Belco or the overall role of foreign capital in the economy.

In early 1986, nevertheless, the Peruvian subsidiary of the Swiss foodstuffs giant, Nestlé, was accused of a variety of abuses that stemmed from its monopoly in the production of milk. After a series of negotiations that occasioned an extensive examination of the detrimental role played by the prevalence of monopolies throughout the Peruvian economy, Nestlé agreed to sell a portion of its milk production to competing firms.

The initial program of the García administration, then, was both highly contrary to orthodox economic theory, as well as ardently nationalistic and anti-imperialistic in the spirit of early *aprista* ideology. Unfortunately, it was also anachronistic; García's idealistic world view pertained less to the conservative world of the late 1980s than to APRA's revolutionary period during the 1920s, or perhaps the late 1960s. "I don't mind that García has so many people at work trying to remake the international economy to his liking," a Peruvian banker was quoted as saying in late 1985, "but I wish he'd have one or two working on the way the economy works today—just in case he fails."[7] These words were soon to prove prophetic.

García's Dominant Political Position

In the meantime, however, Alan García was a brightly shining star in an otherwise dimly lit political universe. A widely quoted public opinion poll taken in August 1985, shortly after the inauguration of his emergency economic plan and the announcement of his 10 percent limitation on debt repayment, gave García an incredible 96 percent public approval rating. This extraordinary popular appeal, coming on the heels of one of the most successful electoral campaigns in Peruvian history, left the APRA party faithful (who held 32 of the total of 60 Senate seats, 105 of the 180 seats in the Chamber of Deputies, and untold thousands of appointed positions in the new government) greatly indebted to García. His authority as undisputed party chief was thus vastly magnified, and a new party post—president of APRA—was created especially for "Alan" (as he was affectionately referred to) in recognition of his elevated position of authority.

García's public appearances and proclamations during these early months in office were highly orchestrated to be in the populist style— bypassing the institutional political framework and the powers-that-be to communicate directly with *el pueblo* (the common people)—frequently found in Peru's past political leaders. The president was a highly effective orator, and his recurrent *balconazos* (unannounced speeches from the second-floor balcony of the National Palace) became familiar to a populace anticipating the declaration of further measures promising to improve its fortune. Frequent proclamations were made, such as lowering his own government salary allotment (and, in turn, that of the ministers and thousands of top managers in government because no government official could, by law, receive a higher salary than the president), and announcing the sale of the palacial ambassadorial residence in Washington, D.C. Both were welcomed with delight by the masses yearning for symbols of responsible and ethical acts by their elected officials. García's critics, nevertheless, viewed them as acts of demagoguery.

The Peruvian president is expected, by custom if not by law, to remain above direct participation in partisan electoral politics. During the November 1986 municipal elections, however, García used his considerable personal popularity (public opinion polls still gave him an approval rating of some 70 percent) to give a last-minute boost to the campaign of Jorge del Castillo, APRA's mayoral candidate in Lima. A little-known mayor of the Lima district of Barranco, del Castillo waged an uphill campaign— promising to build an electric train to alleviate Lima's growing deficiency in mass transit—against the incumbent mayor of Lima and leader of IU,

Alfonso Barrantes, and Luis Bedoya Reyes, the head of PPC who had been a very popular mayor of Lima during two consecutive terms in the 1960s, when he had been credited with greatly expanding the capital city's beachfront as well as building its only expressway. AP, after the disaster of its 1985 vote, decided to sit out the 1986 local elections.

In an unmistakeable bid to further strengthen the power of the governing party, President García appeared on television with del Castillo the night before the elections to exhort APRA victories nationwide. This appearance was widely criticized, although not technically illegal. The open electoral propaganda of the *aprista* newspaper *Hoy* on election morning, however, was blatantly illegal (partisan media propaganda is prohibited for a full week before all Peruvian elections), and the paper was fined as a result. Del Castillo's narrow victory, gaining 38.8 percent of the vote against 33.7 for Barrantes and 25.4 for Bedoya, was also marred by allegations of PAIT workers being bribed, coerced, or tricked into voting for APRA candidates and of outright fraud in the vote tally. Outside Lima, APRA had an easier time of it, gaining nearly 48 percent of the total nationwide vote and winning an impressive 20 of 24 mayoral races in departmental capitals.[8]

García's status within APRA, though never attaining the revered, almost godlike stature that Haya de la Torre retained throughout the decade following his death, was nevertheless imposing. In 1986, a movement developed inside the party to amend the constitution to do away with the prohibition against presidential reelection in order to permit García to run again for the presidency in 1990. This movement, which was reportedly encouraged discreetly by the president himself, never gained the support necessary to have the proposal discussed in the Senate, however.

García's domination of the political scene during 1985 and 1986 was to such an extent, nevertheless, that he monopolized many of the powers that the Peruvian president typically shares with his party and with his cabinet ministers. García's use of non-*aprista técnicos* (experts in technical matters) in many top advisory positions pointed to the deficiency of technical skills within the APRA party leadership, as well as to García's personalistic leadership style.[9]

President García personally made all major (and many minor) political and economic decisions; consultations with personal friends and advisors such as Luis Gonzáles Posada, Daniel Carbonetto, and Hugo Otero were much more important in this respect than were the regular Thursday cabinet meetings.[10] The president's top economic advisors, known as *los audaces* (the bold ones), included a number of foreigners (Carbonetto, an Argentine in Peru under a U.N. contract, headed *los audaces* until his resignation in September 1988; Pierre Vigier was a Frenchman on loan from the European Economic Community), together with Daniel Schydlowsky, a Peruvian-born professor of economics at Harvard, and youthful *aprista* ministers—Gustavo Saberbein of economy and finance, Manuel Romero Caro of industry, and Remigio Morales Bermúdez of agriculture, as well as Javier Tanteleán of the National Planning Institute.[11] Not surprisingly, many longtime party leaders, including Luis Alberto Sánchez, Víctor Villanuava, and, especially, Luis Alva Castro, García's prime minister and an economist by profession, sustained considerable resentment against García's personal domination of governmental power.

Early Adversity

The initial foreign policy successes of the García administration were tempered by a number of early setbacks in the president's political offensive to ease the burden of the external debt. A public quarrel with Fidel Castro, who had proposed that debtor nations declare a moratorium on repayment, while serving to emphasize the moderation of García's proposal, also highlighted the absence of the unity among debtor nations that García sought. Ultimately much more damaging was the Reagan administration's October launching of the Baker Plan to increase lending by multilateral and commercial banks. In time, it was to prove highly successful in taking the wind out of the sails of García's bid to sway other debtors to limit their payments. Although a declaration issued at the close of a December 1985 foreign ministers' meeting in Montevideo, Uruguay, coincided in a number of respects with García's debt posture, including its criticism of the Baker Plan as "insufficient," it fell far short of openly supporting Peru's unilateral declaration on limiting debt service payments.

Having failed to win adequate international support, García was left at the mercy of Peru's creditors. The president offered no policy revision or loan payment to appease the IMF in August 1986, and Peru thereafter joined a small group of less than illustrious nations—Vietnam, Zambia, Somalia, Guyana, Sudan, and Liberia—whose failure to make external loan payments had ostracized them from the international financial community. Shortly thereafter, Peru's failure to stay current on loans with the World Bank led it to be declared unworthy to receive new loans and, in 1989, the same fate befell Peru with respect to the Inter-American Development Bank. The early response of the economy to the García administration's heterodox economic program, as measured by a number of standard indicators, was highly favorable. The expansion in output, 9.5 percent of the GDP in 1986 and 6.9 percent in 1987, was unparalleled in living memory. As unused industrial capacity became utilized, employment in the formal sector grew by 10 percent during those two years. At the same time, inflation fell from a 200 percent annual rate to 63 percent in 1986, but then it turned back up to 115 percent in 1987.

The refueling of inflation was an indication that fiscal and foreign exchange imbalances, as well as disorder in the relative prices of key commodities, were on the rise. As early as mid-1986, it was apparent that García's economic team faced difficulties in formulating a coherent strategy to succeed its initial short-term policies of price freezes to control inflation and consumption-led growth. A stimulation of private investment, always problematical in Peru, where capital flight was commonly viewed as a safer alternative, would be required if growth were to proceed beyond the full use of the installed productive capacity of the economy. This deficiency, together with the nearly absolute lack of external finance capital, positioned the Peruvian economy squarely on the road to hyperinflation.

ARMED ADVERSARIES: SENDERO LUMINOSO AND COCA TRAFFICKERS

New Government Counterinsurgency Strategies

While the inauguration of Alan García was accompanied by widespread public optimism that the deteriorating economic situation would at last be turned around, the new government also elicited considerable hope with respect to its ability to thwart the mounting insurgency that had plagued the Belaúnde regime. García had been highly critical of Belaúnde's bungling and counterproductive antisubversive policies during the electoral campaign, and in his inaugural address, García promised to attack the root causes of the *sierra*-based rebellion by improving the standard of living of the rural poor and to stem the growing abuse of human rights by both police and military personnel in their prosecution of the war. In September, García named a blue-ribbon Peace Commission charged with seeking a dialogue with Sendero and proposing other measures that would bring an end to the five-year-old insurgency. At about the same time, an emergency development plan for the so-called Andean Trapezoid was announced, which was to triple the government's development budget in the poor southern departments of Ayacucho, Huancavelica, Apurímac, Cuzco, and Puno.

García's commitment to human rights was given an early test when, in September, two massacres by army officers in the department of Ayacucho, at Accomarca and Pucayacu, came to light. After failing to present the requested military report on the incidents, the head of the joint command, General Enrico Praelli, was promptly dismissed, along with the commanding generals of the Lima-based Second Military Zone and of the Ayacucho-based emergency zone. During a subsequent trip to Ayacucho, García's minister of war, General Jorge Torres Flores, reiterated the government's commitment to bettering the army's human rights record.[12] Although abuses by no means ended, reported incidents of massacres, disappearances, torture, and other gross human rights violation did, indeed, decline thereafter. Government authorities also became far more responsive to organizations monitoring the human rights situation. Whereas President Belaúnde had publicly ridiculed Amnesty International, for example, García announced that his government would seriously consider the recommendations of a report it issued in February 1987.[13]

Other aspects of García's initial antisubversion efforts were less encouraging, however. First of all, early suggestions that his government might consider an amnesty for political prisoners and negotiations with Sendero Luminoso were answered with a bloody *senderista* offensive that featured selective assassinations of military and *aprista* officials. Bombings and political murder in Lima reached unprecedented proportions during the weeks prior to February 6, 1986, when García decreed a state of emergency, along with a 1 to 5 A.M. curfew, in Lima and Callao.

Secondly, after being launched with such fanfare, the Peace Commission was largely disregarded by the government. It worked hard, submitting what one member, Diego García-Sayán of the Andean Commission of Jurists, described as "three kilos" of proposals.[14] García's military advisors, however, rejected the recommendations, which reportedly included the restoration of civilian control in Ayacucho, the repeal of the sweeping 1981 antiterrorist law, and steps toward holding military personnel responsible for human rights violations, and the president himself refused to meet with the commission.[15] In January 1986, the entire commission resigned in protest. A new three-man commission, containing no political opponents of the government, was named, but it accomplished little during its short life.

The Prison Massacres

'The least welcome development with respect to García's early counterinsurgency efforts, however, and quite possibly the key event of his entire first year in office, took the form of a horrifying massacre of rebellious prisoners in three Lima prisons on June 19, 1986. On the morning of the 18th, as the government prepared to host a meeting of the Socialist International, accused *senderistas* in Lurigancho Prison, El Frontón Prison, and the Santa Bárbara Women's Prison simultaneously revolted, taking hostages and presenting identical lists of 26 demands. The government quickly transferred responsibility for putting down the revolt to the armed forces, and designated the three prisons as "restricted military zones," closed to civilians. After a brief effort at negotiations, the revolt was ended with the killing of at least 249 prisoners. In the island prison of El Frontón, the navy destroyed the building that housed the rebels, killing at least 123 in the process; the fate of the 30–60 survivors of this operation remained unclear. At Lurigancho, 124 prisoners were shot in cold blood, allegedly after having surrendered. At least two were killed at Santa Bárbara.[16]

Although by no means the first prison massacre in Peru (as recently as October 1985, 30 prisoners had been killed during a protest of a police search for arms at Lurigancho), the brutality and scope of these events shocked even the violence-inured *limeño* population. The newly appointed Peace Commission, powerless to either investigate or seek accountability by responsible military and police officials, promptly resigned. Viewing President García's apparent abdication of authority to the military with considerable dismay, progressive and leftist elements, both at home and abroad, abruptly ended their widespread support for Peru's charismatic young president. While Sendero Luminoso lost hundreds of militants and a number of its top leaders, including the ideologue Antonio Díaz Martínez, in *el masacre de los penales,* it gained just as many martyrs, all of whom were commemorated every June 19 thereafter on *el día de la herocidad* with an upsurge in Sendero's normal level of violent acts in Lima.[17]

Lima-Based Senderista Operations

The overall scope of violence associated with the insurgency, meanwhile, as measured by the total number of deaths annually reported by the Special Commission on Violence of the Peruvian Senate, diminished steadily from a high of 4,319 in 1984 to 697 in 1987.[18] This was not a reflection of a weakening of the insurgent movement, however, but of a change in tactics on the part of Sendero Luminoso to push political work over military confrontation. This new policy was outlined in a 110-page statement of the party's Central Committee—only the third such document published since 1980—entitled "To Develop People's War Serving World Revolution," which urged members to shed Sendero's image of sectarianism and dogmatism and to undertake "much wider political work," including the infiltration of labor unions and government organizations.[19]

This venture into the fringes of the legitimate political arena was designed for purposes of recruitment, particularly in Lima, where Sendero Luminoso sought to challenge the "political space" of Izquierda Unida. Youth were the principal objects of the recruitment drive, and the state-run University of San Marcos was a focal point. Legally "autonomous" in the Latin American tradition, dating from the 1918 Argentine University Reform, and thus traditionally out of the legal reach of the government, the campuses of San Marcos and other universities in Lima were nonetheless "invaded" in February 1987 as well as on several subsequent occasions during García's five years in office by military authorities in search of subversives, weapons, and propaganda materials.

As part of its recruitment effort, Sendero held its first Party Congress, clandestinely although with considerable publicity, in January 1988. It also set up a series of front organizations that, beginning in 1986, operated openly and unabashedly in public to varying degrees. These organizations included the Association of Democratic Lawyers, which defended arrested *senderistas;* Popular Aid, which assisted them while in prison; the Committee of Families of the Prisoners of War and Political Prisoners, which organized public protests and whose first public march was held in downtown Lima on May 1, 1988; the Association of New Culture, which promoted cultural events; and two labor groups, the Class Committee of Labor Unions of the Central Highway and the Movement of Classist Laborers and Workers.[20]

At the same time, public meetings by legitimate IU labor organizations were commonly disrupted by *senderistas;* a January 1988 rally by the IU-affiliated CGTP labor confederation in Lima's Plaza Dos de Mayo, where its headquarters are located, ended in a gun battle between *senderistas* and IU's security personnel. By mid-1988, Peruvian intelligence had detected *senderista* infiltration into scores of Lima-based labor unions, including the teachers' union, SUTEP, and the civil servants confederation, CITE, within which the ministries of Transport and Communication and of Health were singled out as containing workers who were sympathetic to Sendero.[21]

The key to Sendero's bid to penetrate the domain of legitimate political activity was *El Diario,* a newspaper founded by orthodox leftists in 1980 that was taken over by Sendero in 1986 and, subsequently, under the directorship of Luis Arce Borja, became increasingly unabashed as its propaganda organ. Perhaps the most noteworthy exploit of *El Diario* was its publication of a lengthy interview with Abimael Guzmán in July 1988, which analysts believed was aimed at reasserting party authority and morale following the June capture of Sendero's alleged second-in-command, Osman Morote. Over the next 16 months, the offices of *El Diario* were attacked and its personnel were harassed and arrested under the 1981 antiterrorist law as "apologists for terrorism." Arce Borja escaped and undertook propaganda and fund-raising in Europe; he was denied a visa to enter the United States. Sendero Luminoso had recently joined, then quickly become the leading party within, the London-based Revolutionary International Movement, whose U.S. affiliate is the tiny Revolutionary Communist Party.

Borrowing from a successful tactic used in Ayacucho on numerous occasions during 1989 and 1990, Sendero's Lima labor organizations declared one-day "armed strikes" in order to demonstrate their power to intimidate the populace at large. Although these were extremely effective propaganda measures, the most conspicuous effect of these endeavors to clear Lima's streets proved to be the absence of public transportation. The owners of privately owned busses were coerced, through overt threats and the burning of a few busses, into staying home, thus denying transportation to work and school for the vast majority of *limeños.*

Other tried and true actions, such as the blowing up of high-tension electrical towers (over 1,200 in all between 1980 and early 1990) to create blackouts, which provided cover for a variety of operations that included spectacular firebombings of major business enterprises, continued to be valued by Sendero for their high content of propaganda value. In addition to ongoing assassinations of military, police, government, and APRA party officials, Sendero occasionally perpetrated more grandiose forms of violence. In June 1989, for example, a bus carrying troops from the Presidential Guard was attacked by dynamite-wielding *senderistas* only blocks from the National Palace, resulting in 7 soldiers killed and 19 injured. A month later, a bus carrying Soviet fishermen was attacked in Callao, which resulted in some 28 injuries. In July 1990, just two days before García's departure from office, the Palace was struck by a grenade launched from a nearby highway.

Provincial Operations

Outside of Lima, meanwhile, *senderista* activity spread well beyond its original base in Ayacucho to embrace virtually the entire Peruvian *sierra.* The area in which formal political authority was held by the armed forces mushroomed correspondingly: by January 1989, there were five Politico-Military Commands, covering seven entire departments (Ayacucho, Apurímac, Huancavelica, Junín, Pasco, Huánuco, and San Martín) in addition to the Province of Lima and the Constitutional Province of Callao. This represented a total of 56 provinces (almost a third of the total), stretching from Ayacucho in the south-central *sierra* to the edge of the jungle in the north and containing over half the Peruvian population, that were governed under a constitutional state of emergency.[22] Throughout this entire area, save Lima and Callao, all civilian government officials were legally subordinate to the local Politico-Military Command. Ironically, then, an ever-expanding portion of Peru came under *de jure* military rule during the very decade that followed the return of the government to civilian and democratic rule.

Furthermore, there were at least two other areas *not* under military authority, the Azángaro–Ayaviri region in the department of Puno and the environs of Huaráz in Ancash, that were also persistent foci of *senderista* activity. The attempted assassination of Peru's naval attaché in the Bolivian capital of La Paz in early 1989 brought to light the prospect of the insurgency's spreading into Peru's southern neighbor as a troublesome aspect of *senderista* activity near the border in Puno. While providing evidence of Sendero's ability to act in Bolivia, a nation that shares most of the social problems and many of the circumstances surrounding Peru's insurgency, other reports indicated that Bolivia had also become a source of arms and refuge for *senderistas* acting in Peru.[23]

After the Upper Huallaga River valley coca-growing region in San Martín and Huánuco, which will be discussed separately below, the most disturbing growth in subversive activity, nevertheless, was witnessed in the two central *sierra* departments of Pasco and Junín. Sendero Luminoso's concentration in this region was apparently aimed at choking off Lima, which is located only a short distance away, although the descent—through some of the most imposing terrain in the world—is torturously slow. Pasco contains Peru's largest state-owned copper mines, operated by Centromín, while Junín, in addition to being the source of Lima's water and (hydropowered) electrical supplies, is a rich agricultural region that, throughout half the year, is Lima's largest single source of food.

The physical destruction caused by the *senderista* campaign was vast by any measure and, for a poor country in the midst of its worst economic crisis of the century, staggering. In 1989, Centromín's president estimated the company's losses from sabotaged equipment since 1980 to be $48 million. In addition to toppling the high-tension wires mentioned above, Sendero blew up a number of key highway bridges in the region and also destroyed as much as possible of the Lima-Huancayo railway, leaving this most important of Peru's two rail lines nearly inoperative by 1990.

Destruction to agricultural productive capacity was equal to, if not greater than, that to the infrastructure. In its advocacy of farming for subsistence only, a consistent *modus operandi* of Sendero since 1981 was to destroy both regional markets for surplus foodstuffs and the agroindustrial concerns that supplied Peru's cities and its export markets. Its most destructive endeavor in this regard took place in 1989, when it completely destroyed the SAIS Cahuide, one of Peru's largest agricultural cooperatives, having 800 associate members and producing 7,000 liters of milk a day.[24] By 1990, it was estimated that, throughout all Peru, no less than 1.2 million hectares of productive farmland had been abandoned by campesinos fleeing the war-torn countryside.[25] In November 1989, the head of the Special Commission on Violence of the Peruvian Senate, Enrique Bernales, estimated the total cost of the physical damage of nine and one-half years of war at $11.84 billion.[26] The additional loss to the economy in terms of foregone production was untold.

In terms of lives lost, in June 1990 Senator Bernales calculated the cost of a decade of warfare at just over 17,000, with 1,700 additional persons "disappeared."[27] After declining between 1984 and 1987, the death rate began to climb again, reaching 3,200 in 1989 and averaging 9 deaths per day during the first half of 1990.[28] Responsibility for these deaths was shared by the "dirty war" tactics of the government forces and by the ruthlessness of the insurgents. A second *modus operandi* of Sendero Luminoso in the countryside, after all, was the murder of civilians:

On entering a new area Shining Path typically rounds up the inhabitants and kills government officials, landowners and traders, and threatens to kill those who do not support the movement. Age is no consideration: even 10-year-old children are reported to have been seized and "executed" as purported thieves or police informers. Killings are often carried out in public after mock trials, sometimes after torture and mutilation.[29]

Members of so-called *rondas campesinas,* also known as civil defense committees, were particularly liable to be singled out by Sendero Luminoso as "enemies of the people." Since 1983, the armed forces had placed more and more emphasis on organizing these vigilante groups within the campesino communities in their effort to build loyalty among the local population. Numerous critics of this policy argued that the armed forces used the *ronderos,* or members of the *rondas campesinas,* as a front line in the war in order that they might avoid armed confrontation with Sendero, and that the *ronderos* served to aggravate traditional intercommunity rivalries among the *comuneros.* Indeed, the government investigation led by Vargas Llosa linked the tragic events of 1983 in Uchuraccay to the recent armed forces' campaign to organize campesinos in the area into *rondas.* The killings very likely resulted, the investigation concluded, from the journalists having been mistaken for *senderistas.*[30] Despite their being linked to a rising death toll, the *rondas campesinas* received highly visible support from the armed forces and from President García. They thus became even more prevalent, and by mid-1990 they were reported to have numbered 20,000 vigilantes in Junín's Mantaro River valley alone.[31]

In addition to uncooperative campesinos, Sendero also habitually murdered government representatives and other "outsiders" who were seized in zones under *senderista* control. During the late 1980s, agronomists, engineers, educators, administrators working on government projects, and tourists came increasingly under attack. But it was government officials who remained under the greatest threat. A mid-1989 count by *The Peru Report* in 15 of Peru's 24 departments found that, since 1986, a total of 15 mayors and 2 local councilmen had been killed, 116 mayors and 325 councilmen had resigned, and 11 mayors and 74 councilmen had simply abandoned their posts, presumably out of fear for their lives.[32] The U.S. Department of State, in its 1989 human rights report, counted 75 local officials assassinated during 1989 alone, and a total of 590 mayors and councilmen who, since being elected in 1986, had abandoned their posts out of fear.[33] Another well-informed source estimated in early 1990 that fully one-third of the total of some 4,000 positions as local judges were vacant due to a lack of candidates.[34]

Students of the phenomenon of Sendero Luminoso commonly argued that Sendero's intent in these assassinations was to create a power vacuum within the Peruvian *sierra*. In truth, however, the rural areas of the Peruvian *sierra* have been suffering from a vacuum of state power since the Spanish conquest. Historically, this had been partially filled by the presence of church officials and large landowners—called *hacendados* or, in the pejorative, *gamonales*—who, in their paternalistic role, fulfilled many of the functions of the modern state. The decades surrounding the mid-twentieth century witnessed the wholesale decline of the traditional *hacienda,* however, and the Velasco government's agrarian reform put the final nail in the coffin of this traditional sociopolitical structure in rural Peru. In large part, then, a power vacuum was already a fact of rural Peru when Sendero came onto the scene. Thus a more suitable analogy might be that Sendero filled a power vacuum throughout much of the Peruvian *sierra,* and that the war represents the government's effort to recover its lost authority.

Other Sources of Political Violence

In October 1987, meanwhile, the MRTA dramatically entered the fray by taking military control of the city of Juanjuí, in the heart of the Upper Huallaga valley in the department of San Martín, with a column of some 60 guerrillas, led by Víctor Polay Campos, accompanied by a film crew. The sudden reappearance of this more traditional, Ché Guevara–style guerrilla force was viewed the following day on nationwide television, much to the embarrassment of a government that had persistently dismissed the MRTA as of little military consequence. The MRTA column was, in fact, dispersed in short order, although its forces continued to be present in San Martín, albeit less active and in smaller numbers, throughout the remainder of the decade. In February 1989, Polay was captured after having rented a room in the state-run Hotel de Turistas in Huancayo.

The most spectacular endeavors of the publicity-oriented *emerretistas*— followers of the MRTA—during those three years took place in Lima, and included the October 1989 kidnapping of Héctor Delgado Parker, president of Lima's Channel 5 television station, an *aprista* and a close friend of President García, and the January 1990 assassination of Enrique López Albújar, who had only recently stepped down as minister of national defense. Delgado Parker was released in April 1990, following a number of television appearances by *emerretistas* on Channel 4 and, allegedly, the payment of a substantial ransom. But the most sensational action undertaken by the MRTA was the escape, through an elaborate tunnel some 300 meters in length, of 48 of its members, including Polay and several other top leaders, from Lima's Canto Grande prison in July 1990. Suspicion that prison and/or government officials had "looked the other way," if not actively aided in the escape, stemmed in part from the notorious corruption of the Guardia Republicana police officials in charge of guarding Peru's prisons (see below). More worrisome suspicions arose—over the complicity of important government officials—because the escape took place less than three weeks before the end of the APRA government, and because Polay was a former *aprista* and had been a confidante of both Haya de la Torre and Alan García, and he thus had extremely vital government connections.[35]

The appearance of paramilitary death squads, allegedly having links to the armed forces and to top government officials, topped off the alarming growth of political violence under the García administration. Responsibility for the majority of the death squad activity was claimed by the Comando Rodrigo Franco (CRF), named after an *aprista* leader and the head of the government food marketing agency ENCI who had been brutally assassinated by Sendero Luminoso in 1988. Since shortly after first appearing in July 1988, when it claimed responsibility for the murder of Osman Morote's defense lawyer, there were consistent allegations that the CRF was covertly led by the minister of the interior, Agustín Mantilla, an *aprista* militant and personal friend of the president.[36] Government spokesmen, of course, denied the charge, countering that it held no responsibility or control over the death squad activity. Amnesty International found evidence that linked CRF activity to military authorities in Ayacucho and San Martín and to the antiterrorist division of the National Police, known as DIRCOTE, in Lima. They concluded that "CRF is a masquerade, a methodology to obscure responsibility for the elimination of government opponents."[37]

Military Discontent

A major segment of the armed forces had indeed been dissatisfied, ever since García's early efforts to curb the human rights abuses of the military, with what it perceived as the undue limitations placed on its conduct of the war. It lobbied, unsuccessfully, in favor of the restoration of the death penalty for convicted terrorists and, successfully, against efforts to place military personnel accused of human rights abuses under the legal jurisdiction of civilian courts. Discontent was due not only to such attempts by the new administration to hold the armed forces accountable for their abuses of human rights, which by all accounts were widespread, but also to the youthful president's early endeavors to act on his belief that the military received too large a portion of the government budget. García had announced in his inaugural address that he planned to cut back the air force's purchase of 26 Mirage 2000's, recently contracted but not yet delivered. After myriad negotiations, 12 of the highly sophisticated jet fighters were bought. While Peru's military budget is a tightly guarded state secret, all post-1985 estimates showed à marked decline. The decline registered by *The Military Balance* is truly remarkable: from $1.4 billion in 1983 and $1.3 in 1984 to $640 million in 1985 and just over $700 million in 1986.[38]

Such severe budget restraints, coupled with a growing economic crisis, brought about sharp reductions in both equipment purchases and military pay. Well-justified salary grievances, as a result, became perpetual; one report cited the December 1988 monthly salary of a division general as the equivalent of $84 and that of a rear admiral as $71.[39] Morale suffered throughout the armed forces as a consequence; requests for early retirement grew significantly, while recruitment figures likewise suffered dramatically.[40]

As a consequence of these and other grievances within the armed forces, there were persistent rumors of coups d'état throughout much of García's presidency. The most forceful of these rumors, during late 1988 and early 1989, were related to widespread reports of the president being in a deep depression over the failure of his political and economic programs (see "Economic Collapse," Chapter 7 in this volume). It was also widely reported that officers approached the U.S. embassy on numerous occasions, asking for—and the request being firmly rebuffed—U.S. support for a coup.[41] In early October 1988 army General Víctor Raúl Silva Tuesta, who was the commander of the Piura-based First Military Region and one of García's strongest allies within the armed forces, was suddenly ousted for "questioning the loyalty of the high command" after he began mobilizing senior army officers to block what he believed to be an incipient coup attempt.

A second documented mobilization of military forces against García took place in April 1987 and was related to the creation of the Ministry of National Defense to replace the three ministries (War, Aeronautics, and the Navy) that heretofore had represented the three armed services. All three services were reportedly against the project, but the commander of the air force, General Luis Abram Cavallerino, openly voiced his opposition and, when García signed the law, sealed off Las Palmas air force base in Lima and ordered jets to buzz the National Palace in a clear attempt to intimidate the president. His efforts earned him an early retirement, but they apparently also contributed to García's decision to name, not a civilian as he had preferred, but the military's highest-ranking active-duty general, Enrique López Albújar, to be the first minister of national defense in October 1987.[42]

The prevalence of such levels of discontent greatly impaired the military, of course, in its prosecution of the war against Sendero Luminoso. Reports of low morale and the desertion of troops stationed in the emergency zones were not uncommon. The poor performance of the government's war effort could also be attributed to the utter failure of President García's highly touted plans to attack the root causes of the insurgency through agricultural development programs in the Andean Trapezoid. Although the government's budget for such projects indeed tripled in the months after García entered office, the value of these funds was rapidly decimated by inflation and, furthermore, millions of dollars of these funds that were earmarked for projects in Ayacucho were reported to have been embezzled by corrupt local officials.[43]

Agricultural Failure, Coca, and the Growth of Judicial Corruption

García administration policies that were designed to stimulate food consumption by urban dwellers proved to be highly detrimental to agricultural interests. The enforcement of low, controlled prices for many basic foodstuffs was reinforced by the importation of agricultural products at artificially low prices through the maintenance of multiple exchange rates. Both policies served as a brake on local farm output, and, as a result, per capita production of every (legal) agricultural product, save rice and chicken, witnessed a decline between 1985 and 1990.[44] Thus, the lot of the campesino, instead of improving as García had aspired to in 1985, clearly deteriorated—by a number of measures at least—in terms of both physical and economic security. Rather than making a positive contribution to a counterinsurgency campaign that acknowledged the importance of social causes of the rise of Sendero Luminoso, then, the overall effect of García administration policies was to contribute further to the problem.

The singular realm in which agriculture witnessed an immense growth was, of course, in the production of coca. One study found that the area under coca cultivation in Peru had grown from 18,000 hectares in 1978 to a "conservative" estimate of 200,000 hectares by 1989.[45] Throughout much of this interim, the area under coca culture grew at a rate of some 10 percent from one year to the next, as new jungle land was cleared by a flood of new immigrants, proceeding largely from the *sierra* into the high jungle areas that were suitable for coca growing. Fully half of Peru's coca crop was grown in the Upper Huallaga River Valley that stretched northward from Tingo María, in the department of Huánuco, and into the eastern portions of the department of San Martín. Other high jungle valleys where coca cultivation thrived included the Marañón (in the north bordering the departments of Cajamarca and Amazonas), the Apurímac (bordering the departments of Ayacucho, Cuzco, and Junín), and the Urubamba, in Cuzco.

Estimates on the annual income earned in Peru during the late 1980s from the cultivation of coca ranged between $600 million and $1.2 billion. The most commonly used figure, $800 million, represented about a third of the value of all of Peru's legal exports at the time, and more than the combined earnings of its two top legal exports, copper and petroleum. The rush to participate in the "coca boom" was little wonder, given the crisis state of most of the Peruvian agricultural sector and the inescapable fact that coca was several times more profitable than the region's next most remunerative crop, cocoa. The extent of the migration into coca-growing regions had not been measured, although estimates on the total number of people involved in growing coca and processing it into the semirefined coca paste that is exported ranged upward from 70,000.[46] One study estimated the population of the province Tocache, in the heart of the Upper Huallaga Valley, to have grown 500 percent between 1980 and 1986.[47] Another put the total number of Peruvians that make their living from coca, either directly or indirectly, at an astounding 10 percent of the population, or over 2 million.[48]

The ramifications of such vast growth in the production of coca were, of course, multiple. In addition to the enormous social problems caused by hundreds of thousands of addicts and the variety of economic consequences of the numbers cited above, the rapid growth of coca culture also greatly exacerbated the corrupt practices endemic throughout Peru's judicial system. Even more worrisome were the intertwining of Peru's coca culture with Sendero Luminoso and the consequences of this for a U.S. government that, at the close of the 1980s, had placed the "war on drugs" near the top of its foreign policy agenda.

Long before the explosion in coca production, Peru's judicial system had been beset by seemingly intractable difficulties. These included a sorry lack of professionally trained judges; a debilitating case overload, which was linked to the tortuously slow pace of the judicial process; partisan political biases in the naming of judges and at virtually every stage of the legal process; miserable levels of government funding for the police and prisons as well as for the courts, yielding, of course, miserable wages for all personnel involved; and inherent biases against Peru's poor majority.[49]

As many of these problems were directly related to a lack of money, it should be no surprise that the infusion of a vast amount of illicit coca-dollars carried a great power to corrupt. The temptation for a judge or police official to accept a bribe from a narcotics trafficker, who could easily offer them the equivalent of several years' wages to have a legal procedure "overlooked" or a crucial piece of evidence "lost," all too often proved irresistible. Bribery of this sort was commonplace; perhaps the most notori-

ous such case involved the release by the Supreme Court of convicted cocaine trafficker Pericles Sánchez Paredes in August 1988.

This problem was compounded by the power of the drug traffickers as
well as subversives from MRTA and Sendero Luminoso to evade legal
conviction through the use of physical intimidation. The fact that judges
were increasingly under threat by both elements was an important part of
the explanation of the extremely low conviction rate of alleged terrorists,
estimated at 20 percent by the U.S. Department of State in 1988.[50]

In an effort to confront these growing problems, special civilian tribu-
nals were created in 1987 in order to try accused terrorists. Despite the
salary benefits and greater security offered judges and witnesses in these
courts, however, no judges were found who were willing to undertake such
hazardous duty, and the idea of special terrorism courts was soon abandoned. It resurfaced in mid-1988, however, when García once more proposed their creation but, again, no action was undertaken to put his
recommendation into effect.

The low conviction rate for accused terrorists was also a consequence of
the flimsy cases being presented to the courts by the police and the state
prosecutors. These key institutions within the judicial system were also
deeply troubled by myriad problems, including organizational ineptness,
a lack of funding, and rampant corruption. The García administration's
reorganization of Peru's police forces, which had long been notorious in
all three regards, was, in large part, an effort to improve their operational
capability. While remaining under the Ministry of Interior, the three separate forces—the Civil Guard, the Republican Guard (in charge of security
at prisons and other public institutions as well as at border crossings), and
the plainclothes Peruvian Investigative Police—were put under a single
National Police command. Their names were subsequently changed to
the General Police (Policía General), the Security Police (Policía de
Seguridad), and the Technical Police (Policía Técnica), respectively. At
the same time (early 1986), several thousand officers were forced into retirement in an effort to weed out some of the most corrupt elements
within the top-heavy officer corps. Subsequent improvements in the cooperation among the three forces and in the levels of their honesty were
barely noticeable, however.

Prisons, where fully 75 percent of the inmates were commonly awaiting
trial and conditions were generally unfit for human beings, were the focus
of possibly the most notorious of all corrupt activity. It was not uncommon, for example, for an inmate to buy his freedom from his Republican
Guard jailers. Furthermore, it was not only petty criminals and drug bar-
ons who were thus allowed to "escape": the August 1988 jailbreak by
Dennis Martínez Sarmiento ("Cojo Dennis"), a convicted kidnapper considered to be extremely dangerous, was later found to have been the result
of a payoff. The spectacular tunnel-escape of MRTA leader Víctor Polay

and 47 of his comrades-in-arms was also believed to have involved bribery.

Sendero, Coca Traffickers, and the U.S. Government Meet in the Upper Huallaga

Both the MRTA and Sendero Luminoso were interested in maintaining a presence in the coca-ridden Upper Huallaga Valley during the late 1980s. After being dispersed in the wake of its spectacular foray into Juanjuí in October 1987, however, the presence of the MRTA in Peru's principal coca-growing region was only slight. On the other hand, following Sendero Luminoso's brutal armed attacks during March and April 1987 on both MRTA guerrillas and on the gangs of narcotics-related thugs, known locally as *sicarios,* in the vicinity of Tocache, and the first of its two assaults on the Uchiza police post the following June, Sendero was left "virtually unchallenged as the de facto government of the Huallaga Valley."[51]

Sendero's relationship with the drug producers and traffickers who manufactured coca paste and flew into the Huallaga on small planes to buy it was the subject of as much misunderstanding as concern. The Peruvian government long held that they worked hand-in-hand in the Huallaga Valley, even using the term *narcoterroristas* to erase all distinction between the two. U.S. State Department officials called their relationship a "marriage of convenience," with both parties interested in keeping the government presence in the Upper Huallaga Valley to a minimum. Sendero was *not* an advocate of the *narcos,* however; on the contrary, it acted as a "bargaining agent of sorts for the region's coca farmers, forcing drug producers to pay fair prices for the leaves."[52] Together with their having brought the wanton violence associated with the *sicarios* to bear, this role legitimized Sendero's overt presence among the populace of the Upper Huallaga Valley.

Another aspect of Sendero's relationship with the *narcos* was equally, if not more, disturbing. As de facto political authority, it levied a "tax" on the shipment of coca paste out of the area. Estimates of Sendero's annual "tax revenues" varied between $10 and $40 million. Speculation as to what Sendero Luminoso did with these funds included the payment of subsistence wages to its estimated 3,000 to 7,000 militants, the purchase of weapons (although as of mid-1990, there was little evidence of this), and placing it in overseas banks for later use.

Under the State of Emergency put into effect in mid-1984, de jure control over the Upper Huallaga Valley was held by the armed forces. Military patrols only seldom ventured outside their barracks in Juanjuí, Tingo María, and Huánuco, however, and their commanders publicly contended that their mission was counterinsurgency, while narcotics trafficking was a police matter. Privately, military officers worried about the tremendous power of coca to corrupt their troops.

Sendero Luminoso's second assault on the Uchiza police post, in March 1989, was particularly disturbing to authorities for at least two reasons. First, the military's failure to respond to repeated pleas for support by the besieged police underscored both the inability of the military to mobilize in an emergency situation and the wretched state of its relations with the police. Second, after the post had been taken, Sendero shot the commanding officers it had captured, but then freed the low-ranking officers, and thus delivered a powerful message in its campaign to encourage defections among police and military rank and file.

A few days later, 400 troops were stationed in Uchiza under the command of Brigadier General Alberto Arciniega. While continuing to insist that the armed forces would not get involved in antinarcotics operations, Arciniega pursued a more aggressive stance against the *senderistas* in the vicinity. Six months later, he claimed to have killed between 700 and 1,000 armed insurgents in the area around Uchiza, where he was also credited with having destroyed two major *senderista* facilities, one a training camp and the other a communications base. For his stance against coca eradication, Arciniega was highly popular among the local population, and equally unpopular among U.S. government personnel. A U.S. Senate subcommittee heard testimony in September 1989 that Arciniega "protects coca growers and traffickers in return for their help in fighting guerrillas" and that he received "payoffs from the traffickers."[53]

The police force with the major responsibility to combat narcotics traffic in the Upper Huallaga was a 400-man Civil Guard unit known as UMOPAR, or Rural Mobile Patrol Unit. UMOPAR (whose name was later changed to the Narcotics Police Division of the National Police, or DIPOD) was created in the early 1980s to support two U.S.–government-funded antinarcotics programs: the Special Project for the Control and Eradication of Coca in the Upper Huallaga (CORAH) and the Upper Huallaga Special Project (PEAH). CORAH was essentially an eradication project, whereas PEAH was designed to both improve local educational and transportation infrastructure and encourage farmers to grow alternative crops. Confronted with myriad difficulties, including the virtually universal hostility of the local population, these programs struggled throughout the 1980s while the production of coca skyrocketed.

The United States also funded militarized antinarcotics campaigns, one called Operation Bronco in 1984 and another, a series of seven maneuvers, called Operation Condor that took place between 1985 and 1987. U.S. Drug Enforcement Agency (DEA) personnel and contracted pilots, using aircraft on loan from the United States and from the Peruvian air force, took part alongside UMOPAR personnel in several of these operations. Similar operations, which were designed to destroy the land-ing strips used by the narcotics traffickers and the laboratories where the coca paste was manufactured, were carried out under the name of Operation Snowcap after Condor was terminated. Twenty-five to 30 DEA agents also trained UMOPAR personnel.

The personnel of these programs were under constant threat from *senderistas* and *emerretistas,* as well as from drug traffickers: at least 30 Peruvian CORAH workers were killed during the decade, and two U.S. government agents were known to have been wounded. On more than one occasion, the danger level caused the programs to be temporarily suspended. A program of aerial spraying, designed to be safer and more efficient than the CORAH eradication project, had to be jettisoned in 1989 after the U.S. manufacturer of the herbicide SPIKE refused to sell it to the U.S. government on environmental grounds. In January 1990, Peru's minister of the interior inaugurated a fortified police base, located in the heart of the Upper Huallaga at Santa Lucía, in an effort to better protect the DIPOD and DEA agents in the region.

Shortly thereafter, as the "war on drugs" became a key issue in Washington, the United States proposed increasing the level of its antinarcotics assistance to Peru to $65 million, $36 million of which was to equip and train six infantry battalions of the Peruvian army that were stationed in the Upper Huallaga. Part of the proposal, which was not accepted by the García administration, was to station 24 Green Beret trainers and another 12 or so support personnel in Peru.[54] At the time, concern was on the rise in both Washington and Lima of the growing prospect of the United States becoming involved in an inextricable war against both narcotics traffickers and Sendero Luminoso.

NOTES

1. All figures in this paragraph are from the World Bank; one major study was dated December 17, 1985, and another, from late 1988, was reprinted in *The Peru Report* (Lima), Vol. 2, No. 12 (December 1988).

2. A valuable discussion of President García's position on the foreign debt can be found in Cynthia McClintock, "Peru: A New, Determined Leader Tackles Old, Large Problems," in *The Latin American and Caribbean Contemporary Record: Vol. 5, 1985–86,* Abraham F. Lowenthal, ed. (New York: Holmes and Meier, 1988), pp. B169–B188.

3. James L. Rowe, Jr., "Peru Creditors Wary of García Strategy of Confrontation," *The Washington Post,* November 3, 1985, pp. F1, 10, 12.

4. "President Addresses U.N. General Assembly," *Foreign Broadcast Information Service—Latin America,* September 26, 1985, p. J4. See also James Brooke, "Peruvian President, at the U.N., Warns I.M.F. That Debt Repayment Must Be Eased," *The New York Times,* September 24, 1985.

5. "President Addresses U.N. General Assembly," p. J8.

6. James D. Rudolph, "Peru and Contadora: A Matter of Principles," a paper

126   Peru

presented at "Contadora, the United States and Central America," a conference organized by the School of Advanced International Studies, Johns Hopkins University, in Washington, D.C., in February 1986.

7. Rowe, "Peru Creditors Wary," p. F12.

8. Fernando Tuesta Soldevilla, *Perú político en cifras: elite política y elecciones* (Lima: Fundación Friedrich Ebert, 1987), pp. 191–96. Also see Henry A. Dietz, "Electoral Politics in Peru, 1978–1986," *Journal of Inter-American Studies and World Affairs,* Vol. 28, No. 4 (Winter 1986–1987), pp. 156–57.

9. Pedro Planas, "La alanización del estado," *Debate* (Lima), Vol. 8, No. 42 (December 1986), pp. 20–22.

10. See Jonathan Cavanagh's report on top-level decision-making under García in *The Peru Report* (Lima), Vol. 2, No. 4 (April 1988), pp. 7-1 to 7-8.

11. *The Peru Report* (Lima), July 1987.

12. A good account of the counterinsurgency politics during the early years of the García administration is in Philip Mauceri, *Militares: insurgencia y democratización en el Perú, 1980–1988* (Lima: Instituto de Estudios Peruanos, 1989), pp. 50–59.

13. The report mentioned is Amnesty International, *Peru: "Disappearances," Torture and Summary Executions by Government Forces after the Prison Revolts of June 1986* (London, 1987).

14. Raymond Bonner, "Peru's War," *The New Yorker,* January 4, 1988, p. 58.

15. David P. Werlich, "Debt, Democracy, and Terrorism in Peru," *Current History,* January 1987, p. 32.

16. Amnesty International, *Peru: "Disappearances," Torture, and Summary Executions,* is the most complete account of these events. See also Washington Office on Latin America, *Peru in Peril: The Economy and Human Rights, 1985–1987* (Washington, D.C., 1987), pp. 32–33.

17. On the thought of Díaz Martínez, see Colin Harding, "Antonio Díaz Martínez and the Ideology of Sendero Luminoso," *Bulletin of Latin American Research* (London), Vol. 7, No. 1 (1988), pp. 65–74.

18. República Peruana. Comisión Especial del Senado sobre las Causas de la Violencia y Alternativas de Pacificación en el Perú, *Violencia y Pacificación* (Lima: DESCO y la Comisión Andina de Juristas, 1989), p. 375.

19. Bradley Graham, "Peruvian Rebels, in Policy Shift, Extend List of Assassination Targets," *The Washington Post,* April 14, 1987. See also *The Andean Report* (Lima), March 1987, pp. 38–42, 47–49.

20. Alan Riding, "Peruvian Guerrillas Emerge as an Urban Political Force," *The New York Times,* July 17, 1988.

21. *The Peru Report* (Lima), Vol. 2, No. 5 (May 1988), p. 7-5.

22. Amnesty International, *Peru: Human Rights in a State of Emergency* (New York, August 1989), p. 5

23. *The Peru Report* (Lima), Vol. 3, No. 7 (July 1989), p. 7B-2.

24. See Michael Reid's report in *The Peru Report* (Lima), Vol. 3, No. 6 (June 1989), pp. 7-1 to 7-7.

25. *La República* (Lima), October 22, 1990.

26. *El Comercio* (Lima), November 29, 1989.

27. *El Comercio,* June 8, 1990.

28. *La República,* May 13, 1990, p. A9. Numbers are from the Bernales Commission (Comisión Especial del Senado).

29. Amnesty International, *"Caught between Two Fires": Peru Briefing* (New York, November 1989), p. 5.

30. Mario Vargas Llosa, "Inquest in the Andes: A Latin American Writer Explores the Political Lessons of a Peruvian Massacre," *The New York Times Magazine,* July 31, 1983, pp. 18–56.

31. *El Comercio,* July 18, 1990, p. A9. A good discussion of the *rondas campesinas* is in Americas Watch Committee, *A New Opportunity for Democratic Authority: Human Rights in Peru* (New York, September 1985), pp. 12–18.

32. *The Peru Report* (Lima), Vol. 3, No. 7 (July 1989), pp. 7B-3–4.

33. From a summary of the Department of State's 1989 human rights report in *La República* (Lima), March 25, 1990, p. 28.

34. David Scott Palmer, "Peru's Persistent Problems," *Current History,* January 1990, p. 32.

35. These suspicions grew when, two weeks after the escape, Polay was seen on nationwide television in a clandestine, 10-minute interview. On Polay's *aprista* connection, see *The Peru Report,* Vol. 1, No. 12 (December 1987), p. 7-6, and Carol L. Graham, "APRA 1968–1988: From Evolution to Government—the Elusive Search for Political Integration in Peru" (D.Phil. thesis, Oxford University, January 1989), p. 269.

36. This connection was confirmed in hearings held in the Chamber of Deputies. See *The Andean Report* (Lima), August 1989, pp. 181–3 and *Oiga* (Lima), August 21, 1989, pp. 18–24.

37. Amnesty International, *"Caught between Two Fires,"* p. 13.

38. *The Military Balance, 1986–1987* (London: International Institute for Strategic Studies, 1987) for 1983 and 1984 figures; 1985 and 1986 figures are from *The Military Balance, 1988–1989.*

39. *The Peru Report* (Lima), Vol. 3, No. 2 (February 1989), p. 7A-3.

40. On requests for early retirement, see *The Peru Report,* Vol. 3, No. 2 (February 1989), p. 7A-3. The recruitment information is from an interview with Henri Favre published in *La República.*

41. See, for example, Bonner, "Peru's War," p. 58.

42. David P. Werlich, "Peru: García Loses His Charm," *Current History,* January 1988, p. 15. See also *The Peru Report,* Vol. 1, No. 11 (November 1987), pp. 7-4 to 7-6.

43. Riding, "Peruvian Guerrillas Emerge."

44. *El Comercio,* July 24, 1990, p. A16.

45. These and many other useful data on coca are reported in *The Peru Report,* Vol. 3, No. 7 (July 1989), n.p.n. The 10 percent annual growth figure is from U.S. Undersecretary of State Ann Wrobleswki, reported in *El Comercio,* March 5, 1988, p. B4.

46. Palmer, "Peru's Persistent Problems," p. 32.

47. Scott L. Malcomson, "Cocaine Republic," *The Village Voice,* August 26, 1986, p. 15.

48. *El Nacional* (Lima), September 3, 1989, citing Lima-based sources in the French Press Agency (AFP).

49. The myriad difficulties within the judicial system are often discussed, but rarely tackled. Two useful English-language sources are Americas Watch Committee, *Abdicating Democratic Authority: Human Rights in Peru* (New York, October 1984), and the annual *Country Report on Human Rights Practices* of the U.S. Department of State. In Spanish, see the report of the findings of a study by the West German Friedrich Neumann Foundation in *El Comercio,* December 2, 1985; F. Eguiguren, et al., "La primera década de la Constitución," *Debate* (Lima), Vol. 11, No. 56 (July-August 1989), p. 64, and Ivan Jara and Martín Carrillo, "Poder judicial: faustos y misterios," *Que Hacer* (Lima), No. 40 (April-May 1986), p. 58.

50. "U.S. Human Rights Report for 1988," in *The Peru Report,* Vol. 3, No. 4 (April 1989), p. 7B-9.

51. Raúl González, "Coca's Shining Path," *NACLA Report on the Americas,* Vol. 22, No. 6 (March 1989), pp. 23–24.

52. Jo Ann Kawell, "Going to the Source," *NACLA Report on the Americas,* Vol. 22, No. 6 (March 1989), p. 15.

53. *The Peru Report,* Vol. 3, No. 10 (October 1989), p. 7B-4.

54. *Newsweek* (international edition), May 21, 1990, p. 41.

7

THE DECLINE OF ALAN GARCÍA PÉREZ: 1987–1990

Inflation, which at 63 percent in 1986 had been lower than during any year since 1980, took a sudden leap upward in early 1987, along with the government's fiscal deficit. Foreign reserves began to nosedive at about the same time. The emergence of these danger signals within the previously booming economy highlighted the García administration's difficulties in shifting from its highly successful short-term program for economic recovery to an economic agenda more suitable for the longer term (see Chapter 6 in this volume). This impasse coincided with the rise of a variety of adverse political circumstances that were both causes and effects of the looming economic troubles.

EMERGENT POLITICAL PROBLEMS

García's earlier domination of the political landscape had been nearly total. On the right, the president had maintained a dialogue with the business community through periodic meetings with a group, known popularly as the "12 apostles," of the most influential members of Peru's financial and industrial elite, and alloted business significant tax breaks in order to promote the economic recovery. The cooperation of the 12 apostles—who included Dionisio Romero, Juan Francisco Raffo, Guillermo Wiese, and Pedro Brescia—was key to the confidence of the business community in García's early program. On the left, García's strong Third World orientation in foreign affairs, and his external debt stance in particular, had enamored him to much of the legal left within IU. This infatuation began to wear thin after the June 1986 prison massacres, however, and a massive general strike in May 1987, during which the police also walked off, placed the affair between García and the left in great jeopardy.

The key to García's command of the political setting, though, lay

within the leadership of his own party. Ironically, it was this constituency
that proved the most problematical for the president. Under the 55-year
hegemony of Haya de la Torre, APRA had prided itself on having clearly
delineated lines of authority and strict discipline among the rank and file.
After the death of the party founder and ideologue in 1979, however, this
rigid party hierarchy and discipline began to break down, and the party's
coming to power in 1985 only served to make matters worse. Under
García, according to a major study of APRA at the time, "party activities
were relegated to secondary priority, and most party leaders opted for
government-related posts. The party mechanism as such virtually ceased
to function."[1] In an oblique reference to how little influence was wielded
by APRA, as a political party, some analysts referred to the "Alanization"
of the government apparatus under García.[2]

Under García's leadership, APRA was so riddled with generational and
ideological factions that "the party function[ed] more like an electoral
front than ... an organized mass party."[3] APRA's chronic generational
rifts were aggravated by the fact that García only placed party militants of
his own generation, such as Luis Gonzáles Posada, Hugo Otero, Remigio
Morales Bermúdez, and Rómulo León Alegría, into close advisory positions. Older *aprista* militants, such as octogenarian Luis Alberto Sánchez
and Guillermo Larco Cox, obtained important congressional and cabinet
positions, but were rarely consulted by García on major policy issues.[4]

Ideological positions were so diverse within APRA that it was perhaps
more accurate to refer to the party's ideological pluralism than to distinct
factions. Nonetheless, for the sake of analysis, it could be said that
apristas ranged from leftist revolutionaries among the party youth, many
of whom left the party in the 1980s to join ex-*aprista* Víctor Polay
Campos in the MRTA, to ultraconservative anticommunists who held
many high party and government positions, especially outside Lima and
within the National Police force. Three of the most identifiable forces between these two extremes were the "pragmatic centrists," which included
Deputy José Barba Caballero and Luis Alberto Sánchez; the "center leftists," among whom was found Senator Javier Valle Riestra; and the "radicals," led by Deputy Carlos Roca Cáceres.

Ever since the death of Haya, the top echelon within APRA had been
characterized by rivalries for leadership, first between Villanueva and
Townsend and then, after 1985, between García and Luis Alva Castro.
Under García, Alva Castro held multiple positions: he was elected second
vice-president on García's ticket and to the Chamber of Deputies in his
own right. Furthermore, he held appointed positions as García's prime
minister and minister of economy and finance until June 1987 when, seeing the economic writing on the wall, he resigned with a view toward his
own 1990 presidential bid.

Born in 1945 and, like García, a member of the youthful leadership bureau trained by Haya during the 1970s, Alva Castro became an economist with an expertise in matters surrounding the external debt. In his increasingly bitter rivalry with García after 1985, Alva Castro used his position as prime minister to build up a personal power base within the party, appointing fellow *mocheros* (people from Moche, a town near Trujillo in the heart of APRA's *norte sólido*) to many key government positions. He was also awarded patronage over the government's Support Program for Temporary Income (PAIT), which hired some 75,000 urban poor on a part-time basis between 1985 and 1987, and thereby was able to build a small army of loyalists.[5]

The key to Alva Castro's ascent within APRA, however, took place in July 1987, only weeks after he resigned from García's cabinet. Much to the chagrin of President García, Alva Castro was elected president of the Chamber of Deputies, a position that he was to use as a counterweight to García's power of the presidency. It was no coincidence that the movement among *aprista* congressmen to amend the constitution so that García might be allowed to be reelected in 1990 also collapsed in mid-1987. The dismay of the president was such that it led him to make a ruinous mistake.

THE BANK TAKEOVER BID AND MORE
POLITICAL DIFFICULTIES

García's announcement, during his annual state of the union address on July 28, 1987, of his government's takeover of the 16 banks and finance companies (*financieras*) and the 17 insurance companies that remained in the hands of domestic private investors came as a surprise to almost everyone, even many of his fellow APRA party leaders. Vice President Luis Alberto Sánchez reportedly found out about the measure one hour before its announcement, and then not from García but from former President Belaúnde.[6] Although the reasons for the measure given by García were economic (to "democratize credit" within the nation's financial system and to force the business community to invest in Peru instead of sending its profits abroad in the form of capital flight), informed analysts concurred that these explanations were unpersuasive and that the real motives behind García's attempted bank takeover were political.

As an attempt to regain the initiative following the multiple economic and political difficulties of early 1987, García's attempt to take over the banking and insurance industries was, indeed, to cause a political firestorm. In nearly every respect, it proved to be a major miscalculation on the part of the president, however. The mass media, siding overwhelmingly with the bankers, were soon replete with unsightly images—such as tanks breaking through the locked entranceways of banks and bank owners sleeping on cots in their offices to ward off the forced seizure by government troops—that conjured up the confiscatory military dictatorship.

Within APRA, Alva Castro continued to hold onto the high ground, using his position of authority over the 105 *aprista* representatives in the Chamber of Deputies to enable him to easily defeat Rómulo León Alegría, whom García openly promoted, in the party's internal elections for the top position of secretary general in December 1988. Thereafter, Alva Castro was able to coast to the nomination as APRA's 1990 presidential candidate. It was a tribute to the immensity of García's ego that he did not repudiate the reelection campaign until July 1988, nor did he resign his position as party president until a few short days before the party's December elections.[7]

The right, meanwhile, was almost instantly resuscitated, under the leadership of novelist Mario Vargas Llosa, from its moribund status of the previous four years (see "The 1990 Electoral Campaign," this chapter). The attempted bank grab only played well among those on García's left flank. As a direct blow to Dionisio Romero and others among the business elite whose conglomerate empires were capped by financial institutions, the left saw García's advance on the banks as a fitting move to break the back of Peru's post–Velasco-era monopoly capitalists.

DESGOBIERNO AND ECONOMIC COLLAPSE

García's perfidy toward the 12 apostles, many of whom were owners of the confiscated financial institutions, cost him the confidence he had built within the business community over the previous two years. Rather than promote capital investment, as García had fashioned, his attempted bank grab yielded a widespread reluctance by domestic business concerns to put their capital at risk in Peru. Few believed García's assurances that further expropriations were not in the offing. Foreign investment had already dried up in the wake of García's debt stance and the expropriation of Belco Petroleum.

In part because of the pervasive lack of investor confidence, economic output was stagnant throughout mid- and late 1987. The 6.9 percent growth in the GDP registered for 1987 was a statistical anomaly, due to the comparatively low average level of output in 1986, a year of rapid growth. The Peruvian economy was, in fact, on the edge of its most profound depression of the twentieth century: the World Bank would measure declines in the GDP of 8.8 percent in 1988 and 14 percent in 1989.[8] According to the Lima-based firm Macroconsult, between 1985 and 1989, the GDP experienced an overall decline of 4.5 percent.[9]

Real wages, which had increased significantly during 1986, were ravaged during the post-1987 depression. Between July 1985 and July 1990 the purchasing power of the minimum wage declined 49 percent, while that of the average salary in the private sector dropped 52 percent and that in the public sector dropped an astounding 62 percent.[10] The percentage of the economically active population with adequate employment declined during those years from 27 to only 18 percent.[11]

If a lack of private capital investment helped to trigger a depression, Peru's post-1987 economic debacle could also be traced to the erratic, inappropriate, and incompetent behavior on the part of the government. Widely known by the Spanish term *desgobierno,* this phenomenon was prevalent in Peru (as indeed throughout much of Latin America) during the 1980s. But there are few better examples of *desgobierno* than that offered by Peru during the second half of the administration of Alan García.

The bloated state-owned enterprise sector offered, perhaps, the most glaring examples of *desgobierno* in Peru (see "Economic Reform," Chapter 4 in this volume). By 1988 the government owned, either wholly or partially, a total of 100 financial and 135 nonfinancial enterprises. Only 30 of the financial and 90 of the nonfinancial enterprises were truly functional, however; the remaining enterprises were phantoms, existing only on paper.[12] Peru's 10 largest companies, however, were also among the state-owned enterprises at the time, according to the World Bank, when the state's nonfinancial firms employed a total of some 130,000 people.

Created, for the most part, under the Velasco government for reasons that were not always clear or consistent, the state enterprises came to be used by the civilian regimes of the 1980s for a variety of reasons that suited their short-term political wishes. These included the placing of party loyalists into high-paying positions as company directors, managers, or consultants, for which they were rarely qualified. President García severely criticized the Belaúnde regime for this practice and drastically lowered the salaries of high-ranking officials early in his regime, but then nullified this achievement by markedly increasing the number of persons employed by the state enterprises. García also used the state enterprises for anti-inflationary and public welfare purposes by subsidizing the public consumption of products marketed by public firms, particularly food and petroleum products.

The state enterprises were notoriously inefficient as a result of such practices, and nearly all of them operated at a financial loss. During the 1970s, deficits had been hidden by the firms' easy access to foreign credits, but the inaccessibility of foreign loans during the 1980s exposed the state enterprises to fiscal reality. By the late 1980s, the state enterprises' combined deficit of hundreds of millions of dollars annually had become a major contributor to the government's chronic fiscal deficit. The biggest loser by far was the state petroleum firm, Petroperú, which sold its products far below their cost of production throughout the late 1980s.[13] In 1988, the combined financial losses of the state enterprises totaled almost U.S. $1.2 billion, according to a bicameral congressional commission,

and even more, according to other sources.[14] The deterioration of the
state enterprises could also be measured by the precipitous decline in
their revenues from 36 percent of the GDP in 1980 to 26 percent in 1985,
and a mere 10 percent in 1990.[15]

The state's fiscal deficits, which had grown significantly during the
Belaúnde administration, increased to unprecedented heights under
García. Revenues dropped precipitously, with the tax burden dropping
from an already low 15 percent of the GDP in 1985 to less than 4 percent
by 1989; total state spending, in a figure that incorporated the deficit
from state enterprises, was around 11 percent of the GDP at that time,
making for a total fiscal deficit of about 7 percent of the GDP.[16] The increase in state expenditures was also due in part to an increased wage bill.
According to the Colombian newsmagazine *Visión,* employment grew
from 20 to 50 percent throughout the state enterprises and public agencies during García's first four years in power.[17]

This growing fiscal deficit was, in turn, a principal cause of the
hyperinflation that took off in 1988. After nearly doubling to 115 percent
in 1987, the consumer price index skyrocketed to 1,722 percent in 1988
and 2,778 percent in 1989.[18] According to the government's National Institute of Statistics, whose measurements were consistently below those of
private research institutes, cumulative inflation between July 1985 and
July 1990 (García's term in office) was an extraordinary 2,200,000
percent.[19] Hyperinflation ravished the inti, the currency that had replaced the old sol at a rate of 1,000 to 1 in early 1986, to such an extent
that in late 1990 it was announced that the inti was soon to be replaced by
the new sol at an exchange of 1,000,000 to 1.[20]

Hyperinflation also reflected *desgobierno* insofar as policymaking in
the economic sphere was both inconsistent and poorly designed. The
problem was, on the one hand, a lack of consistency among the three principal economic policymaking bodies—the Ministry of Economy and Finance, the Central Bank, and the National Planning Institute. Under
García, each operated with its own particular leadership and theoretical
orientation, mirroring the ideological factionalization within the APRA
party, and with only minimal policy coordination from above.[21]

Virtually every major economic decision, on the other hand, was made
by García personally. Above all else, García was determined to counter
inflation with measures other than the radical "shock treatment" routinely prescribed by the IMF. His obstinant objection to the "economic
imperialism" of the IMF, as well as his eye toward his own political future,
led García to pursue a policy of gradual adjustment that proved relatively
painless, but highly ineffective. Beginning in March 1988, the government announced a series of so-called economic packages (*paquetazos*),
which were really price adjustments designed to lower government consumer subsidies. Although each bit deeply into the public's purchasing

power, none was severe enough to significantly lower the fiscal deficit and thus curb the galloping inflation. Three ministers of economy and finance resigned during 1988 alone, each after having proposed an adjustment more severe than the president was willing to impose.[22]

Exchange rate policy was another area of *desgobierno*. A poorly conceived system of multiple exchange rates that made foreign currency available to importers at unrealistically low prices was instituted principally to promote the consumption of imports. This policy hurt competing local industries as well as Peruvian exporters, who received unrealistically low amounts of local currency for their earned dollars. Even more damaging, however, was the drain it caused on the nation's net foreign currency reserves, which fell from almost $1.5 billion at the end of 1985 to a negative $350 million three years later, then rose to nearly $500 million by late 1989, only to fall again to minus $70 million at the end of García's term in July 1990.[23]

Peru's external debt had little to do with its foreign exchange crisis of 1990. Only token payments had been made on the foreign debt since early 1988; by the end of 1989 Peru was some $8.7 billion in arrears in its payments on an external debt of nearly $17 billion, for a total debt of over $25 billion. The secondary market for Peru's foreign debt stood at a mere 6 cents on the dollar, against an average for Latin America at the time of 27.5 cents.[24]

Peru's economic crisis was thus comprehensive—simultaneously battering its population through economic depression, hyperinflation, and an all-out foreign exchange crisis. This crisis was essentially self-imposed, caused by unparalleled levels of *desgobierno*. External factors, by comparison, held little of the blame. Peru's terms of trade, indeed, declined some 20 percent between 1985 and 1987, and Peru was ignored by much of the international financial community, furthermore, in the wake of García's limitation of Peru's debt payments. The preponderance of responsibility for Peru's economic crisis of 1990, nevertheless, must be borne by the García government's mishandling of the economy.

CENTRALIZATION AND REGIONALIZATION

Another type of *desgobierno*—centralization—was not due to the García administration per se but, rather, was systemic in Peru, as it was throughout much of Latin America. In Peru, the centralization of governmental authority goes back to the founding of Lima—on the coast, far from major population centers at the time, but with good access to overseas shipping—during the early years of Spanish colonial rule. Since then, local governments have rarely been more than the appointed representatives of the Lima-based central government. Elections for local government officials were held during the first Belaúnde presidency—in 1963 and 1966—then resumed with the return of democratic rule in 1980, with municipal and provincial contests taking place every three years.

Although the institution of municipal elections brought a degree of political autonomy to local governments, authority continued to be highly concentrated within the Lima-based central government. A vital cause of this was the minimal power of taxation held by municipal authorities and the pitifully low level of central government funds alloted to local officials. These grew from about 2 percent of total central government expenditures in 1980 to 4 percent in 1989, but continued to compare very poorly with those of neighboring countries, such as Chile, Ecuador, Colombia, Bolivia, and Brazil, where some 40 percent of central government funds were commonly distributed to local officials. In Peru, as a result, a wide range of services often found under local jurisdiction, such as health, education, road building and repair, and police, remained completely dependent on Lima. The well-known disdain of bureaucrats for living outside the comforts of the capital city (more than half of Peru's government employees were in Lima) added to these difficulties.

The decentralization of governmental authority, in order to improve the responsiveness of such services to local needs, has long been recognized as a necessary innovation in Peru. Even the military regime, which perhaps did more to increase the concentration of governmental functions and authority in Lima than any other administration in recent history, called for a gradual process of decentralization in its 1977 Plan Túpac Amaru. The Belaúnde administration, on its part, had promoted department-level development corporations, known by the Spanish acronym Cordes (Corporaciones del Desarollo), in order to channel development funds through the departmental governments, but they proved to be less responsive to local authorities than to the central bureaucratic authority in Lima. Early in his term García proposed that a number of Lima-based agencies, including Petroperú and the Ministry of Agriculture, be moved into outlying provinces where they would be closer to their clientele and to their resources. In 1986, he even floated the idea of moving the capital from Lima into the Mantaro Valley in the central *sierra*. Neither of these worthwhile projects were ever undertaken, however.

Chapter 12 of the 1979 Constitution calls for the creation of administratively and economically autonomous regional governments consisting of regional presidents, councils, and assemblies. In 1984, Congress approved of a regionalization plan that was to be implemented in 1988. The subsequent APRA-led Congress did not act on the AP plan, however, but in 1986 outlined its own, which called for 12 regional, as well as a number of subregional and microregional, governments to be created over the upcoming years. Power within the regional governments was to be centered in regional assemblies, which consisted of (a) each of the elected provincial mayors within the region, (b) a number of representatives designated by the various productive sectors found in the region, and (c) a number of representatives popularly elected by the voting inhabitants of the region. The first popular elections for assemblymen, in 4 of the 12 regions, took place in November 1989; others were held during 1990 (see map of Peru's regional subdivisions at beginning of this book).

Although 11 regional governments were thus established during García's term in office, they were not yet functional in 1990 and their future effectiveness remained in doubt. Flagrant examples of *desgobierno* continued to prevail, meanwhile, as health, education, road building and maintenance, police and other public services commonly provided by local governments deteriorated noticeably. Despite widespread rhetorical support for decentralization, then, such hard-bitten realities as the high costs involved, bureaucratic inertia, and entrenched interests in the centralized status quo left its future problematical.

THE 1990 ELECTORAL CAMPAIGN AND THE TRIUMPH OF THE "INDEPENDENTS"

The Decline of the Left

Starting in mid-1987, when García's mounting difficulties had made it clear that the APRA party would be incapable of winning the 1990 electoral contest, public opinion polls showed IU's Alfonso Barrantes with a commanding lead in the race for the presidency. Even after he resigned as IU's president later in 1987—as an independent not actively seeking the presidential bid—Barrantes continued for more than a year to be the favored candidate. His lead had evaporated, however, by 1989, when the formal schism within the IU coalition was followed by Barrantes's pitting himself against his former vice mayor, Henry Pease García, for the 1990 presidential contest. The voting public, which since 1978 had consistently rewarded the left when it was united and punished it when it was divided, sent the same message in 1990, when the two leftist slates received a mere 13 percent of the vote between them. After having grown with such promise between 1978 and 1983, this electoral failure spelled an unhappy denouement of the 1980s for the electoral left. What happened during the latter half of the decade to so weaken the electoral left?

First of all, IU found itself up against runaway electoral victories by APRA in 1985 and 1986 and what looked like, throughout all but the final days of the 1990 presidential contest, a similarly decisive victory by the Democratic Front (FREDEMO). Beyond the outstanding successes in the electoral efforts of its worthy opponents, however, IU itself faced a number of unresolved problems. The most salient of these was the persistent sectarianism that divided the parties to the electoral front. Rooted in ideology since the Sino-Soviet split of the mid-1960s, by the 1980s the Peruvian left's sectarianism was based less on arcane ideological debates reflecting those within the international Marxist community than on questions of personal style and the control over party and labor union organizations.[25] If electoral success had initially brought, then held, these diverse elements of IU together, subsequent electoral defeat threatened to split them asunder.

Barrantes's closeness to President García, both personally and in terms of ideology, compounded IU's problems of self-definition. Beyond mutual expressions of admiration and more than one report of the two leaders dining together in private, Barrantes's 1985 presidential platform—which had included a selective moratorium on the external debt, the nationalization of the nation's largest private bank, and the review of oil contracts held by foreign firms—was carried out nearly in its entirety during García's term in office (see "Party Politics and the 1985 Electoral Campaign," Chapter 5 in this volume). Widespread criticism of Barrantes's failure to back the CGTP's first general strike against the García government was instrumental in his resignation as IU's president in mid-1987.

Another major problem within the parties of the electoral left was their doubts, as parties with revolutionary aspirations, with respect to the viability of the electoral path to power. Sendero Luminoso's success in its violent pursuit of revolution, while expressing its contempt for "bourgeois democracy" and the "cretins" of the electoral left, was perhaps the major cause of doubt. As a result, Sendero was denounced with varying degrees of clarity by the leadership within IU, and a portion of the rank and file, contrasting Sendero's apparent effectiveness with IU's mediocre prospects, forsook the electoral path during the 1980s in favor of either Sendero or the less dogmatic MRTA.

Further sources of doubts within the IU leadership as to the viability of the electoral road had their origins in the historical lessons learned from Latin America's two recent experiences in rule by broad Marxist-dominated fronts—Chile's Popular Unity government under Salvador Allende and Bolivia's Popular Democratic Unity government under Hernán Siles. The Bolivian example planted doubts as to whether an IU government would be able to govern effectively in the name of such a diverse coalition, whereas the Chilean example planted doubts that the military would allow an IU government to remain in power to pursue a revolutionary program. If voters were concerned with these lessons, so was the IU leadership. During the 1980s there were persistent reports that Barrantes's campaigns for the presidency were less than animated due to his anxiety over the prospective causes for the failure of his government.[26]

Another problem experienced by the electoral left during the late 1980s might best be described as growing pains. IU's early success had been closely identified with Barrantes's electoral appeal. As the decade wore on, in contrast, the moderate Barrantes became an ever less appealing figure among the radicalized leadership of IU. After Barrantes resigned as president of IU in 1987, the position was rotated every six months among the front's various party leaders, who made numerous attempts to "democratize" the decision-making process within IU away from the personalism that had prevailed under Barrantes. Two important meetings were organized in this effort: a National Popular Assembly of some 2,500 representatives of popular organizations, which was held in November 1987, and IU's first National Congress, which took place in January 1989. Barrantes's failure to attend either function, or to recognize the National Executive Committee that was selected at the 1989 congress, made a split in the electoral front, which had endured nearly the entire decade, inevitable.[27]

The following October, the left presented two presidential planks. Barrantes was the candidate of the more moderate Socialist Accord among the Left (ASI) coalition (whose name was changed shortly afterward to Izquierda Socialista [IS]), which consisted of the Revolutionary Socialist Party (PSR), the Revolutionary Communist Party (PCR), and the Non-Party Socialists. The latter group had been hastily put together by Barrantes's closest independent supporters. The IU coalition was left with the PCP–U, the PUM, the UNIR, FOCEP, the Socialist Revolutionary Action (ARS), and the newly formed Movement of Socialist Affirmation (MAS) of Henry Pease García, who was named the presidential candidate for the diminished IU. Less than a year after Barrantes had been the clear favorite in presidential polls, then, this split of the electoral left all but assured its defeat in the 1990 presidential contest (see Figure 4.1 on p. 73).

The Rise and Fall of the Right

While the left moved steadily downward during the late 1980s, the right, which had been moribund since 1983, was resurrected in 1987 under the leadership of Peru's world-class novelist, Mario Vargas Llosa. His Movimiento Libertad, commonly known as simply Libertad (Liberty), was born in Lima's Plaza San Martín on August 21, 1987, at a massive protest demonstration against President García's attempt to expropriate the private banking and insurance industries. The demonstration's organizers claimed to have attracted more than 100,000 people, a number previously unheard of in Peruvian political rallys. The demonstration culminated in a march to the nearby Palace of Justice, where a manifesto against the bank grab, signed by some 40,000 people, was presented by the demonstration's organizers. These included novelist Mario Vargas Llosa; Hernando de Soto of the Instituto Libertad y Democracia, best known as the author of a highly influential study of Peru's informal sector titled *The Other Path;* artist Fernando de Szyszlo; and Miguel Cruchaga Belaúnde, AP activist and nephew of the former president. But that evening attention was unmistakably focused on Vargas Llosa.

Mario Vargas Llosa was born in Arequipa in 1936, spent much of his youth in Cochabamba, Bolivia, but also lived for a time in Piura in the north of Peru. He moved to Lima to attend the University of San Marcos during the early 1950s, a period of his life that is the setting of his finest novel, *Conversation in the Cathedral.* Vargas Llosa became sympathetic with the left during these late years of the Odría dictatorship, when he briefly joined the PCP. Ever since a series of highly publicized debates with leftist Colombian Nobel Prize–winning author Gabriel García Márquez during the early 1970s, however, he had been identified with the conservative side of the political spectrum. Having long lived in Europe (maintaining an apartment in London), though, Vargas Llosa had had little direct association with Peruvian politics until 1983, when President Belaúnde had asked him to lead a blue-ribbon commission to investigate the massacre of eight journalists in Uchuraccay, near Ayacucho.[28] The following year, Belaúnde offered Vargas Llosa the post of prime minister, which he discreetly declined (see Chapter 5 in this volume).

In 1987 Vargas Llosa said that he saw Libertad as a civic movement to support individual liberty in the face of the threat of state tyranny posed by García's sudden bank takeover; his claim that he held no personal political ambitions was widely seen as ingenuine. In fact, his political course had been set; Libertad was quickly and unabashedly transformed into a movement that, although it did not call itself a political party, nonetheless acted very much like a party whose central purpose was the promotion of the candidacy of Vargas Llosa for the 1990 presidential elections.

Vargas Llosa forcefully and eloquently expressed the liberal ideology of the Movimiento Libertad with the zeal and extremism of a convert. Individual liberties, of both the political and economic variety, were praised almost without limit, while communism and big government were disparaged as the evils whose historical failures in governing were paralleled by their roles in crushing individual liberties. Hernando de Soto's analysis of Peru's economy, in which he saw it afflicted by centuries of the state's playing the central economic role within a system of mercantilism and in need of an infusion of free-market capitalism, was perhaps Libertad's primary theoretical premise.

Libertad's top leadership was dominated by close friends of Vargas Llosa who had initially helped found the movement.[29] Cruchaga, a militant Catholic, remained a central figure in Libertad and, according to some sources, was second only to Vargas Llosa. Miguel Vega Alvear, whose Instituto Pro-Desarrollo was the nexus between Libertad and the business community, was a key figure in Libertad's fund-raising as well as its policy coordination with its allied political parties. Also among the movement's founders were Vargas Llosa's son Alvaro and Luis Bustamante Belaúnde, both of whom remained important political advisors, as did architect Federick Cooper Llosa, who acted as coordinator of Libertad's press campaign. Felipe Thorndike Beltrán, another founder, was in charge of fund-raising.

Hernando de Soto left Libertad in 1988, arguing that it was a mistake to assume an antileftist stance, but his associate and coauthor of *The Other Path*, Enrique Ghersi, remained on as Libertad's standard-bearer of liberal ideology.[30] Among the handful of influential "newcomers" in Libertad at that time were lawyer Raúl Ferrero Costa, who became national policy coordinator in mid-1989, ex-*aprista* Alfredo Barnachea, and Rafael Villegas, former president of CONFIEP, Peru's most important business association. By late 1989, the fledgling Movimiento Libertad was said to have gained some 70,000 adherents nationwide, including a considerable number of defectors from other parties, especially the PPC.

In February 1988, Libertad joined forces with the traditional rightist parties, AP and PPC, under the banner of the Democratic Front (FREDEMO). Beneath its three party leaders, FREDEMO was initially governed by a nine-member commission that consisted of three representatives from each party. After the alliance was joined by two small parties, Solidarity and Democracy (SODE) and the Independent Civic Union (UCI) in 1989, FREDEMO's executive council was increased to 23 members, 5 from each of the large parties and 3 from each of the small ones, who met once a month.

Former President Belaúnde did not cede overall leadership of the rightist coalition to Vargas Llosa without a tussle. Active campaigning by Belaúnde for FREDEMO's presidential candidacy kept the outcome in doubt until just before Vargas Llosa's official proclamation in June 1989. Shortly afterward, in an attempt to limit the scope of FREDEMO's authority, Belaúnde named Eduardo Orrego Villacorta to be AP's candidate for mayor of Lima for the November 1989 municipal elections. In order to impose his view that FREDEMO should present a single list of candidates in November, Vargas Llosa then withdrew his presidential candidacy. Belaúnde was thus forced to back down; Orrego's candidacy was withdrawn in favor of Juan Inchaustegui, an AP member who ran as the FREDEMO candidate, before Vargas Llosa resumed his presidential campaign. Although it was subsequently decided to allow AP and PPC to run candidates under their party names in districts where FREDEMO had no local organization, this power play left no doubt as to Vargas Llosa's leadership of FREDEMO.

Nevertheless, Inchaustegui was unable to overcome the early lead held by Ricardo Belmont Cassinelli, the popular proprietor of Lima's television Channel 11, who ran for mayor as an independent under the Movimiento Cívico Obras. Belmont gained some 44 percent in the November 12 vote, against 28 percent for Inchaustegui. Overall, however, FREDEMO was the big winner, garnering 28 of Lima's 41 district mayoralties and fully half of the leadership posts in other major cities nationwide. APRA, which in 1986 had been swept into local offices nationwide, was the big loser, being defeated in every major city save Trujillo, Chimbote, and Cajamarca in the heart of the *norte sólido.*

The campaign for the presidency then got under way in earnest. Vargas Llosa continued to hold a solid lead, according to public opinion polls, of between 40 and 50 percent of the projected popular vote; Henry Pease and Luis Alva Castro, who held second and third places in the polls, were both weak candidates. With virtually all observers confident of a Vargas Llosa victory, the campaign was less an electoral contest than a massive promotion of, and a debate fostered by his opponents over, the FREDEMO candidate's radical platform for change.

Vargas Llosa's short-term economic goal was to bring inflation rapidly down to a level of 10 percent per annum through a radical, orthodox adjustment program supported by the IMF and the reopening of Peru to the international financial and business communities. His longer term goal was to transform the Peruvian state from the large, inefficient, and weak apparatus it had become in recent years into one that would be small, efficient, and strong. Central to this latter goal was the wholesale privatization of Peru's state-owned enterprises, which Vargas Llosa said would become the property of their workers.

Vargas Llosa's costly campaign was waged not so much against his opponents as in an effort to surpass 50 percent in the April 8 vote and thus avoid a second-round electoral contest against the runner-up. Giving further reassurance to Vargas Llosa was his sound belief that, in case he should fail to gain 50 percent and so a second round were to be held, each of his two likely opponents—Pease and Alva Castro—was disliked so intensely by the other's supporters that he would generate a significant number of new votes for Vargas Llosa that were cast against his opponent. Having Alberto Fujimori as his second-round opponent, however, in which case Vargas Llosa could not count on this negative vote, did not figure in his calculations.

The Tsunami Fujimori

Fujimori, an agricultural engineer and professor at Lima's National Agrarian University who in 1988 had founded the Cambio 90 (Change 90) political movement to promote his presidential candidacy, was a virtual unknown only a few short weeks before the election. One not atypical public opinion poll, taken nationwide by a respected firm between mid-

February and mid-March, showed Fujimori as the preference of a mere 4.8 percent of the voters.[31] In what became known as "the Fujimori phenomenon" or the "Fujimori tsunami [tidal wave]," his position in the polls rose spectacularly during the last three weeks of the campaign. Only in the final days before the election, when Peruvian law prohibits the publication of election polls, did the polls show him as likely to gain second place behind Vargas Llosa and, more importantly, to deny Vargas Llosa a first-round victory. The final results showed Vargas Llosa with a disappointing 32.6 percent of the valid vote, while Fujimori gained 29.1 percent.[32] Third place went to Alva Castro, with 22.6 percent, and fourth, with a paltry 8.2 percent, went to Pease; Barrantes came in fifth, with only 4.8 percent (see Table 5.1 on p. 94).

After failing to convince Fujimori to concede the presidency, Vargas Llosa reportedly wanted to concede the second round to his opponent, but he was convinced by his devout supporters within Libertad, nonetheless, that victory in the second round was within reach. In truth, however, a Fujimori victory in the second-round election, slated for June 10, was all but a foregone conclusion. All he had to do to defeat Vargas Llosa was to avoid any major blunder, particularly one that would so alienate the Marxist or *aprista* voters that they would vote against him en masse.

The campaign for the runoff election quickly turned nasty, with Senator Enrique Chirinos Soto, acting as a spokesman for Vargas Llosa at a news conference held at U.N. headquarters in New York, stated that "Peru is very old, with a tradition dating back to the Incas, and I don't believe that the country is ready to have a president who is first-generation Peruvian."[33] This reference to the fact that Fujimori's parents had immigrated to Peru from Japan was criticized, correctly, by Vargas Llosa's opposition as racist, and it proved quite detrimental to the novelist's uphill battle.

Worse still was the extent to which religion became an issue in the campaign. Fujimori is Catholic, but his running mate for second vice president, Carlos García García, was a highly active Baptist minister who at the time was president of the National Evangelical Council of Peru, while no less than 49 of Cambio 90's 180 congressional candidates were either ministers or members of some Protestant sect. Circulars, whose origins remained in doubt, began to appear shortly after the first electoral round in which both the Catholic church and the cult of the Virgin Mary were objects of criticism. Lima's newly appointed Archbishop Augusto Vargas Alzamora then led a campaign in defense of the church, culminating in a massive rally in downtown Lima, that looked suspiciously like a disguise for an overt campaign by the church in favor of Vargas Llosa. If this was, in fact, an attempt by either the new archbishop or by people associated with the Vargas Llosa campaign to associate a vote for Vargas Llosa with a vote for Catholicism (Peru is virtually entirely Catholic; Protestants were estimated at between 2.5 and 5 percent of the population at the time), it failed to have the desired effect.

Fujimori's wide margin of victory in the second round, 62.5 percent versus 37.5 percent for Vargas Llosa, was not difficult to foresee. As in the first round, negative votes (votes cast against a particular candidate) were the key. A vast majority of Peruvians, convinced that Vargas Llosa represented the white elite and that his program would place an unfair burden of the economic adjustment onto the poor, voted against Vargas Llosa. Since before the first electoral round, APRA had undertaken this negative campaign quite openly, sponsoring highly emotional television ads that tied the Vargas Llosa campaign to widespread suffering by the poor under an IMF-mandated "shock" program. Vargas Llosa's sophisticated and extensive campaign, which cost several times the resources spent by all his opponents combined, proved unable to overcome the negative image created by APRA's clamor to "Vote No al Shock."[34]

PERU IN CRISIS: SOME CONCLUDING REMARKS

Alan García's disastrous performance in office was a painful disappointment for a variety of reasons. His leadership, talent, and youthful energy had borne false promises to many that the social democratic and Third World issues, which he promoted so vigorously in 1985 and 1986, would, at last, receive the hearing they justly deserved. Champions of democratic rule saw hope, in the form of Peru's second consecutive constitutional period of civilian rule, turn to fear that a weakening democratic structure might become the victim of a military coup or even a *senderista* victory. Perhaps most disturbing was the dashed hope, nurtured over the previous six decades, that the coming to power of APRA—the most viable of Peru's modern, mass-based political organizations—would precipitate long-postponed structural changes in Peru's social and economic landscape. Despite all of this disillusionment, only the shortsighted would pin all the blame on García for Peru's predicament in 1990.

La crisis was a term that Peruvians had employed to describe their nation's plight ever since the mid-1970s, when the Velasco-initiated reform program sputtered out, leaving the expectations of socioeconomic betterment that it had created among Peru's poor and middle classes unfulfilled. Peru's military-led "revolution from above" left, instead, a legacy of poorly-managed state enterprises, fiscal and balance of payments deficits, and external debt that was to vex succeeding governments.

Austerity measures that accompanied agreements signed with bank creditors in 1976 and with the IMF in 1978 triggered a prolonged series of strikes, the most widespread in the nation's history, and a drastic decline in the standard of living, particularly among the poor, during the regime of Francisco Morales Bermúdez. After Fernando Belaúnde's return to power, new letters of intent signed with the IMF in 1982 and again in 1984 were also widely associated with a growing economic crisis. The Peruvian population, thus living for six years under the watchful eye of the IMF, had become convinced that its government had lost control over the formulation of national economic policy.

It is little wonder, then, that by the time that García entered the National Palace, the international economic order, enforced by the IMF, was widely perceived in Peru as the underlying cause of *la crisis.* García's economic advisors believed that Peru had become caught in what they termed a "debt trap," a vicious circle in which new loans were required in order to ease the burden of payments on past loans. Foreign borrowing had thus become a stopgap to ease one year's balance of payments crisis, only to make next year's worse. Foreign borrowing also caused the economic crisis to be self-perpetuating, they believed, because neoliberal policies dictated by creditors inhibited the economic growth necessary to overcome the need to request new loans. Therefore, the status quo was in acute need of reform, it was said, before Peru could benefit from its relationship with the international financial community.

The status quo within the international economic order witnessed little change in five years, but the breadth and magnitude of the economic failures of the García administration served, nonetheless, to widely discredit these ideas by the time President Fujimori was inaugurated on July 28, 1990 (Peru's independence day and also, by chance, Fujimori's fifty-second birthday). The disarray of the economy, with inflation raging out of control at some 30 percent monthly and production in its deepest depression of the twentieth century, was near total. With an estimated 7 million Peruvians, almost one-third of the total population, unable to supply its basic nutritional needs, and some 3 million of these, or more than one of every eight Peruvians, suffering from malnutrition, the social reality of widespread and deepening poverty was likewise nothing short of a raging crisis. Peru's economic crisis had aggravated these tenacious social problems; a 1989 study under the auspices of the United Nations and the Peruvian government found a "truly worrisome deterioration of Peru's income distribution" between 1985 and 1988.[35]

Peru's governing institutions, meanwhile, had become increasingly ineffectual; by 1990 they were largely unable to provide Peru's citizens— even those in the capital city—with police protection, judicial and educational services, or adequate electrical and water supplies. *Desgobierno,* discernible throughout the inefficient and centralized bureaucracies of government agencies and state enterprises, had even more serious consequences, however. It was not surprising, to give perhaps the most disturbing example, that the government proved incapable of meeting the growing guerrilla challenge presented by Sendero Luminoso. More than one observer noted that *senderista* activity increased faster during periods, such as 1988 and 1989, when the political and economic tidings were particularly onerous.[36] Sendero Luminoso's apparent ability to act at will during such times, with little if any government counteraction in evidence, served to discredit the government still further.

Few Peruvians believed in 1990 that Sendero Luminoso was in a position to assume power in the near future, but the insurgency had become, nonetheless, a nagging reminder of the gravity of their crisis. Characterized as "Peruvian civil society . . . deteriorating into a state of nature"[37] by one observer, and "not simply a government but an entire society . . . falling apart"[38] by another, Peru's national crisis was not confined to the growing insurgency, to *desgobierno,* or to social and economic decay, but by 1990 it had become generalized, practically without bounds. Data on legal emigration, which jumped from 38,000 in 1986 to some 120,000 in 1988, indicated the extent to which Peruvians believed the crisis to be irrevocable.[39]

The origins of Peru's crisis unquestionably predate the mistaken and irresponsible policy aspects of the government of Alan García, the exigencies of the international economic structure, or even the failures of the military-led "revolution," however. Historical antecedents abound. Peruvian foreign debt crises date back to the immediate postindependence era, when the urgency to repay debt contracted during the war for independence yielded the guano age, whose principal beneficiaries were to be the foreign contractors. Fiscal irresponsibility dates back at least to Nicolás de Piérola, President José Balta's finance minister, who initiated the ruinous Dreyfus contract in 1869 in order to finance the building of railroads and other public works.

Desgobierno also has a long history in Peru; in the republican period one need look no further than the debacle of the War of the Pacific. If the centralization of governmental authority were to be considered under this rubric, then we must go back at least to the colonial era, when the Spanish Crown's requisite of focusing its South American political, military, and economic power in Lima bred myriad distortions of sensible rule and eventually persuaded reasonable men to rebel. While considering *desgobierno,* we must also cast a critical eye on the limited role historically played by the Peruvian state. Is it fair, after all, to expect fully competent management of a complex, modern governmental administration from a state that didn't even collect its own taxes until 1964?

Peruvians customarily trace the roots of their national predicament even further back into their history, whether to the trauma of the Spanish conquest, to the failure of the European and native populations to integrate under colonial rule, or to an inadequate sense of a collective national endeavor in the wake of independence. Each sought to explain the persistence of profound social divisions within Peru. It is these divisions that lay at the core of *la crisis.*

At the close of the twentieth century, Peru remained in many ways what it had been for nearly 500 years: a "dual society" having an extraordinarily skewed income distribution and distinct population groups, each with its own manner of viewing the world. Whether one were to divide Peru between the *costa* and the *sierra,* the traditional and the modern, the indigenous and the transplanted populations, the rich and the poor, or the conquerors and the conquered, it was a population—as noted in the opening chapter—that remained to a large extent unintegrated and lacking a shared sense of the value and meaning of nationhood.

Although *la crisis* had the effect of widening still further the gap between the rich and the poor, others among these cleavages were well on their way toward breaking down during the late twentieth century. Ethnic differences were becoming less pronounced as Peru evolved quite rapidly into an overwhelmingly mestizo society. Traditional rural subsistence culture was disappearing as the self-sufficient *sierra* hacienda became a thing of the past, and all but the most remote peoples became integrated into the modern market economy. Even regional dualism was breaking down as migration brought an ever-greater proportion of the national population into Lima and other coastal cities.

In an article published in the wake of Fujimori's electoral victory, Peruvian sociologist Marcial Rubio noted how his country's traditional, oligarchy-based social order had died during the second half of the twentieth century without, as yet, having generated a replacement. Poorly defined social customs and practices thus resulted in what in 1990 seemed to be widespread chaos, with fixed rules of social conduct replaced by "the law of the jungle."[40]

Peru, indeed, had undergone vast economic and social changes in recent decades. Gone was the traditional social structure, with paternalistic oligarchs enjoying princely sums of wealth entrenched at the top. Its replacement, although poorly defined, was clearly much more fluid than the old social order. By 1990, considerable social mobility was evident, with such values as ambition, audacity, and creativity—traditionally disparaged among the lower social sectors—now customarily being rewarded instead. An optimist, then, might look upon Peru's crisis as a difficult interval in the evolution of a new social order that will be less rigid and more equitable.

NOTES

1. Carol L. Graham, "APRA 1968–1988: From Evolution to Government— the Elusive Search for Political Integration in Peru" (D.Phil. thesis, Oxford University, January 1989), p. 226.

2. Pedro Planas, "La Alanización del estado," *Debate* (Lima), Vol. 8, No. 42 (December 1986), pp. 20–22.

3. Graham, "APRA 1968–1988," p. 410.

4. Ibid., pp. 212–14.

5. Ibid., p. 178. Also see *The Peru Report,* Vol. 2, No. 6 (June 1988), p. 7-4.

6. Ibid., p. 193.

7. *The Peru Report,* Vol. 2, No. 6 (June 1988), pp. 7-4 to 7-5.

8. International Bank for Reconstruction and Development, *World Development Report, 1990* (Washington, D.C., 1990), as reported in *El Comercio* (Lima), April 1, 1990, p. A1.

9. *El Comercio,* August 1, 1990, p. B3.

10. The 1985 figure is from the World Bank (see Chapter 6, note 1); the 1990 figure is from Macroconsult (see note 9 above).

11. The Ministry of Labor measured open unemployment in 1990 at 9 percent and underemployment at 73 percent.

12. Most figures on state enterprises are from the World Bank report reprinted in *The Peru Report,* Vol. 2, No. 12, December 1988. The number of functional enterprises is from José Palomino Roedel, president of the National Development Corporation, as quoted in *El Comercio* (Lima), March 19, 1987, p. A2.

13. The inefficiency of Peru's state enterprises was infamous by the late 1980s. See especially World Bank report referred to in note 12 above. *El Comercio* reported (March 19, 1987, p. A2) a projected 1987 deficit for the state enterprises equivalent to U.S. $500 million.

14. The congressional commission figure is from *El Comercio,* December 7, 1990. Guido Pennano, a well-known Peruvian economist who became minister of industry under President Fujimori, said (*El Comercio,* August 19, 1989, p. A13) that the 1988 subsidy figure was $1.3 billion. Javier Silva Ruete, another respected Peruvian analyst, put the figure at $2.2 billion (*El Comercio,* March 8, 1990).

15. Tax burden figures and 1990 state enterprise revenue figures are from Macroconsult (see note 9 above). Figure on state enterprise revenues for 1985 are from the World Bank report referred to in note 12 above. The 1980 figure is from Fernando Sánchez Albavera, "Política de desarrollo y empresas públicas en el Perú: 1970–80, *Socialismo y Participación* (Lima), No. 26 (June 1984), p. 61.

16. 1989 figures are from Rudiger Dornbush, an economic aide to García, quoted in *The Peru Report,* Vol. 3, No. 11 (November 1989), p. 1–4.

17. *Visión* (Bogotá), July 24, 1989.

18. These are government figures. Other estimates of Peru's inflation are generally higher. *El Comercio* (May 9, 1990) reports, for example, that the International Monetary Fund measured Peru's 1989 inflation at 3,399 percent.

19. *El Comercio,* August 2, 1990, p. A1.

20. *El Comercio,* November 15, 1990, p. A1.

21. Carol Wise, "Democratization, Crisis, and the APRA's Modernization Project in Peru," in *Debt and Democracy in Latin America,* Barbara Stallings and Robert Kaufman, eds. (Boulder, Colo.: Westview Press, 1989).

22. See Alan Riding, "As Peru's Crisis Grows, Drastic Change Is Urged," *The New York Times,* November 30, 1988.

23. World Bank figures quoted in *El Comercio,* May 17, 1990. The July 1990 figure is from the Peruvian Central Bank, reported in *El Comercio,* July 27, 1990.

24. Payment arrears and secondary market prices are from the "Reporte económico trimestral" of the Grupo Crédito, as reported in *El Comercio,* November 17, 1990. The total external debt figure is obtained by adding this figure on arrears to the debt figure ($16.7 billion) cited by David Scott Palmer in "Peru's Persistent Problems," *Current History,* January 1990, p. 6.

25. The work of Sandra Woy-Hazleton has followed the intricacies of the alliances and schisms among Peru's electoral left.

26. See, for example, Barrantes's comments while he was in Mexico: "Barrantes admite existencia de grave crisis en coalición 'Izquierda Unida'," *El Comercio,* March 7, 1989, p. B2.

27. The slow-motion division of IU was quite public. Two journals in which it extensively was reported were *Que Hacer,* the quasi-official bimonthly magazine of Izquierda Unida, and the English-language *The Peru Report.* See, in particular, *The Peru Report,* Vol. 1, No. 11 (November 1987) (pp. 7-3 and 7-4) and Vol. 3, No. 5 (May 1989) (pp. 7-1 through 7-6).

28. The commission's report was translated and published as a cover story in *The New York Times Magazine:* Mario Vargas Llosa, "Inquest in the Andes: A Latin American Writer Explores the Political Lessons of a Peruvian Massacre," July 31, 1983, pp. 18–23, 33–37, 42, 48–51, 56. Its conclusions, that guilt for the crimes most likely fell on the frightened and unweary *comuneros* of Uchuraccay, was widely interpreted at the time as an apology for the military forces that had recently been given political authority over the region.

29. Information on the Libertad's leadership comes from *The Andean Report* (Lima), May 1989 and September 1989, and from the Lima daily newspaper, *La República,* October 29, 1989.

30. Carlos Monge, "The Political Eclipse of Mario Vargas Llosa," *Hemisphere,* Vol. 1, No. 1 (Fall 1988), pp. 8–10, presents an interesting discussion of de Soto's departure from Libertad, Libertad's alliance with the traditional right, and their negative effects on Vargas Llosa's political prospects.

31. This poll was published in *El Comercio,* March 24, 1990, p. A6.

32. An interesting description of the campaign leading to Fujimori's extraordinary first-round showing is José María Salcedo, *Tsunami Fujimori* (Lima: La República and Arte & Comunicaciones, April 1990).

33. Quoted from *El Comercio,* April 13, 1990. Translation by author.

34. An interesting discussion of the bizarre 1990 election results is Marcial Rubio C., "Peru: antes y despues de Fujimori?," *Que Hacer* (Lima), No. 65 (July-August 1990), pp. 4–10.

35. Instituto Nacional de Planificación y Programa de las Naciones Unidas para el Desarrollo, "Pobreza en el Perú," reprinted in *The Peru Report,* Vol. 3, No. 4 (April 1989), p. 5A-12.

36. See, for example, Cynthia McClintock, "The Sendero Luminoso Insurgency in Peru," in *The Latin American and Caribbean Contemporary Record: Vol.*

8, 1988-89, James M. Malloy, ed. (New York: Holmes and Meier, 1991), and Palmer, "Peru's Persistent Problems," p. 8.

37. Susan C. Bourque and Kay B. Warren, "Democracy without Peace: The Cultural Politics of Terror in Peru," *Latin American Research Review,* Vol. 24, No. 1 (1989), p. 25.

38. Alan Riding, "Peru Fights to Overcome its Past," *The New York Times Magazine,* May 14, 1989, p. 40.

39. *The New York Times,* January 21, 1989.

40. Marcial Rubio C., "Hacia un nuevo orden social," *Debate* (Lima), May-July 1990, p. 19.

Postscript

On August 6, 1990, less that two weeks after taking office, President Alberto Fujimori instituted the most drastic economic adjustment ever witnessed in Peru. In an attempt to put an end to hyperinflation once and for all, prices of consumer goods were increased between 300 and 1,000 percent overnight.

The "Fuji-shock" laid the foundation for a remarkably successful effort to stabilize an economy that had been left in ruins by the government of Alan García. Inflation subsequently declined steadily, reaching 4 percent monthly in early 1992, and Peru made rapid progress in its effort to reenter the international financial community after half a decade of being regarded as an international pariah as a result of García's stance on debt. However, the "Fuji-shock" also demonstrated disturbing aspects of the character of the man whose campaign slogan had been *Vote No al Shock!*" A considerable number of militants within Fujimori's political party, Cambio 90, became disillusioned with the anti-popular economic policies of the president who, in turn, came to rely increasingly on the armed forces for political support.

Twenty months later, on the night of April 5, 1992, Fujimori once again "shocked" Peru—and the world—with his announcement that he was closing Congress and the judicial branch of government. As a justification he cited their widespread corruption as well as their inefficiency in combatting narcotics trafficking and the ever-spreading insurgency spearheaded by Sendero Luminoso. The international outcry, led by the United States, was nearly unanimous in holding that, though the sins of Peru's legislators might be widely recognized, they did not justify doing away with Peru's constitutional order.

The initial reaction of the Peruvian population, in marked contrast, was one of overwhelming support of President Fujimori. This reaction supports the assertion made in the preface to this volume that, with the escalation of *la crisis,* the preservation of democratic institutions has ceased to be of primary importance to Peruvians. Another explanation of the widespread popular support for Fujimori's assumption of dictatorial powers lies in the president's ongoing ability to capitalize—as he did during his election campaign—on the rampant disillusionment with the political establishment. Whereas in 1990 the establishment had been represented by Mario Vargas Llosa, in 1992 the establishment was embodied by a Congress made up in large part of the leaders of the traditional political parties.

The Fujimori dictatorship, installed with the backing of the high commands of the armed forces and the police, added a new dimension to *la crisis.* On top of a growing insurgency and long-term social and economic decay, Peru now had a de facto government. This loss of democratic political legitimacy cost the government its most potent weapon in combatting its many problems. Meeting in the auditorium of the Peruvian Bar Association on April 21, the recently dismissed Congress swore in Máximo San Román, the first vice president who had been elected in 1990 along with Fujimori, as the legitimate president of Peru. Initially, however, this shadow government received no foreign diplomatic recognition.

On the same day, under intense international pressure to restore Peru's democratic order, Fujimori announced a timetable for a return to democratic rule within 12 months. Within that framework, constitutional amendments drafted by the government were to be debated in a "National Dialogue for Peace and Development," while a series of municipal, regional, and congressional elections were to culminate in the installation of a new Congress on April 5, 1993. Given the ongoing opposition emanating from the international community and from the Peruvian Congress, it was difficult to envision how this timetable could be adhered to unless the dictatorship, which had been remarkably mild during its initial days, were to become much more repressive.

Selected Bibliography

Alba, Victor. *Peru*. Boulder, Colo.: Westview Press, 1977.

Alexander, Robert J., ed. *Aprismo: The Ideas and Doctrines of Víctor Raúl Haya de la Torre*. Kent, Ohio: Kent State University Press, 1973.

Alisky, Marvin. *Peruvian Political Perspective*. 2d ed. Tempe: Arizona State University, Center for Latin American Studies, 1975.

Americas Watch Committee. *Abdicating Democratic Authority: Human Rights in Peru*. New York, October 1984.

_____. *A New Opportunity for Democratic Authority: Human Rights in Peru*. New York, September 1985.

Amnesty International. *"Caught between Two Fires": Peru Briefing*. New York, November 1989.

_____. *Peru: Amnesty International Briefing*. London, January 1985.

_____. *Peru: Human Rights in a State of Emergency*. New York, August 1989.

_____. *Peru: Torture and Extrajudicial Executions*. New York, August 1983.

Angell, Alan. "Peruvian Labour and the Military Government since 1968." Working Paper No. 3. London: University of London, Institute of Latin American Studies, 1980.

Angell, Alan, and Rosemary Thorp. "Inflation, Stabilization and Attempted Redemocratization in Peru, 1975–1979." *World Development,* Vol. 8, November 1980, pp. 865–86.

Arce Borja, Luis and Janet Talavera Sánchez. "La entrevista del siglo: el Presidente Gonzalo rompe el silencio," *El Diario* (Lima), July 31, 1988.

Astiz, Carlos A. *Pressure Groups and Power Elites in Peruvian Politics*. Ithaca, N.Y.: Cornell University Press, 1969.

Astiz, Carlos A., and José Z. García. "The Peruvian Military: Achievement, Orientation, Training, and Political Tendencies." *Western Political Quarterly,* Vol. 25, No. 4, December 1972, pp. 667–85.

Avery, William P. "Origins and Consequences of the Border Dispute between Ecuador and Peru." *Inter-American Economic Affairs,* Vol. 38, No. 1, Summer 1984, pp. 65–77.

———. "The Politics of Crisis and Cooperation in the Andean Group." *Journal of Developing Areas,* Vol. 17, No. 2, January 1983, pp. 155–84.

Becker, David G. *The New Bourgeoisie and the Limits of Dependency: Mining, Class, and Power in "Revolutionary" Peru.* Princeton, N.J.: Princeton University Press, 1983.

Bollinger, William. "Peru Today—the Roots of Labor Militancy." *NACLA Report on the Americas,* Vol. 14, No. 6, November–December, 1980, pp. 2–35.

Bonner, Raymond. "Peru's War." *The New Yorker,* January 4, 1988, pp. 31–58.

Booth, David, and Bernardo Sorj, eds. *Military Reformism and Social Classes: The Peruvian Experience.* New York: St. Martin's Press, 1983.

Bourque, Susan C., and Kay B. Warren. "Democracy without Peace: The Cultural Politics of Terror in Peru." *Latin American Research Review,* Vol. 24, No. 1, 1989, pp. 7–34.

Bourricaud, François. *Power and Society in Contemporary Peru.* New York: Praeger, 1970.

Burgess, Stephen. "The Communal Kitchens of Lima: An Analysis of Women's Organizations in the Barriadas." M.Phil. thesis, Oxford University, October 1986.

Carey, James Charles. *Peru and the United States, 1900–1962.* Notre Dame: University of Notre Dame Press, 1964.

Centro de Estudios y Promoción del Desarrollo (DESCO). *Violencia política en el Perú. 1980–1988.* Lima, 1989.

Chaplin, David, ed. *Peruvian Nationalism: A Corporatist Revolution.* New Brunswick, N.J.: Transaction Books, 1976.

Child, Jack. "Historical Setting." In Richard F. Nyrop, ed., *Peru: A Country Study.* Washington, D.C.: U.S. Government Printing Office, 1981.

Cleaves, Peter S., and Martin J. Scurrah. *Agriculture, Bureaucracy, and Military Government in Peru.* Ithaca, N.Y.: Cornell University Press, 1980.

Collier, David. *Squatters and Oligarchs: Authoritarian Rule and Policy Change in Peru.* Baltimore: Johns Hopkins University Press, 1976.

Cotler, Julio. *Clases, estado y nación en el Perú.* Lima: Instituto de Estudios Peruanos, 1978.

———, ed. *Para afirmar la democracia.* Lima: Instituto de Estudios Peruanos, 1987.

Davies, Thomas M., Jr. *Indian Integration in Peru: A Half Century of Experience, 1900–1948.* Lincoln: University of Nebraska Press, 1974.

———. "Víctor Raúl Haya de la Torre and the APRA: The Politics of Ideology." Paper presented at the conference "APRA as Party and Government: From Ideology to Praxis," University of California, San Diego, March 21, 1988.

de Soto, Hernando. *The Other Path: The Invisible Revolution in the Third World.* New York: Harper and Row, 1989.

del Pilar Tello, María. *Golpe o revolución: hablan los militares del 68.* Lima: Ediciones Sagsa, 1983.

Díaz Martínez, Antonio. *Ayacucho: hambre y esperanza.* 2d ed. Lima: Mosca Azul Editores, 1985.

Dietz, Henry A. "Electoral Politics in Peru, 1978–1986." *Journal of Inter-*

American Studies and World Affairs, Vol. 28, No. 4, Winter 1986-1987, pp. 139–63.

————. *Poverty and Problem-Solving under Military Rule: The Urban Poor in Lima, Peru.* Austin: University of Texas Press, 1980.

Dobyns, Henry F., and Paul L. Doughty. *Peru: A Cultural History.* New York: Oxford University Press, 1976.

Durand, Francisco. "Los empresarios y la primavera democrática." *Que Hacer,* No. 44, December 1986–January 1987, pp. 34–38.

Durr, Barbara. "Peru: Economic Policy Submerged by Politics." *The Financial Times,* March 22, 1988.

Einaudi, Luigi R. *The Peruvian Military: A Summary Political Analysis.* Santa Monica, Calif.: Rand Corporation, 1969.

————. *Peruvian Military Relations with the United States.* Santa Monica, Calif.: Rand Corporation, 1970.

Ferris, Elizabeth G. "The Andean Pact and the Amazon Treaty: Reflections of Changing Latin American Realities." *Journal of Inter-American Studies and World Affairs,* Vol. 23, No. 2, May 1981, pp. 147–75.

Figueroa, Alejandro. "The Impact of Current Reforms on Income Distribution in Peru." In Alejandro Foxley, ed., *Income Distribution in Latin America.* London: Cambridge University Press, 1976.

Fitzgerald, E. V. K. *The Political Economy of Peru, 1956–1978: Economic Development and the Restructuring of Capital.* Cambridge: Cambridge University Press, 1979.

————. *The State and Economic Development: Peru since 1968.* Cambridge: Cambridge University Press, 1976.

Fried, Mark, ed. "Fatal Attraction: Peru's Shining Path." *NACLA Report on the Americas,* Vol. 24, No. 4, December 1990–January 1991, pp. 9–39.

Friedman, Douglas. *The State and Underdevelopment in Spanish America: The Political Roots of Dependency in Peru and Argentina.* Boulder, Colo.: Westview Press, 1984.

García Pérez, Alan. *El futuro diferente: la tarea histórica del APRA.* Lima: Editorial Imprenta DESA, 1982.

García Sayán, Diego, ed. *Coca, Cocaína, y narcotráfico: laberinto en los andes.* Lima: Comisión Andina de Juristas, 1989.

Gilbert, Dennis. "The End of the Peruvian Revolution: A Class Analysis." *Studies in Comparative International Development,* Vol. 15, No. 1, Spring 1980, pp. 15–38.

González, Raúl. "Ayacucho: por los caminos de sendero." *Que Hacer,* August 1984, pp. 38–77.

————. "Coca's Shining Path." *NACLA Report on the Americas,* Vol. 22, No. 6, March 1989, pp. 22–24.

————. "La cuarta plenaria del Comité Central de Sendero Luminoso." *Que Hacer,* No. 44, December 1986–January 1987, pp. 49–53.

Goodsell, Charles T. *American Corporations and Peruvian Politics.* Cambridge, Mass.: Harvard University Press, 1974.

Gorman, Stephen M., ed. *Post-Revolutionary Peru.* Boulder, Colo.: Westview Press, 1982.

Graham, Carol L. "APRA 1968–1988: From Evolution to Government—The Elusive Search for Political Integration in Peru." D. Phil. thesis, Oxford University, January 1989.

Guerra García, Francisco. *Velasco: del estado oligárquico al capitalismo del estado.* Lima: CEDEP, 1983.

Handelman, Howard. "Peasants, Landlords and Bureaucrats: The Politics of Agrarian Reform in Peru." *American Universities Field Staff Reports,* South America series, No. 1, 1981.

_____. "Peru: The March to Civilian Rule." *American Universities Field Staff Reports,* South America series, No. 2, 1980.

_____. *Struggle in the Andes.* Austin: University of Texas Press, 1975.

Harding, Colin. "Antonio Díaz Martínez and the Ideology of Sendero Luminoso." *Bulletin of Latin American Research* (London), Vol. 7, No. 1, 1988, pp. 65–74.

Haya de la Torre, Víctor Raúl. *El antimperialismo y el APRA.* Lima: Ediciones Culturales Marfil, 1985.

_____. *Treinta años del APRA.* Mexico: Fondo de Cultura Económica, 1956.

Hemming, John. *The Conquest of the Incas.* London: Macmillan, 1970.

Hilliker, Grant. *The Politics of Reform in Peru: The Aprista and Other Mass Parties of Latin America.* Baltimore: Johns Hopkins University Press, 1971.

Iguiñez, Javier. "Las chances y las restricciones de la política del APRA." Paper presented at the conference "APRA as Party and Government: From Ideology to Praxis." University of California, San Diego, March 21, 1988.

Jaquette, Jane S. *The Politics of Development in Peru.* Ithaca, N.Y.: Cornell University, Latin American Studies Program, 1971.

Kantor, Harry. *The Ideology and Program of the Peruvian Aprista Movement.* Washington, D.C.: Saville Books, 1966.

Kawell, Jo Ann. "Going to the Source." *NACLA Report on the Americas,* Vol. 22, No. 6, March 1989, pp. 13–21.

Klaiber, Jeffrey L. *Religion and Revolution in Peru.* Notre Dame: University of Notre Dame Press, 1977.

Klarén, Peter F. *Modernization, Dislocation, and Aprismo: Origins of the Peruvian Aprista Party.* Austin: University of Texas Press, 1973.

Korovkin, Tanya. *Politics of Agricultural Co-operativism: Peru, 1969–1983.* Vancouver: University of British Columbia Press, 1990.

Kuczynski, Pedro-Pablo. *Peruvian Democracy under Economic Stress: An Account of the Belaúnde Administration, 1963–1968.* Princeton, N.J.: Princeton University Press, 1977.

_____. "The Peruvian External Debt: Problem and Prospects." *Journal of Inter-American Studies and World Affairs,* Vol. 23, No. 1, February 1981, pp. 3–27.

Larson, Everette E., ed. "Sendero Luminoso: A Bibliography," *Hispanic Focus,* No. 3. Washington, D.C.: Library of Congress, 1985.

Letts, Ricardo. *La izquierda peruana: organizaciones y tendencias.* Lima: Mosca Azul Editores, 1981.

Lowenthal, Abraham F., ed. *The Peruvian Experiment: Continuity and Change under Military Rule.* Princeton, N.J.: Princeton University Press, 1975.

Malloy, James M. "Authoritarianism, Corporatism, and Mobilization in Peru." *Review of Politics,* Vol. 36, January 1974, pp. 52–84.

_____. "Peru's Troubled Return to Democratic Government." *UFSI Reports,* South America series, No. 15. Hanover, N.H.: UFSI, 1982.

Mariátegui, José Carlos. *Seven Interpretive Essays on Peruvian Reality.* Trans. Marjory Urquidi. Austin: University of Texas Press, 1971.

Matos Mar, José. *Desborde popular y crisis del estado.* Lima: Instituto de Estudios Peruanos, 1985.

_____, ed. *La oligarquía el el Perú.* Lima: Instituto de Estudios Peruanos, 1969.

Mauceri, Philip. *Militares: insurgencia y democratización en el Perú, 1980–1988.* Lima: Instituto de Estudios Peruanos, 1989.

McClintock, Cynthia. "APRA and the Peruvian Army since the Constituent Assembly." Paper presented at the conference "APRA as Party and Government: From Ideology to Praxis," University of California, San Diego, March 21, 1988.

_____. "Democracies and Guerrillas: The Peruvian Experience." *International Policy Report.* Washington, D.C.: Center for International Policy, 1983.

_____. *Peasant Cooperatives and Political Change in Peru.* Princeton, N.J.: Princeton University Press, 1981.

_____. "Peru: A New, Determined Leader Tackles Old, Large Problems." In Abraham F. Lowenthal, ed., *The Latin American and Caribbean Contemporary Record.* Vol. 5. *1985–1986.* New York: Holmes and Meier, 1988.

_____. "Peru: Precarious Regimes, Authoritarian and Democratic." In Larry Diamond, Juan J. Linz, and Seymour Martin Lipset, eds., *Democracy in Developing Countries.* Vol. 4. *Latin America.* Boulder, Colo.: Lynne Rienner, 1989.

_____. "Peru's Sendero Luminoso Rebellion: Origins and Trajectory." In Susan Eckstein, ed., *Power and Popular Protest.* Berkeley: University of California Press, 1989.

_____. "The Sendero Luminoso Insurgency in Peru." In James M. Malloy, ed., *The Latin American and Caribbean Contemporary Record, Vol. 8, 1988-89.* New York: Holmes and Meier, 1991.

_____. "Sendero Luminoso: Peru's Maoist Guerrillas." *Problems in Communism,* September-October 1983, pp. 19–34.

_____. "The War on Drugs: The Peruvian Case." *Journal of Inter-American Studies and World Affairs,* Vol. 30, Nos. 2–3, Summer-Fall 1988, pp. 127–42.

_____. "Why Peasants Rebel: The Case of Peru's Sendero Luminoso." *World Politics,* Vol. 37, No. 2, October 1984, pp. 48–84.

McClintock, Cynthia, and Abraham F. Lowenthal, eds. *The Peruvian Experiment Reconsidered.* Princeton, N.J.: Princeton University Press, 1983.

Medianero, David. "Ayacucho: pobreza y distribución." *Socialismo y Participación,* No. 26, June 1984, pp. 99–109.

Middlebrook, Kevin J. and David Scott Palmer. *Military Government and Political Development: Lessons from Peru.* Beverly Hills: Sage Publications, 1975.

Miller, Rory. "The Coastal Elite and Peruvian Politics." *Journal of Latin American Studies,* Vol. 14, Part 1, May 1982.

Monge, Carlos. "The Political Eclipse of Mario Vargas Llosa." *Hemisphere,* Vol. 1, No. 1, Fall 1988, pp. 8–10.

North, Liisa. *Civil-Military Relations in Argentina, Chile, and Peru.* Politics of Modernization series, No. 2. Berkeley: University of California, Institute of International Studies, 1966.

Owens, Ronald Jerome. *Peru.* London: Oxford University Press, 1963.

Palmer, David Scott. "The Changing Political Economy under Military and Civilian Rule." *Inter-American Economic Affairs,* Vol. 37, No. 4, Spring 1984, pp. 37–62.

————. "Peru: the Authoritarian Legacy." In Howard J. Wiarda and Harvey F. Kline, eds., *Latin American Politics and Development.* 2d ed. Boulder, Colo.: Westview Press, 1985.

————. *Peru: The Authoritarian Tradition.* New York: Praeger, 1980.

————. "Peru's Persistent Problems." *Current History,* January 1990, pp. 5–8, 31–34.

————. "Rebellion in Rural Peru: The Origins and Evolution of Sendero Luminoso." *Comparative Politics,* Vol. 18, No. 2, January 1986, pp. 127–46.

————. "Terrorism as a Revolutionary Strategy: Peru's Sendero Luminoso." In Barry Rubin, ed., *The Politics of Terrorism.* Washington, D.C.: Johns Hopkins Foreign Policy Institute, 1989.

Partido Comunista del Perú Sendero Luminoso. Comité Central. "Desarrollar la guerra popular sirviendo a la revolución mundial." August 1986.

————. "No votar! Sino, generalizar la guerra de guerrillas para conquistar el poder para el pueblo." February 1985.

Pásara, Luis, and Jorge Parodi, eds. *Democracia, sociedad y gobierno en el Perú.* Lima: Centro de Estudios de Democracia y Sociedad, 1988.

Petras, James. "State, Regime, and the Democratic Muddle." *LASA Forum,* Vol. 18, No. 4, Winter 1988.

Philip, George D. E. *The Rise and Fall of the Peruvian Military Radicals, 1968–1976.* London: Athlone Press, 1978.

Pike, Frederick B. *The Modern History of Peru.* New York: Praeger, 1967.

————. *The Politics of the Miraculous in Peru.* Lincoln: University of Nebraska Press, 1986.

————. *The United States and the Andean Republics.* Cambridge, Mass.: Harvard University Press, 1977.

Pinelo, Adalberto J. *The Multinational Corporation as a Force in Latin American Politics: A Case Study of the International Petroleum Company in Peru.* New York: Praeger, 1973.

Planas, Pedro. "La alanización del estado." *Debate* (Lima), Vol. 8, No. 42, December 1986, pp. 20–22.

"President García's Inaugural Address." *The Andean Report* (Lima), August 1985.

Reid, Michael. *Peru: Paths to Poverty.* London: Latin America Bureau, 1985.

República Peruana. Asamblea Constituyente. *Constitución política del Perú.* Lima, 1979.

República Peruana. Comisión Especial del Senado sobre las Causas de la

Violencia y Alternativas de Pacificación en el Perú. *Violencia y Pacificación.* Lima: DESCO y la Comisión Andina de Juristas, 1989.

República Peruana. Instituto Nacional de Estadística. *Censos nacionales, VIII de población, III de vivienda, 12 de julio de 1981.* 2 vols. Lima, December 1982.

———. *Compendio estadístico.* Lima, 1982.

———. *Perú: algunas caracteristicas de la población. Resultados provisionales del censo del 12 de julio de 1981.* Special Bulletin No. 6. Lima, October 1981.

República Peruana and Centro Latinoamericano de Demografía de los Naciones Unidas. *Estimaciones y proyecciones de población.* Lima, 1983.

Riding, Alan. "Peru Fights to Overcome Its Past." *The New York Times Magazine,* May 14, 1989, pp. 40–44, 100.

———. "Peru Puts Democracy to the Test." *The New York Times Magazine,* July 14, 1985, pp. 23–24, 42–45.

Roett, Riorden. "Peru: The Message from García." *Foreign Affairs,* Vol. 64, No. 2, Winter 1985-1986, pp. 274–86.

Rubio C., Marcial. "Peru: antes y despues de Fujimori?" *Que Hacer,* No. 65, July-August 1990, pp. 4–11.

Rudolph, James D. "Government and Politics." In Richard F. Nyrop, ed., *Peru: A Country Study.* Washington, D.C.: U.S. Government Printing Office, 1981.

———. "The Political Party System and Civilian Rule in Peru." Paper presented at the 12th International Congress of the Latin American Studies Association, Albuquerque, New Mexico, April 18–20, 1985.

Sánchez Albavera, Fernando. "Política de desarrollo y empresas públicas en el Perú: 1970–80." *Socialismo y Participación* (Lima), No. 26, June 1984, pp. 31–65.

Sanders, Thomas G. "Economics and the Peruvian Political Process." *UFSI Reports,* South America Series, No. 28. Hanover, N.H.: UFSI, 1984.

———. "Peru: Alan García's First Two Years." *UFSI Reports,* South America Series, No. 12. Hanover, N.H.: UFSI 1987.

———. "Peru between Democracy and the Sendero Luminoso." *UFSI Reports,* South America Series, No. 21. Hanover, N.H.: UFSI, 1984.

———. "Peru's Economy: Underemployment and the Informal Sector." *UFSI Reports,* South America Series, No. 39. Hanover, N.H.: UFSI, 1984.

———. "Peru's Population in the 1980s." *UFSI Reports,* South America Series, No. 27. Hanover, N.H.: UFSI, 1984.

Scheetz, Thomas. *Peru and the International Monetary Fund.* Pittsburgh, Pa.: University of Pittsburgh Press, 1986.

Sharp, Daniel A., ed. *United States Foreign Policy and Peru.* Austin: University of Texas Press, 1972.

Stein, Steve. *Populism in Peru: The Emergence of the Masses and the Politics of Social Control.* Madison: University of Wisconsin Press, 1980.

Stein, Steve, and Carlos Monge. *La crisis del estado patrimonial en el Perú.* Lima: Instituto de Estudios Peruanos y Universidad de Miami, 1988.

Stepan, Alfred C. *The State and Society: Peru in Comparative Perspective.* Princeton, N.J.: Princeton University Press, 1978.

Stephens, Evelyne Huber. "The Peruvian Military Government, Labor Mobilization, and the Political Strength of the Left." *Latin American Research Review,* Vol. 18, No. 2, 1983, pp. 57–93.

_____. *The Politics of Workers' Participation: The Peruvian Approach in Comparative Perspective.* New York: Harcourt Brace Jovanovich, Academic Press, 1980.

St. John, Ronald Bruce. "The Boundary Dispute between Peru and Ecuador." *The American Journal of International Law,* Vol. 71, April 1977, pp. 322–30.

Tarazona-Sevillano, Gabriela, with John B. Reuter. *Sendero Luminoso and the Threat of Narcoterrorism.* New York and Washington, D.C.: Praeger and The Center for Strategic and International Studies, 1990.

Taylor, Lewis. "Maoism in the Andes: Sendero Luminoso and the Contemporary Guerrilla Movement in Peru." Working Paper No. 2. Liverpool: Centre for Latin American Studies, University of Liverpool, 1983.

Thorp, Rosemary, and Geoffrey Bertram. *Peru, 1890–1977: Growth and Policy in an Open Economy.* New York: Columbia University Press, 1978.

Tuesta Soldevilla, Fernando. *El nuevo rostro electoral: las municipales del 83.* Lima: DESCO, 1985.

_____. *Perú político en cifras: elite política y elecciones.* Lima: Fundación Friedrich Ebert, 1987.

Tullis, F. LaMond. *Lord and Peasant in Peru: A Paradigm of Political and Social Change.* Cambridge, Mass.: Harvard University Press, 1970.

U.S. Department of State. "Peru." *Country Reports on Human Rights Practices* (Annual Report submitted to the Committee on Foreign Affairs, U.S. House of Representatives, and the Committee on Foreign Relations, U.S. Senate).

U.S. Department of State. Embassy in Lima. *Foreign Economic Trends and Their Implication for the United States: Peru.* Washington, D.C.: Department of Commerce, annual.

_____. *Foreign Labor Trends: Peru.* Washington, D.C.: Department of Labor, annual.

Van den Berghe, Pierre L., and George P. Primov. *Inequality in the Peruvian Andes: Class and Ethnicity in Cuzco.* Columbia: University of Missouri Press, 1977.

Vargas Llosa, Mario. "Inquest in the Andes: A Latin American Writer Explores the Political Lessons of a Peruvian Massacre." *The New York Times Magazine,* July 31, 1983, pp. 18–23, 33, 36–37, 42, 48–51, 56.

Washington Office on Latin America. *Peru in Peril: The Economy and Human Rights, 1985–1987.* Washington, D.C., 1987.

Webb, Richard C. "The Distribution of Income in Peru." In Alejandro Foxley, ed., *Income Distribution in Latin America.* London: Cambridge University Press, 1976.

_____. *Government Policy and the Distribution of Income in Peru, 1963–1973.* Cambridge, Mass.: Harvard University Press, 1977.

Weeks, John. *Limits to Capitalist Development: The Industrialization of Peru, 1950–1980.* Boulder, Colo.: Westview Press, 1985.

Werlich, David P. "Debt, Democracy, and Terrorism in Peru." *Current History,* January 1987, pp. 29–32, 36.

———. Peru: García Loses His Charm." *Current History,* January 1988, pp. 13–16, 36–37.

———. "Peru: The Shadow of the Shining Path." *Current History,* February 1984, pp. 78–82, 90.

———. *Peru: A Short History.* Carbondale: Southern Illinois University Press, 1978.

Wise, Carol. "Alfonso Barrantes." *NACLA Report on the Americas,* Vol. 20, September-December 1986.

———. "The Perils of Orthodoxy: Peru's Political Economy." *NACLA Report on the Americas,* Vol. 20, No. 3, June 1986.

———. "Democratization, Crisis, and APRA's Modernization Project in Peru." In Barbara Stallings and Robert Kaufman, eds., *Debt and Democracy in Latin America.* Boulder, Colo.: Westview Press, 1989.

Woy-Hazelton, Sandra L. "Peru," pp. 130–139 in Richard F. Starr, ed., *1990 Yearbook on International Communist Affairs.* Stanford, Calif.: Hoover Institution Press, 1990.

———. "The Return of Partisan Politics in Peru." In Stephen M. Gorman, ed., *Post-Revolutionary Peru: The Politics of Transformation.* Boulder, Colo.: Westview Press, 1982.

Woy-Hazleton, Sandra L., and Stephen M. Gorman. "The Peruvian Left since 1977: Ideology, Programs and Behavior." Paper presented at the American Political Science Association, Denver, Colorado, September 2–5, 1982.

———. "Political Opposition in Peru: Parliamentary and Revolutionary Challenges." Paper presented at the 11th International Congress of the Latin American Studies Association, Mexico City, Mexico, September 30, 1983.

Woy-Hazelton, Sandra L., and William A. Hazleton. "Political Violence and the Future of Peruvian Democracy." Paper presented at the International Congress of the Latin American Studies Association, Miami, December 5, 1989.

Two English-language monthlies, *The Andean Report* and *The Peru Report,* both published in Lima, were also extremely helpful in the preparation of this manuscript.

Index

labor unions, 32–33, 35–36,
64–65, 67, 69; and Sendero
Luminoso, 113. *See also* CGTP,
CTP
language, 10, 78
Leguía, Augusto B., 32–33, 35–39
Libertad. *See* Vargas Llosa, Mario
Lima: founding, 22; population
growth, 14
limited liberal state, 29–33
López Albújar, General Enrique,
117, 119
lower class, 13–14. *See also* informal
economy

Malvinas Islands. *See* Argentina
Mariátegui, José Carlos, 37–38
Marxism, 36–39, 70, 71–74, 93–95,
132, 137–39. *See also* PCP-U, IU
middle class, 12–13
migration, 14–16, 146–47
mining, 24, 32, 44
MIR (Movement of the
Revolutionary Left), 49
Morales Bermúdez Cerrutti,
Francisco, 67–72
Morote, Osman, 113, 118
MRTA (Túpac Amaru Revolutionary
Movement), 91–92, 117–18, 122–23
municipal government, 136

Nestlé, 106
neoliberalism. *See* Ulloa Elías, Manuel
Nicaragua, 105
Nonaligned Movement, 105

OAS (Organization of American
States), 56–57, 105–6
Odría, General Manuel A., 43–47

PAIT (Program for Temporary
Income), 102, 108, 131
Panama, 85
Pardo, José, 32–33
Pardo, Manuel, 29
Partido Civil, 28–33
Partido Constitucionalista, 30

PCP-U (Peruvian Communist
Party-Unity), 38, 41, 44, 65;
origins, 38
PDC (Christian Democratic Party),
47, 50, 65
Peace Commission, 110–12
Pease García, Henry, 94, 137
petroleum industry, 32. *See also*
Belco Petroleum Company;
International Petroleum Company
(IPC)
Pizarro, Francisco, 21–22
Polay Campos, Víctor. *See* MRTA
(Túpac Amaru Revolutionary
Movement)
police reorganization, 122
population, 7–16; growth, 7–8
poverty, 8–9, 54, 78, 132–33, 145; in
Ayacucho, 86–87
PPC (Popular Christian Party), 50,
71–73, 84, 93, 94
Prado, Mariano Ignacio, 28–29
Prado Ugarteche, Manuel, 40–41,
45–46
pre-Hispanic cultures, 19–20
Protestants, 143–44
public sector, 59–62, 83, 133–34,
148 n.14; employees, 12–13, 134

regional governments, 136–37
Revolutionary Government of the
Armed Forces, 53–74, 144;
ideology, 54, 68; Phase Two,
67–72; retreat from office, 70;
structure, 53–54
rondas campesinas, 90, 116

SAIS (agrarian social interest
society), 63; SAIS Cahuide, 115
Sánchez Cerro, Colonel Luis M.,
39–40
San Martín, José de, 25–26
SELA (Latin American Economic
System), 56–57, 104
selva, 5–6; development, 49;
economy, 5–6, 32
Sendero Luminoso (Shining Path),

ABOUT THE AUTHOR

JAMES D. RUDOLPH is a teacher and writer who has lived in Peru since 1986. During that time he has taught political science at Colegio Franklin D. Roosevelt and history at Newton College. Previously, as a senior research scientist at Foreign Area Studies at The American University in Washington, D.C., he co-authored *Peru: A Country Study* and edited or co-authored 20 additional volumes in the Country Study series.